ABANDONED PLANES, TRAINS, AND AUTOMOBILES

CALIFORNIA REVEALED

KEN LEE

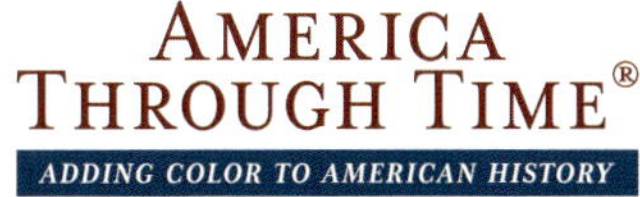

America Through Time is an imprint of Fonthill Media LLC
www.through-time.com
office@through-time.com

Published by Arcadia Publishing by arrangement with Fonthill Media LLC
For all general information, please contact Arcadia Publishing:
Telephone: 843-853-2070
Fax: 843-853-0044
E-mail: sales@arcadiapublishing.com
For customer service and orders:
Toll-Free 1-888-313-2665

www.arcadiapublishing.com

First published 2021

ISBN 978-1-63499-355-5

Typeset in Trade Gothic
Printed and bound in England

CONTENTS

ACKNOWLEDGMENTS

Special thanks to Joe Davis from Eagle Field; Kathleen Dewhurst at Joe Davies Heritage Airpark; Bryan Butler at Motor Transport Museum; Ricardo Iraheta at Golden Cactus; and Michael T. for your kindness.

Night photography friends, including Tim Little, Mike Cooper, Ron Pinkerton, Dave Dasinger, George Loo, and more.

Lance Keimig and Troy Paiva, for your pioneering work, friendship, and inspiration.

Thank you to Lisa Kelly for your editorial help.

www.kenleephotography.com

1

PLANES

EAGLE FIELD

It begins with *Indiana Jones* and thirty-seven open browser tabs. Chasing leads deep into the rabbit holes of YouTube and Google, where I stumble across a photo of an old "Aeropuerto de Nazca" fuel truck from an *Indiana Jones* movie. This was filmed in California, not Peru! After more searching, I discover where it is located and fire off a midnight email to Joe Davis, the owner of Eagle Field. He has been restoring old planes and the airfield out of respect for the men and women who helped win World War II. He responds quickly. I feel like the heavens are smiling upon me when he says yes, we may photograph there at night.

One visit in particular stands out. I am driving through agricultural areas toward the airfield on a late afternoon on a sweltering September day when I see odd dark clouds in the distance. They are insects. Before long, they are bouncing from my windshield, the sound resembling an active Geiger counter. Joe sends a text to warn me about the mosquitos.

Despite the heat, I throw on a hoodie and beanie and apply some Deet before I even get out of the car. During the night, I retreat into the hangar twice to photograph there and escape the ravenous insects. One of my friends is not so fortunate, sustaining so many bites that the next day, he reports that his entire back is massed into one enormous mosquito bite. The only thing I have experienced that compares to this insect insanity was trekking through the Amazon jungle.

Every visit, I stand in reverence of these airplanes. There is something about these airplanes and the people who fly them that inspire me. Whether I see a Bell UH-Huey, the dismembered Lockheed P-2V-3W Neptune, or the epic Lockheed Harpoon that greets you upon entering, there seems to be something noble about these aircraft and the people who fly them.

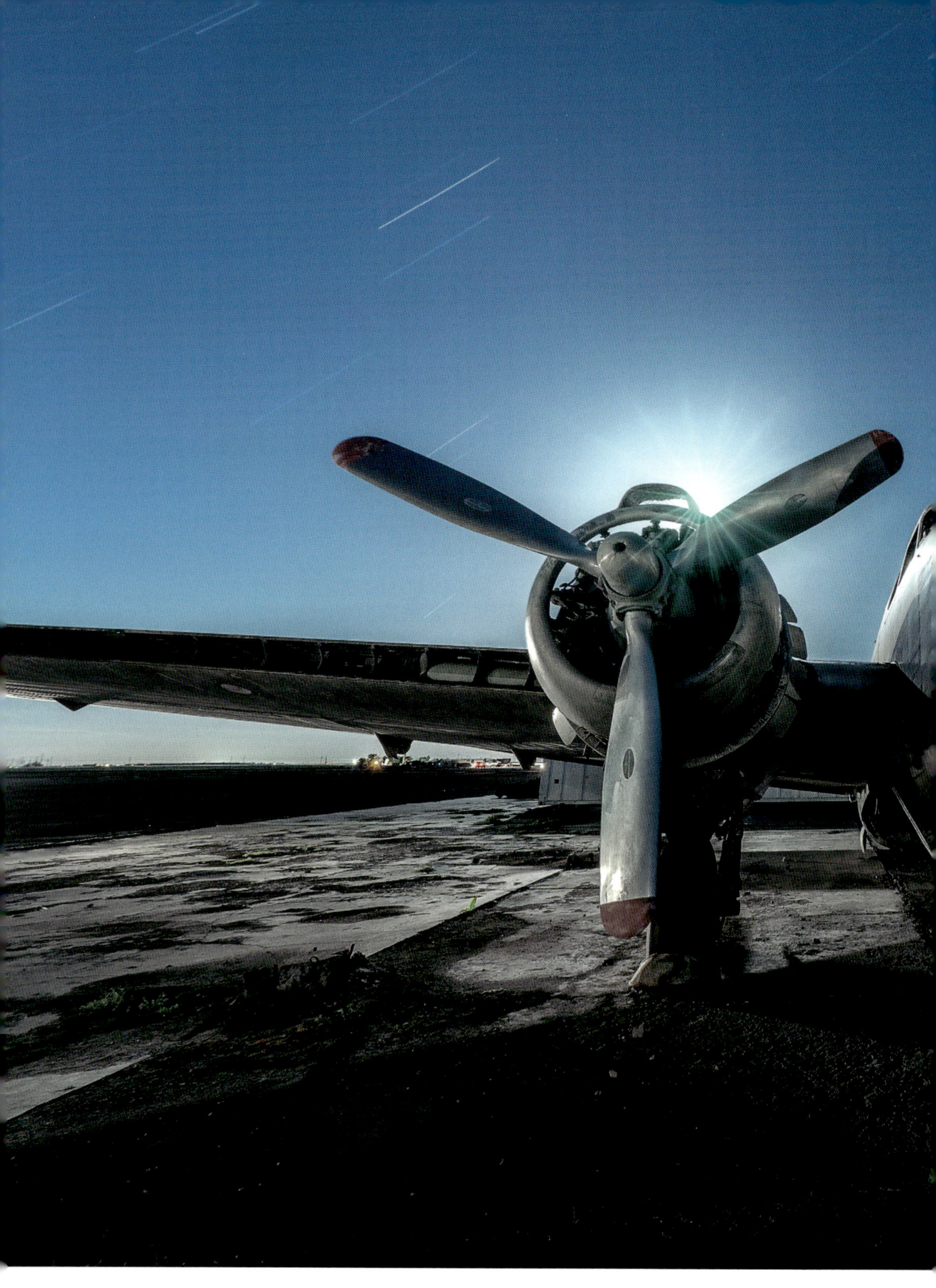

Luna de San Joaquin, Lockheed Harpoon, Eagle Field.
Nikon D750/Nikkor 14–24-mm f/2.8 lens.

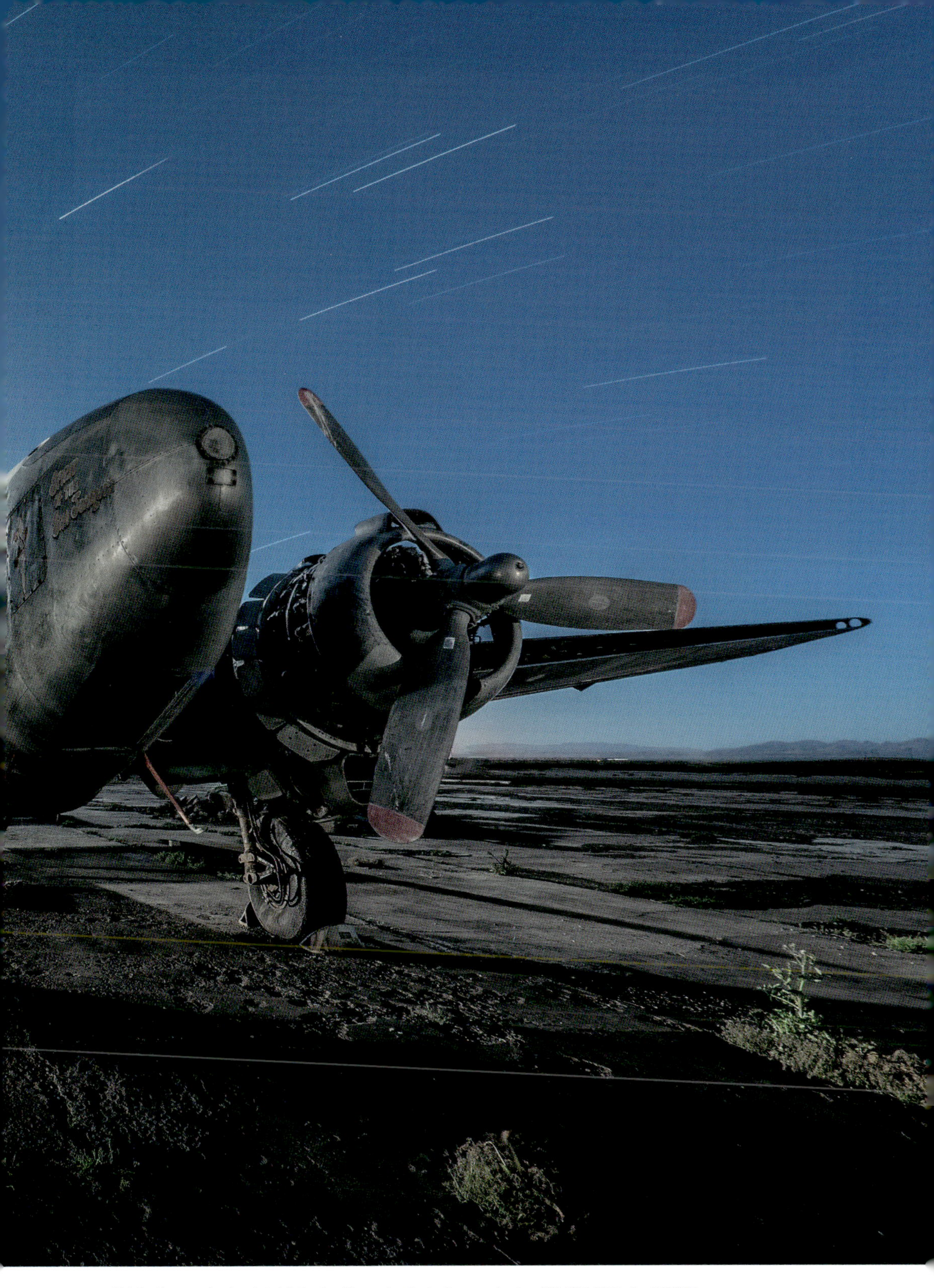

Thirty-three minutes total "stacked"; each photo three minutes f/8 ISO 200. April 2019.
Full moon, warm white light from ProtoMachines LED2.

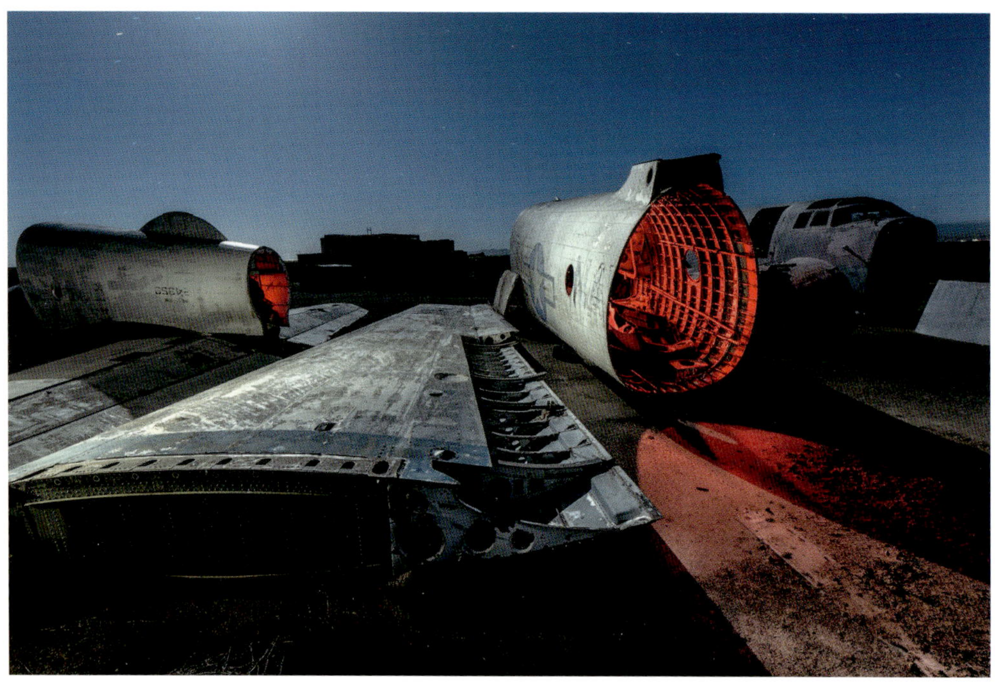

Tearing Us Apart, dismantled P2V-3W Neptune aircraft, Eagle Field.
Nikon D750/Nikkor 14–24-mm f/2.8 lens. One minute fifty-four seconds f/8 ISO 200. April 2019.
Full moon, warm white and red light from ProtoMachines LED2.

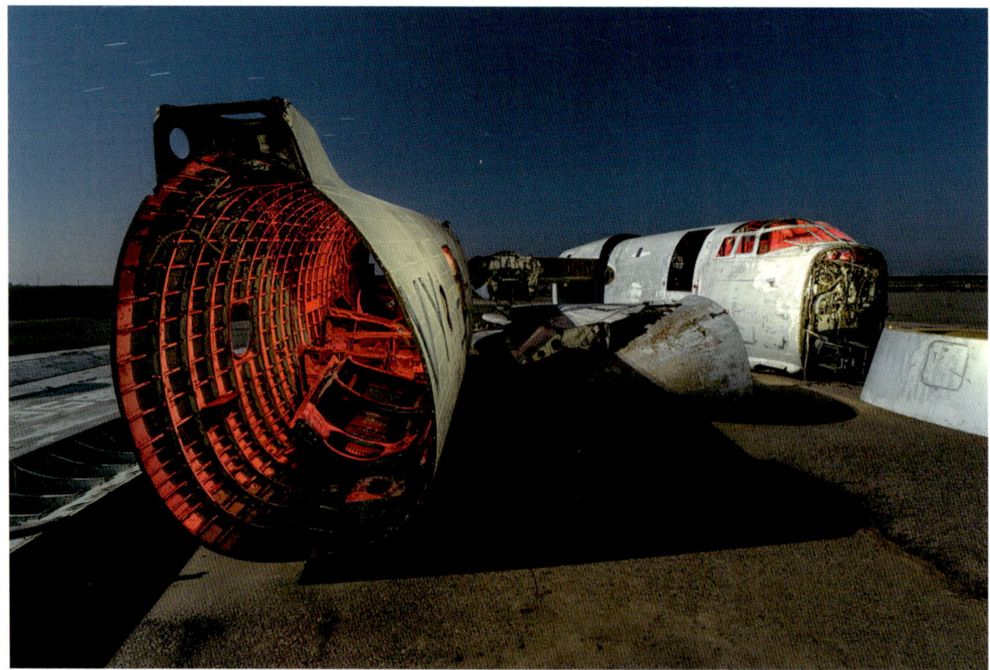

Neptune Breaking, dismantled P2V-3W Neptune aircraft, Eagle Field.
Pentax K-1/15–30-mm f/2.8 lens. Seven minutes total "stacked"; each photo one minute f/8 ISO 200. February 2020.
Full moon, warm white and red light from ProtoMachines LED2.

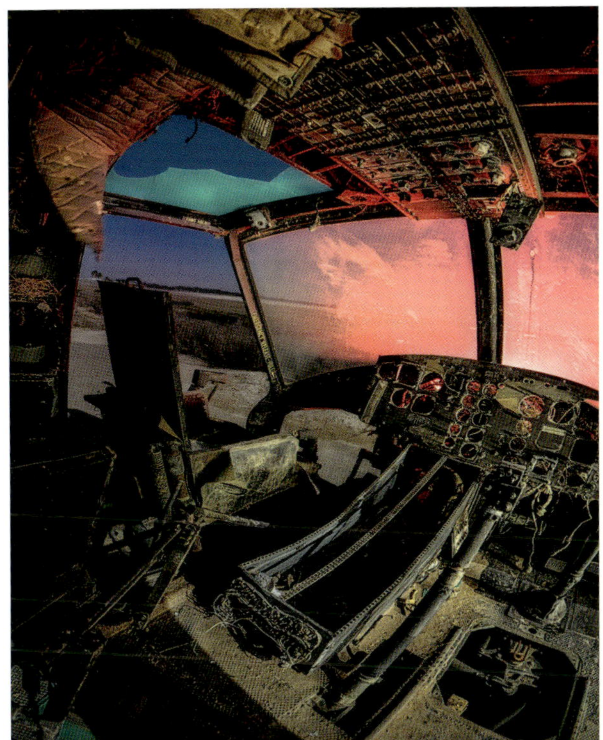

Red Iroquois, cockpit, Bell QUH-1M Iroquois helicopter, often known as "Huey." Designed for medical evacuation, this is the first turbine-powered helicopter produced for the U.S. military. Eagle Field.
Nikon D750/Rokinon 12-mm f/2.8 fisheye lens. One minute thirty-nine seconds f/8 ISO 200. February 2020. Full moon, warm white and red light from ProtoMachines LED2.

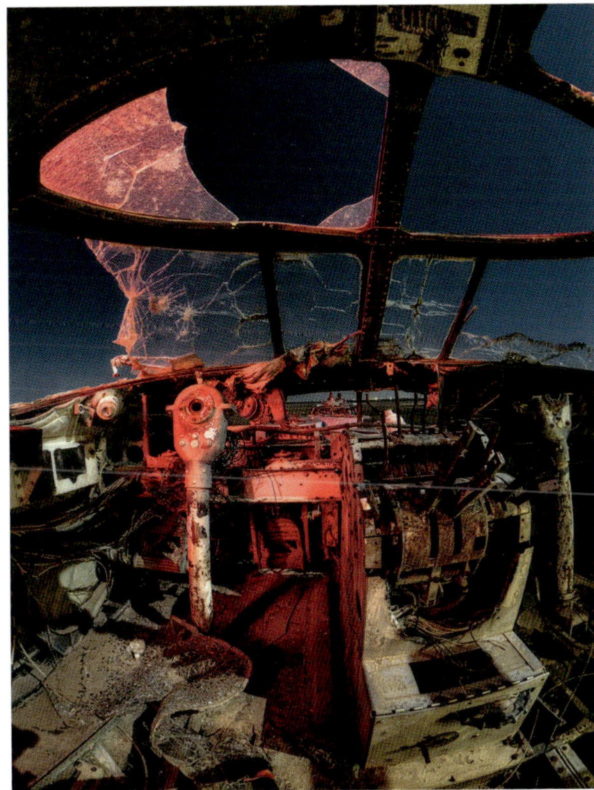

Neptune's Ray, cockpit, dismantled P2V-3W Neptune, Eagle Field. The warm white light was mostly reflected either from my hand or the back of the surprisingly tiny cockpit.
Nikon D750/Rokinon 12-mm f/2.8 fisheye lens. One minute f/8 ISO 200. February 2020.
Full moon, warm white light and red light from ProtoMachines LED2.

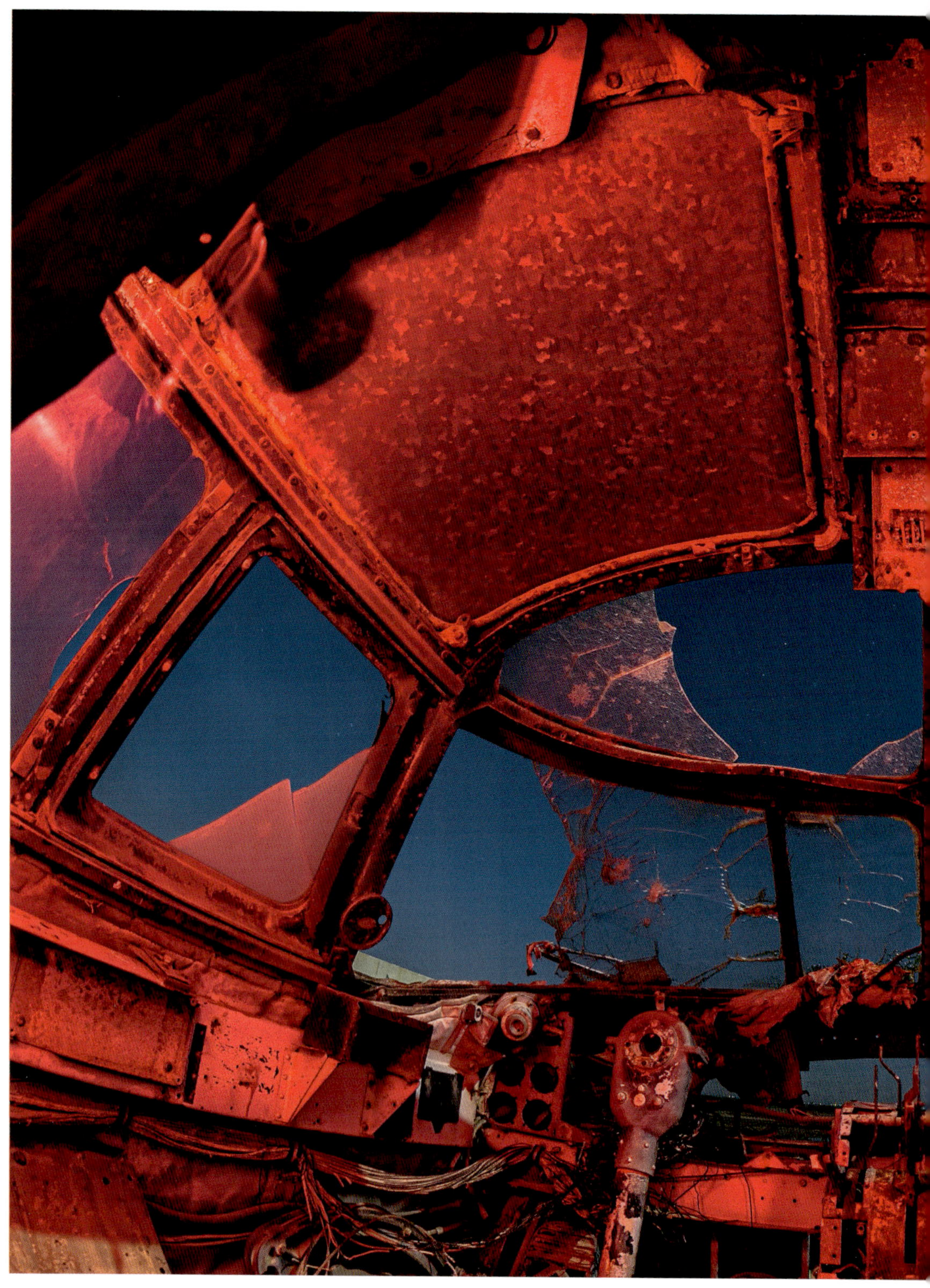

Neptune's Inferno, dismantled P2V-3W Neptune aircraft, Eagle Field. The red light was mostly reflected either from my hand or the back of the surprisingly tiny cockpit.

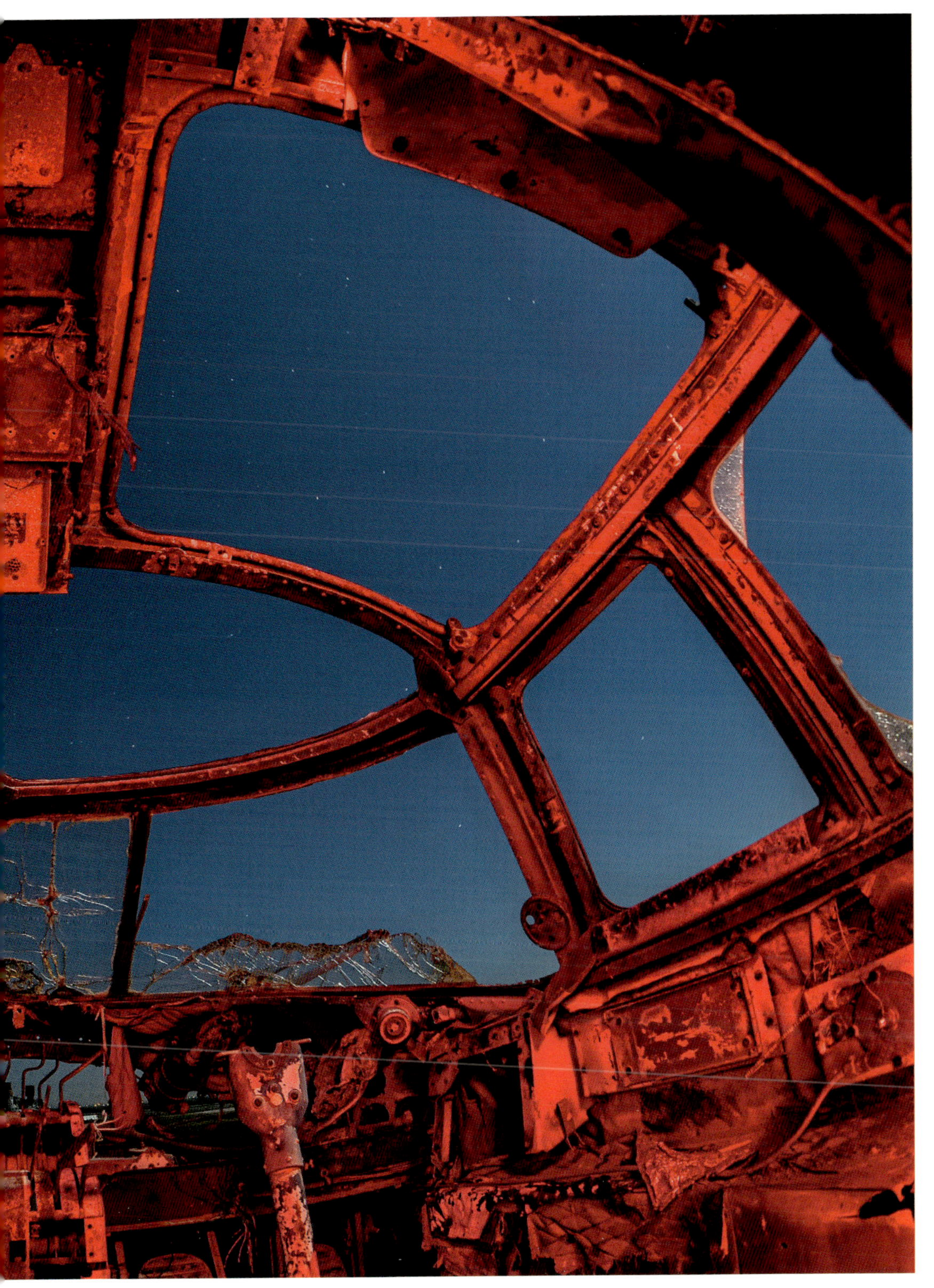

Nikon D750/Rokinon 12-mm f/2.8 fisheye lens. One minute f/8 ISO 200. February 2020. Full moon, red light from ProtoMachines LED2.

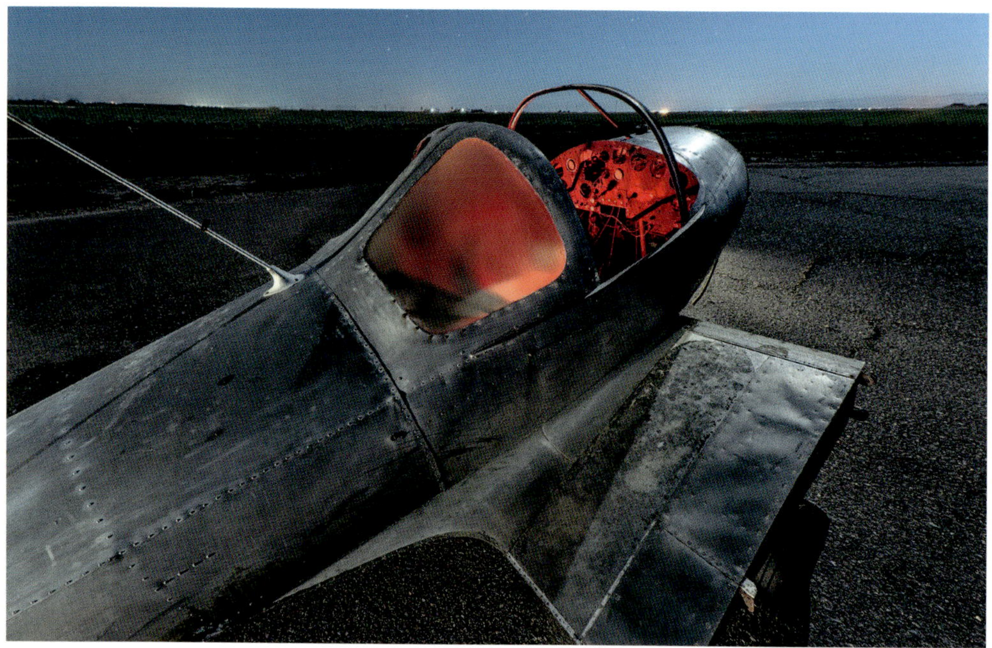

The Plane of Tomorrow, Today, ERCO ErCoupe began rolling off the assembly line around 1937. The Ercoupe was rudderless, flown completely via the control wheel in an attempt to make it virtually incapable of spinning. Eagle Field.
Nikon D750/Nikkor 14–24-mm f/2.8 lens. Thirty-two seconds f/8 ISO 800. April 2019.
Full moon, warm white light and red light from ProtoMachines LED2.

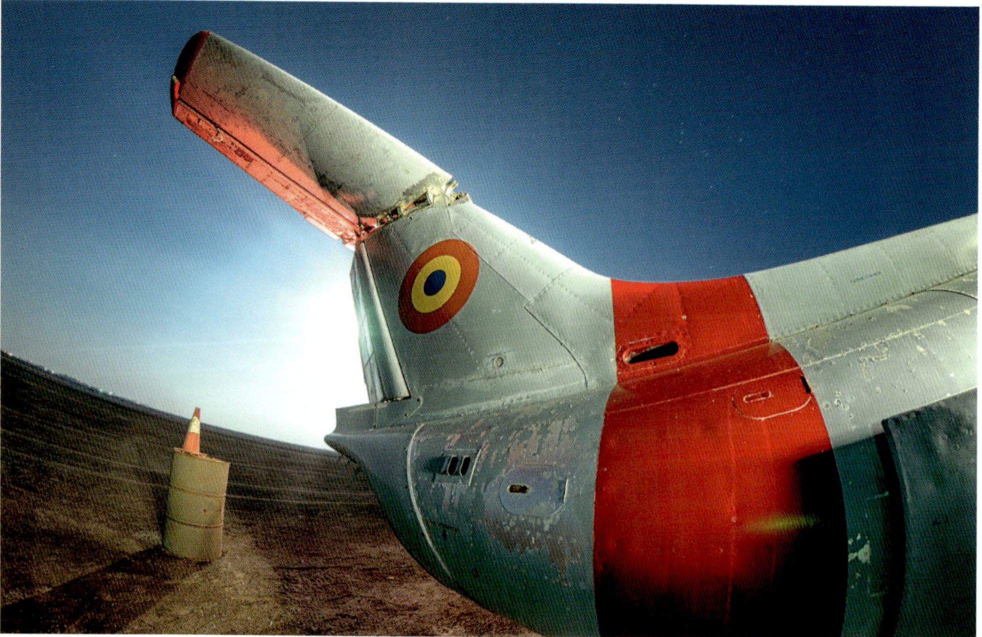

Air Romania, Aero L-29 Delfín, originally by Romania, shipped to the U.S. in pieces and now slowly being reassembled at Eagle Field.
Nikon D750/Rokinon 12-mm f/2.8 fisheye lens. One minute thirty-nine seconds f/8 ISO 200. February 2020.
Full moon, red light from ProtoMachines LED2.

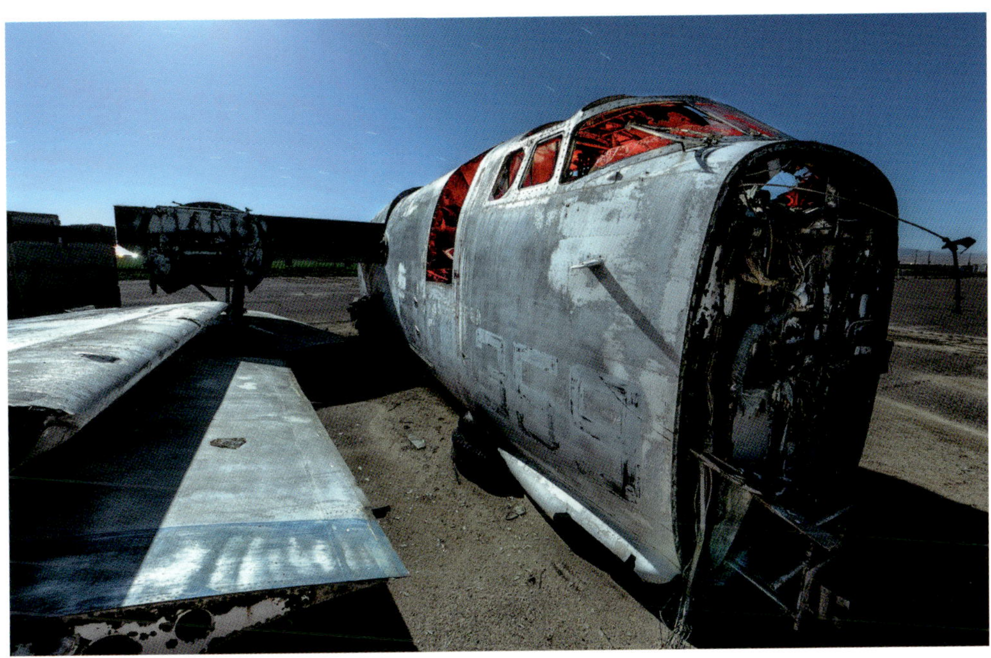

In the Wake of Neptune, dismantled P2V-3W Neptune aircraft, Eagle Field.
Nikon D750/Nikkor 14–24-mm f/2.8 lens. Three minutes f/8 ISO 800. April 2019.
Full moon, warm white light and red light from ProtoMachines LED2.

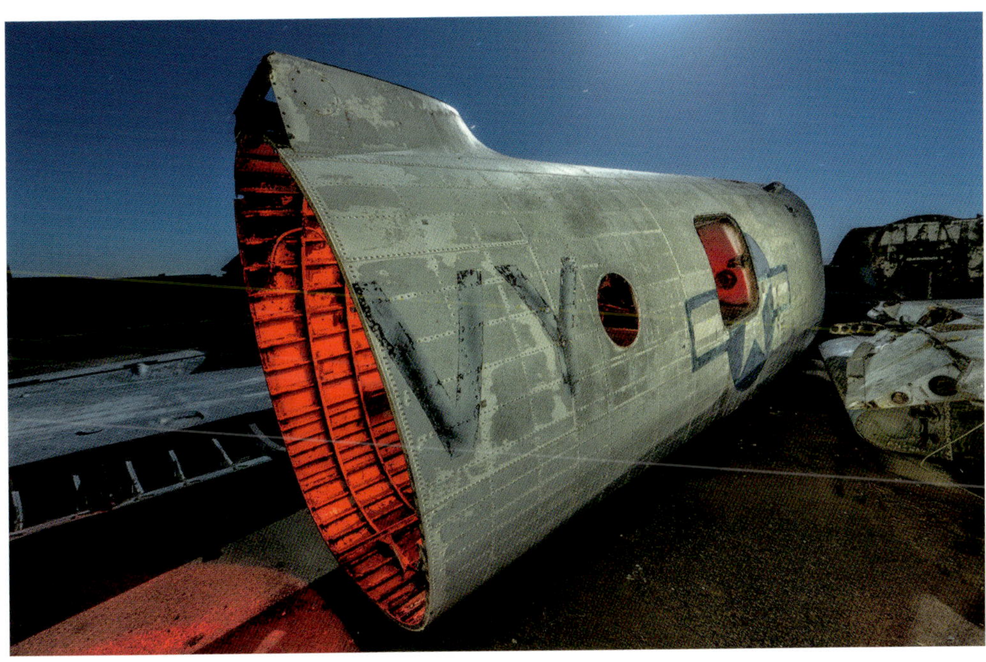

In the Navy, dismantled P2V-3W Neptune aircraft, Eagle Field.
Nikon D750/Nikkor 14–24-mm f/2.8 lens. Two minutes twenty-five seconds f/8 ISO 200. April 2019.
Full moon, warm white light and red light from ProtoMachines LED2.

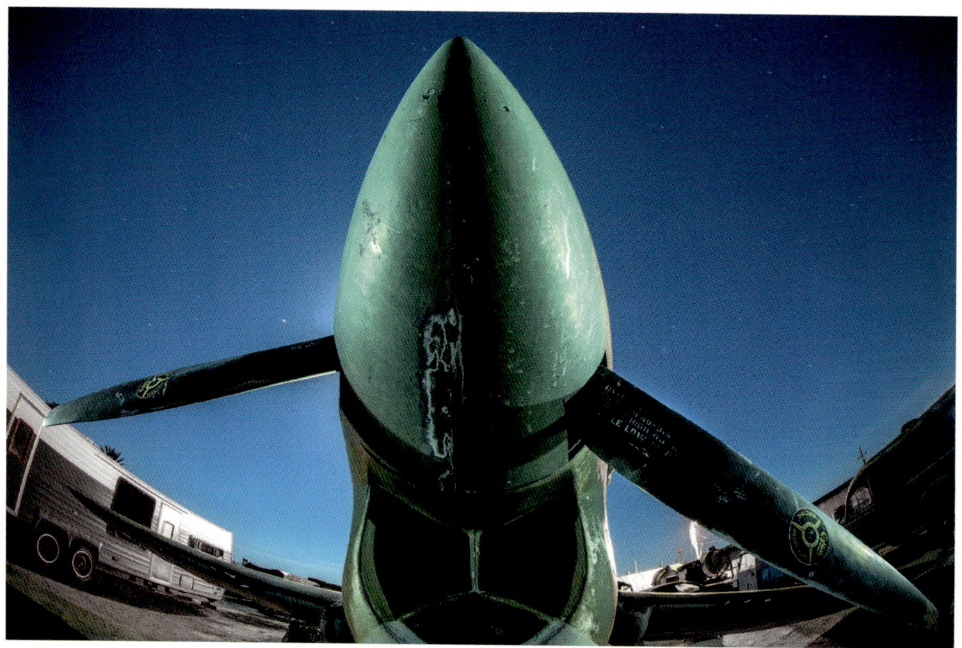

Nose Over Tail, the front nose of a Curtiss P-40 Warhawk, a single-engined, single-seat, all-metal fighter and ground-attack aircraft that first flew in 1938.
Nikon D750/Nikkor 12-mm f/2.8 fisheye lens. Two minutes fifty-one seconds f/8 ISO 200. September 2018. Full moon, lit on both sides with warm white light from ProtoMachines LED2.

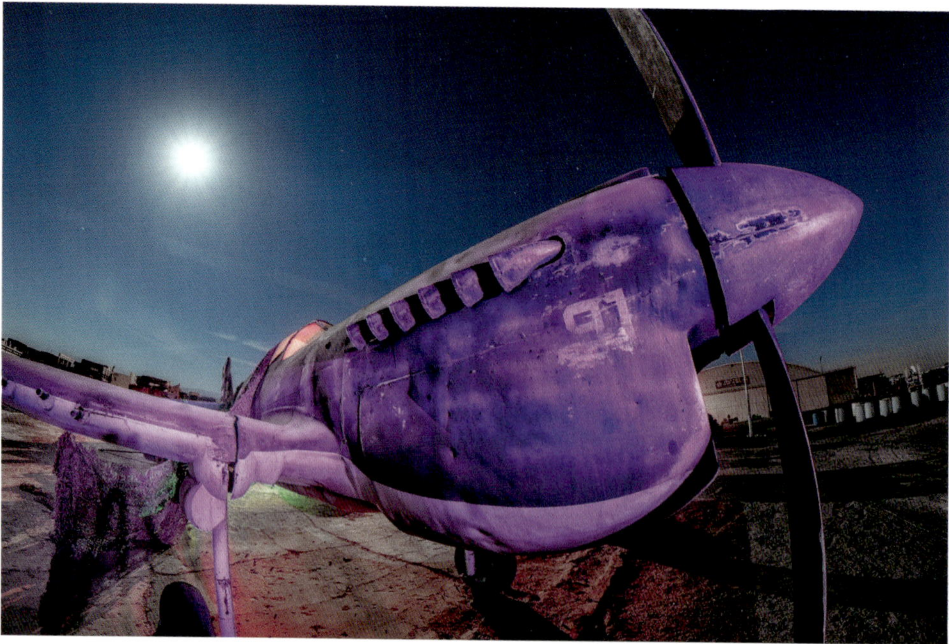

Purple Reign, Curtiss P-40 Warhawk, Eagle Field. I rarely illuminate scenes in purple and yellow, but did so here just to switch it up.
Nikon D750/Nikkor 12-mm f/2.8 fisheye lens. Two minutes fifty-one seconds f/8 ISO 200. September 2018. Full moon, purple light, backlit by a muted yellow light from ProtoMachines LED2.

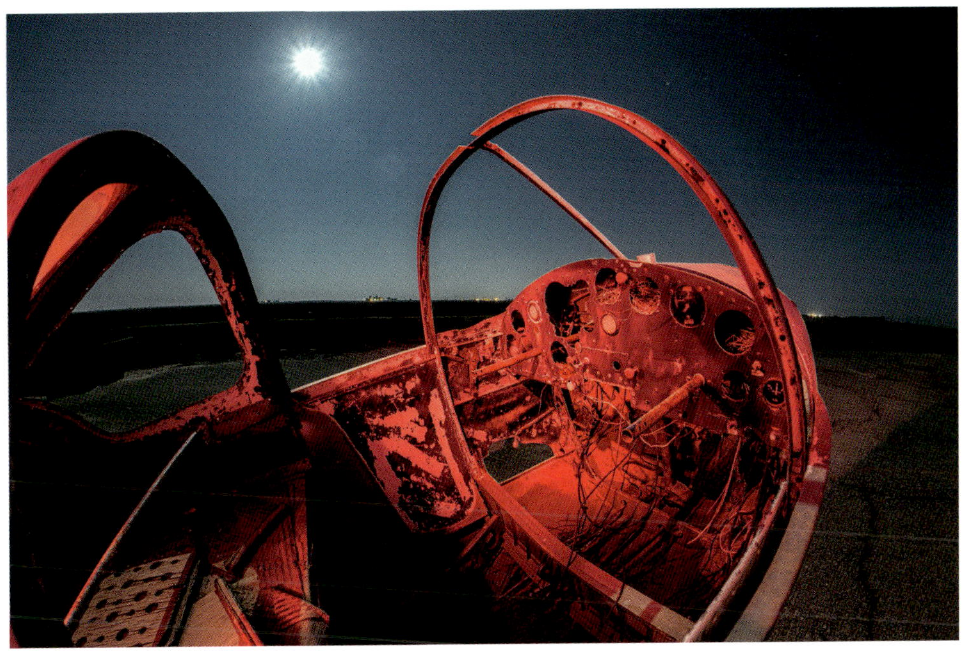

The Plane That Flies Itself, inside the cockpit of an ERCO ErCoupe, a low-wing monoplane trainer. The dream was that anyone could fly it. Eagle Field.
Nikon D750/Rokinon 12-mm f/2.8 fisheye lens. One minute thirty-nine seconds f/8 ISO 200. February 2020.
Full moon, red light from ProtoMachines LED2

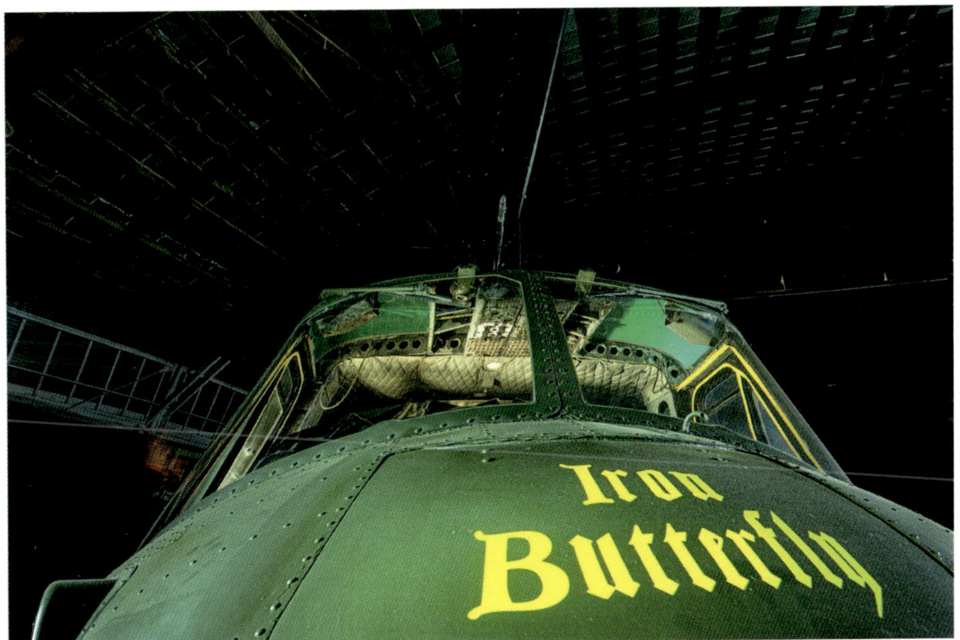

Iron Butterfly, looking up at a Bell UH-1 Huey "Iron Butterfly" helicopter used in Vietnam. Photographed in total darkness inside an airplane hangar, Eagle Field.
Nikon D610/Nikkor 14–24-mm f/2.8 lens. Three minutes f/8 ISO 200. April 2018.
Warm white light from ProtoMachines LED2.

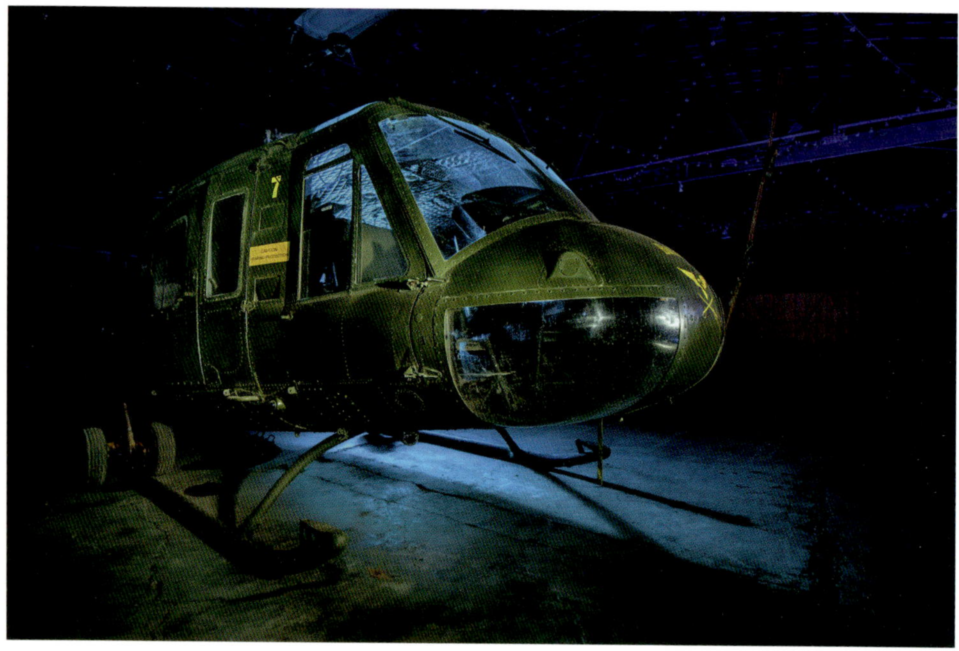

Con Tiki Blue, backlit Cessna L-19A airplane that I keep thinking looks like a helicopter because of the missing wings. Halloween night during a blue moon. Eagle Field.
Pentax K-1/15–30-mm f/2.8 lens. Two minutes f/8 ISO 200. October 2020.
Full moon, streetlight in back, blue light from ProtoMachines LED2.

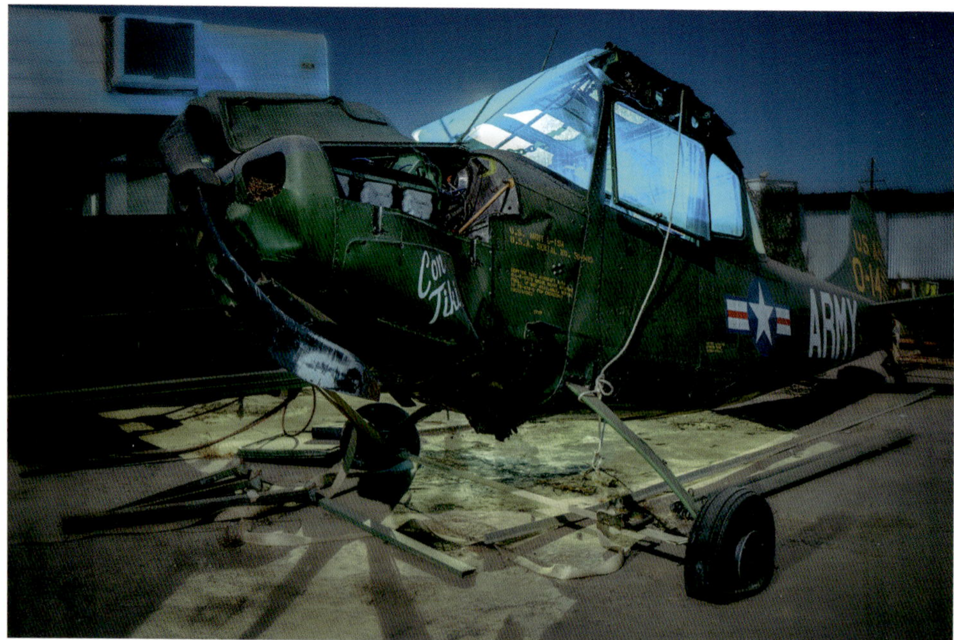

Blue Huey, Bell UH-1 Huey "Iron Butterfly" helicopter used in Vietnam. Photographed in total darkness inside an airplane hangar, Eagle Field.
Nikon D610/Nikkor 14–24-mm f/2.8 lens. One minute forty-seven seconds f/8 ISO 200. October 2020.
Teal (Gas Station Teal) and blue light from ProtoMachines LED2.

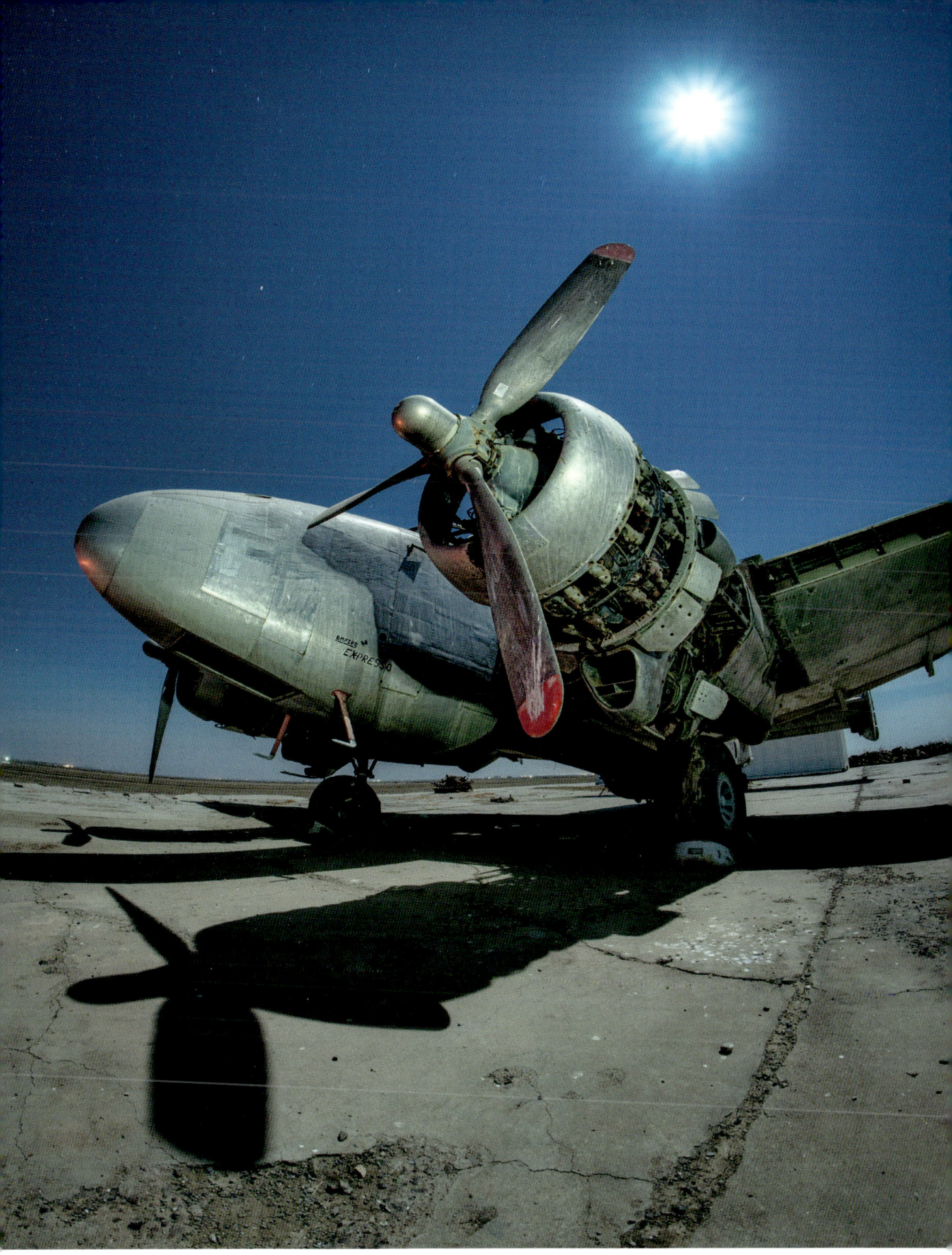

Moon Propeller, a fisheye view of a Lockheed Harpoon on a spontaneous trip to photograph at Eagle Field on a Halloween night featuring a blue moon.
Nikon D750/Rokinon 12mm f/2.8 lens. Two minutes f/8 ISO 200. Halloween 2020.
Full moon, warm white light from ProtoMachines LED2.

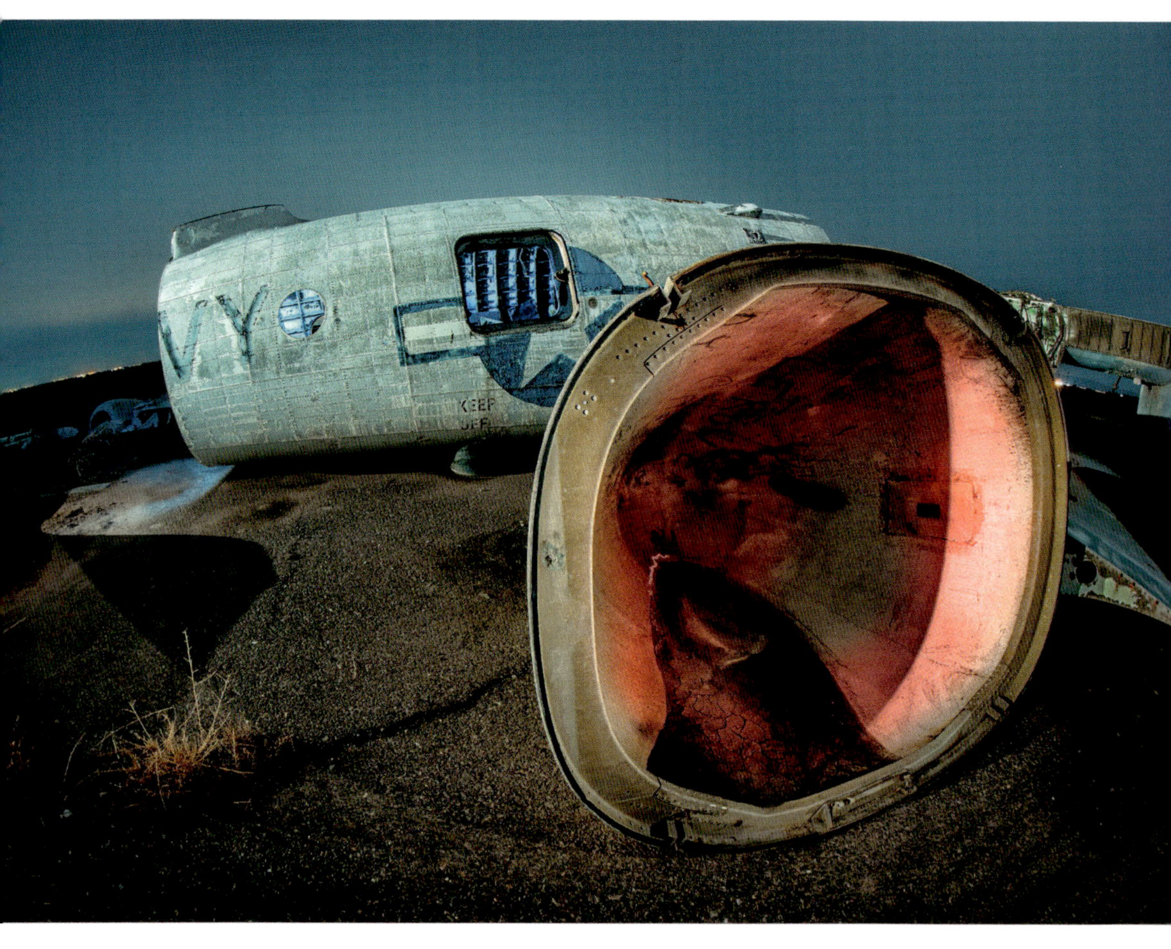

Lorena, dismantled P2V-3W Neptune aircraft, Eagle Field.
Nikon D750/Rokinon 12mm f/2.8 lens. 138 seconds f/8 ISO 250. December 2020.
Full moon, strong ambient light, warm white, blue-green, and red light from ProtoMachines LED2.

Warbirds

I first see the looming dark shape of an aircraft. Even in silhouette, the massive size and presence fill me with wonder. Further on, two more silhouettes, so impossibly massive, I cannot help but think: how did this ever get off the ground? Photographing at night here feels like a peaceful privilege, although this is punctuated occasionally by a sudden loud creak stirred by the desert wind.

At one point, my friend walks up to me, smiling in amazement, mentioning what a tight squeeze it is getting up in the cockpit. I am incredulous. "You can go up in there?" I realize that I am so filled with awe by these monuments of achievement that it never occurred to me that I could go inside. But now I cannot get this out of my head.

I switch to a fisheye lens so I can photograph as much of the cockpit as possible. Then I crawl inside. Thankfully, it is easy to shimmy up. A childhood filled with climbing trees and building treehouses has prepared me for this. Despite being over six feet tall, I squeeze up inside. The interior is filled with jagged metal, so I take extra caution. I manage to squat down carefully and set up my tripod. It seems like it would have been horribly uncomfortable to fly in this small space for hours.

Looking out the broken windows, I feel like I am Captain Nemo inside the *Nautilus*. I try to solve how I am going to illuminate the interior of the cockpit in a pleasing manner when I can barely move. I want the light to look great and accentuate the detail. I hold the ProtoMachines LED2 light painting device so that it bounces off some of the metal in the back. I also reflect some of the light off my hand as well. After numerous attempts, I am satisfied with my approach. I try several different colors, but red feels best. I keep photographing until I have to leave because I need to answer the call of nature. Sometimes, that is how we determine how long we photograph in a particular location.

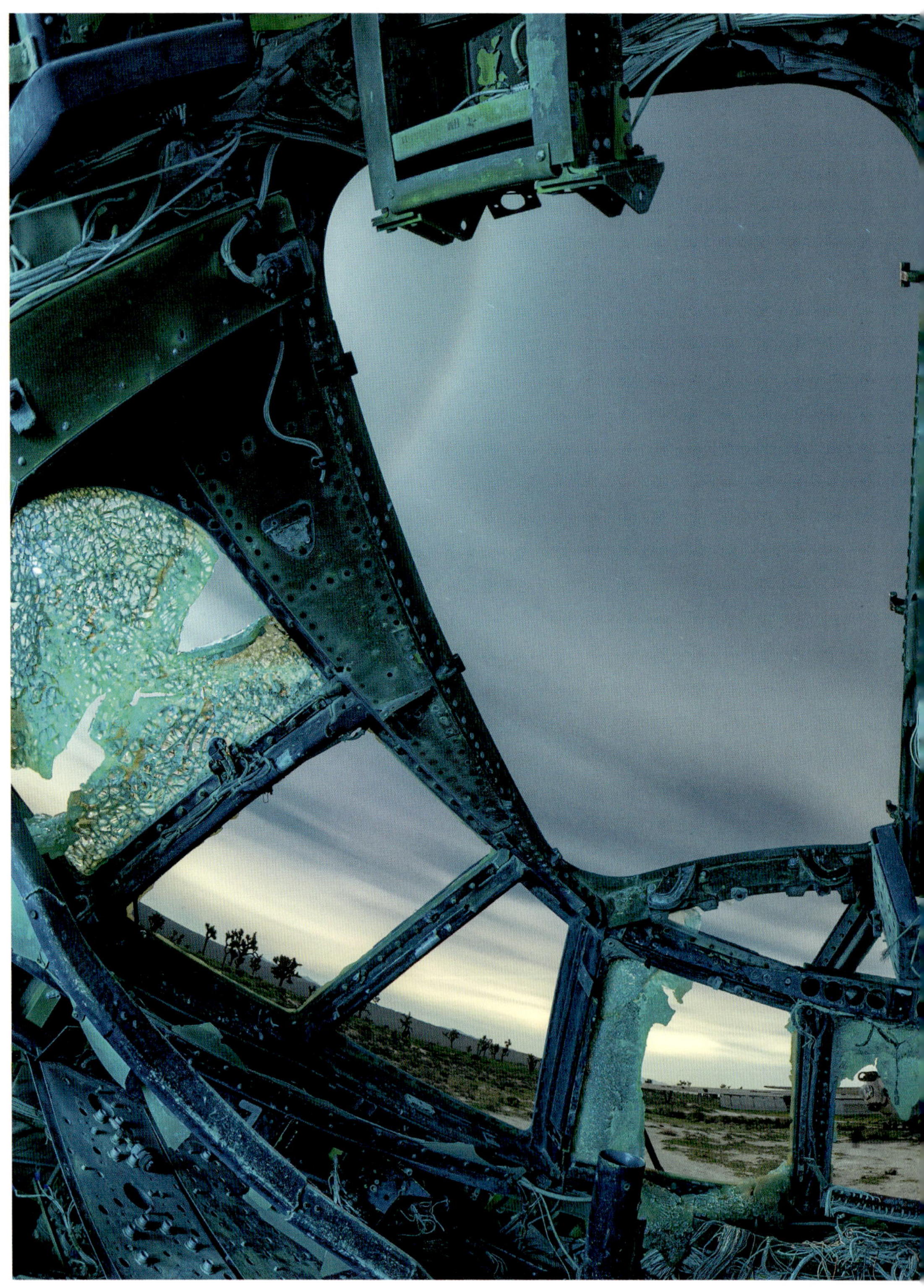

Tales of the Nautilus, inside the cockpit of an abandoned Mojave warbird.

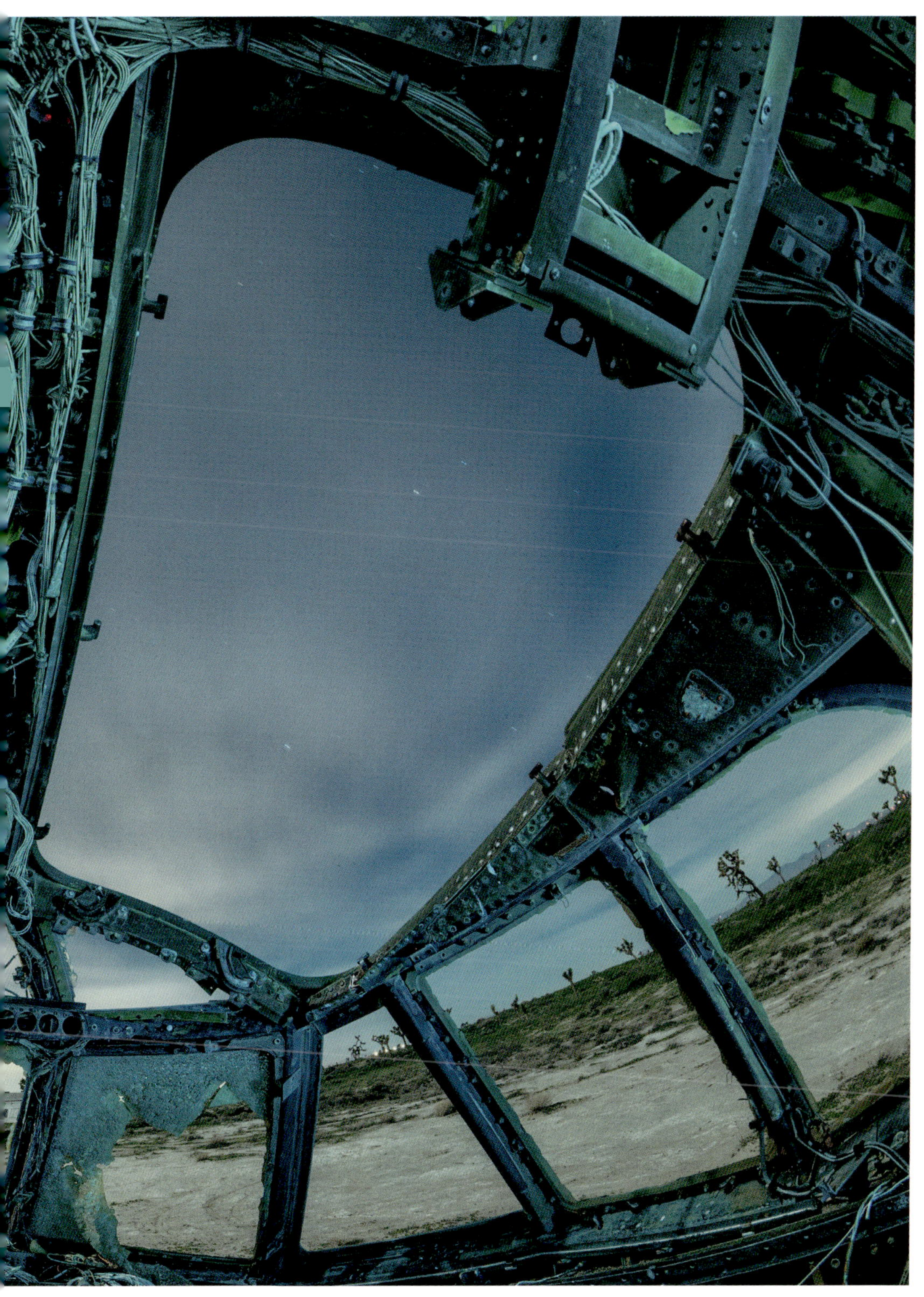

Nikon D610/Rokinon 12-mm f/2.8 fisheye lens. Two minutes f/8 ISO 200. March 2019.
Full moon, green light from ProtoMachines LED2.

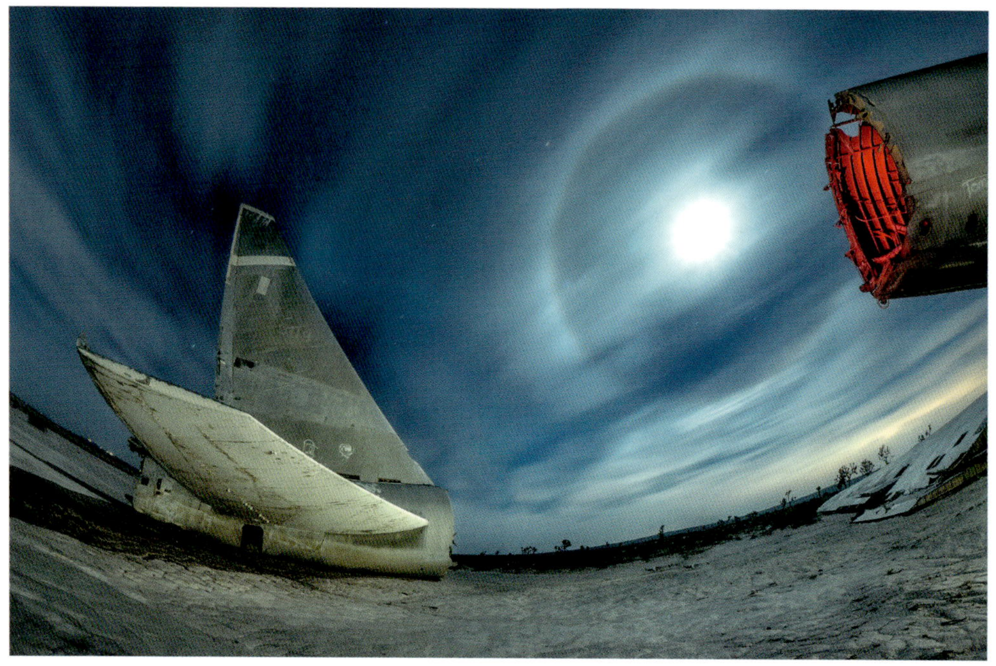

Night of the First Photon Torpedo, Mojave warbird. The severed fuselage looks like it is spitting out a white orb or a photon torpedo.
Nikon D610/Rokinon 12-mm f/2.8 fisheye lens. Two minutes f/8 ISO 200. March 2019.
Full moon, warm white and red light from ProtoMachines LED2.

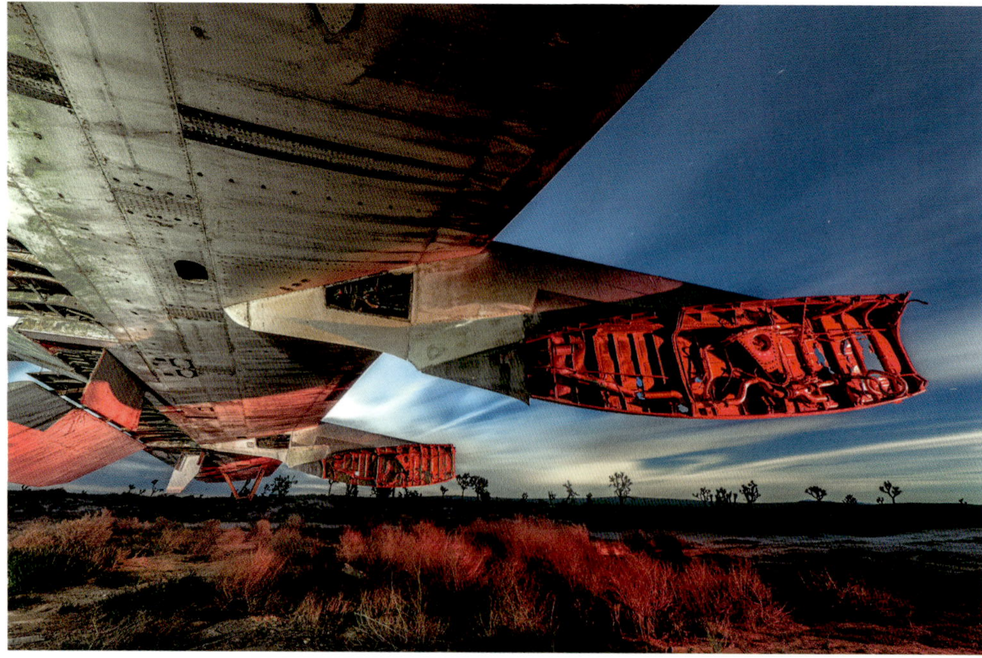

Sun Dragon, underneath the massive wing of a Mojave warbird.
Nikon D750/Nikkor 14–24-mm f/2.8 lens. Two minutes nine seconds f/8 ISO 320. March 2019.
Full moon, warm white and red light from ProtoMachines LED2.

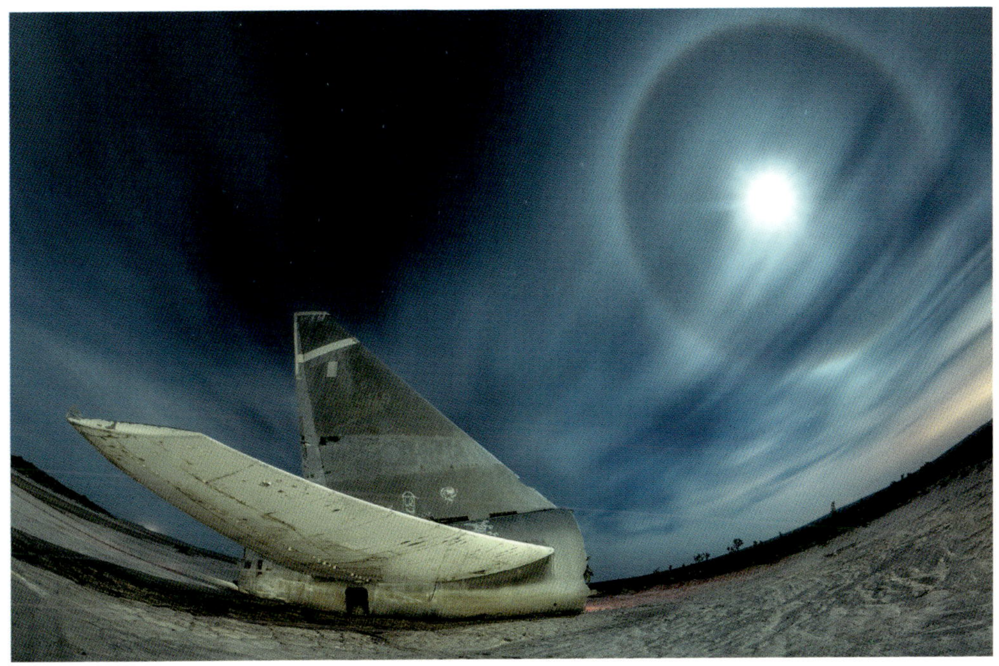

Moon Tail, Mojave warbird and a moon with a halo.
Nikon D610/Rokinon 12-mm f/2.8 fisheye lens. Two minutes f/8 ISO 200. March 2019.
Full moon, warm white light from ProtoMachines LED2.

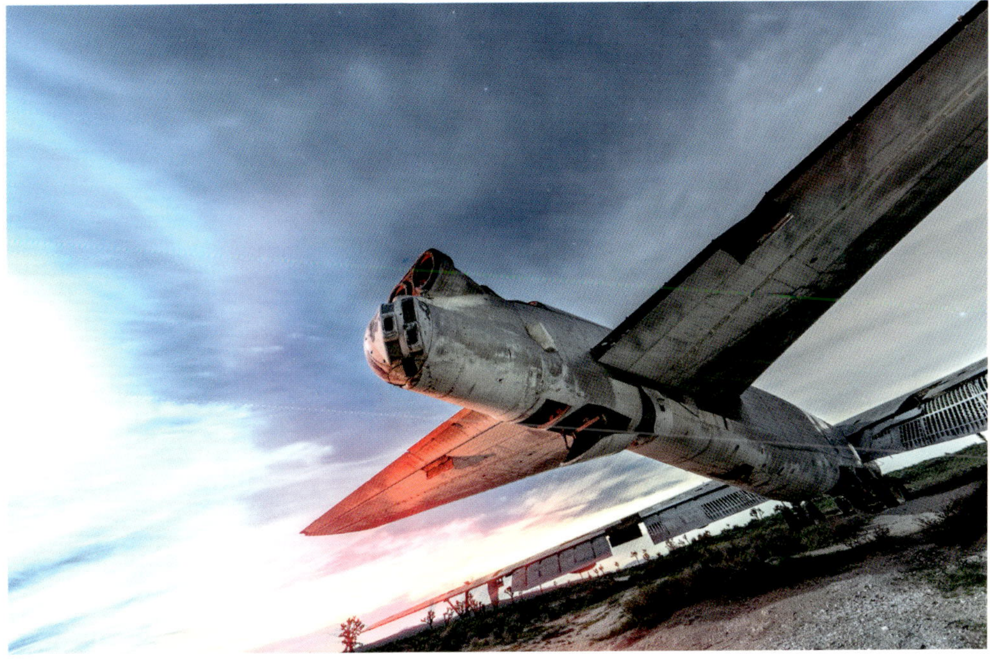

Red Wings, the gun turret of a magnificent Mojave warbird.
Nikon D750/Nikkor 14–24-mm f/2.8 lens. Ten seconds f/8 ISO 1250. March 2019.
Full moon, warm white and red light from ProtoMachines LED2.

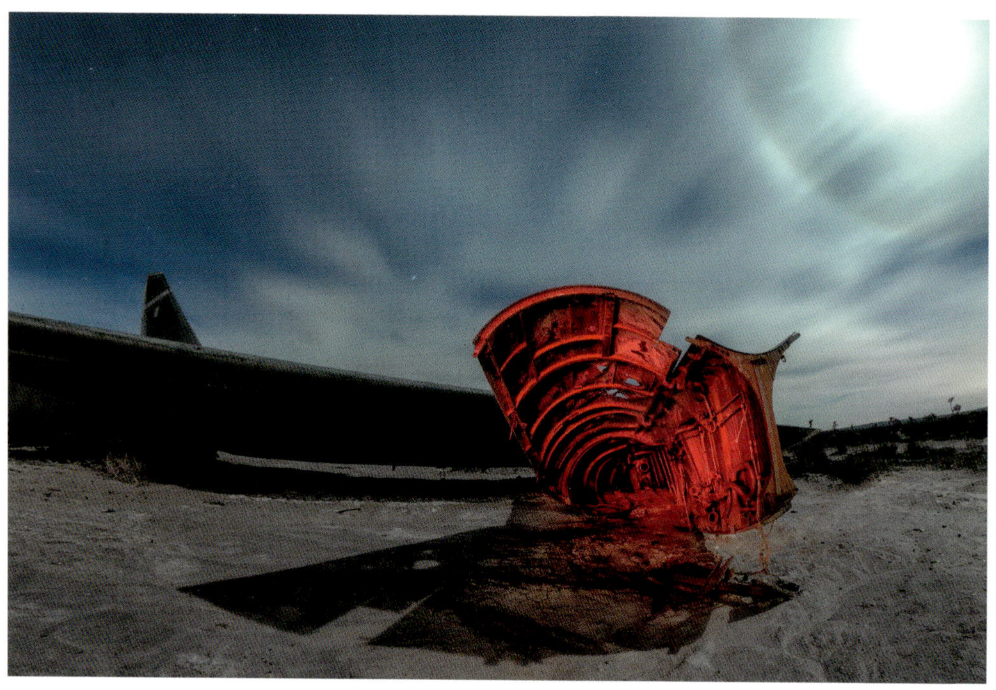

Warp Drive, Mojave warbird with a broken wing.
Nikon D610/Rokinon 12-mm f/2.8 fisheye lens. Two minutes f/8 ISO 200. March 2019.
Full moon, warm white and red light from ProtoMachines LED2.

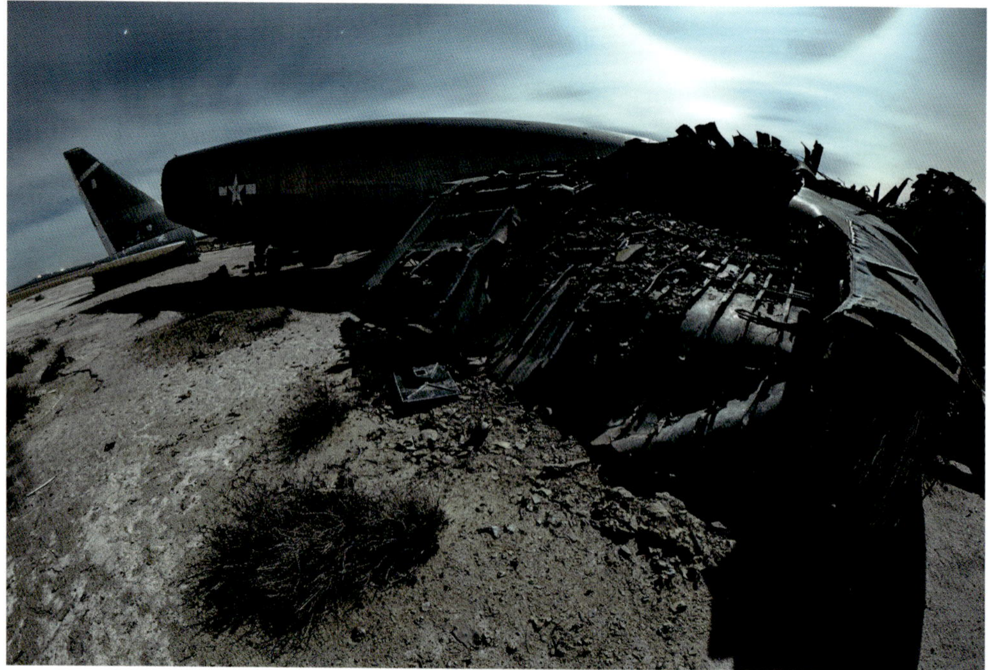

Washed Ashore, Mojave warbird underneath a full moon with a halo.
Nikon D610/Rokinon 12-mm f/2.8 fisheye lens. Two minutes f/8 ISO 320. March 2019.
Full moon.

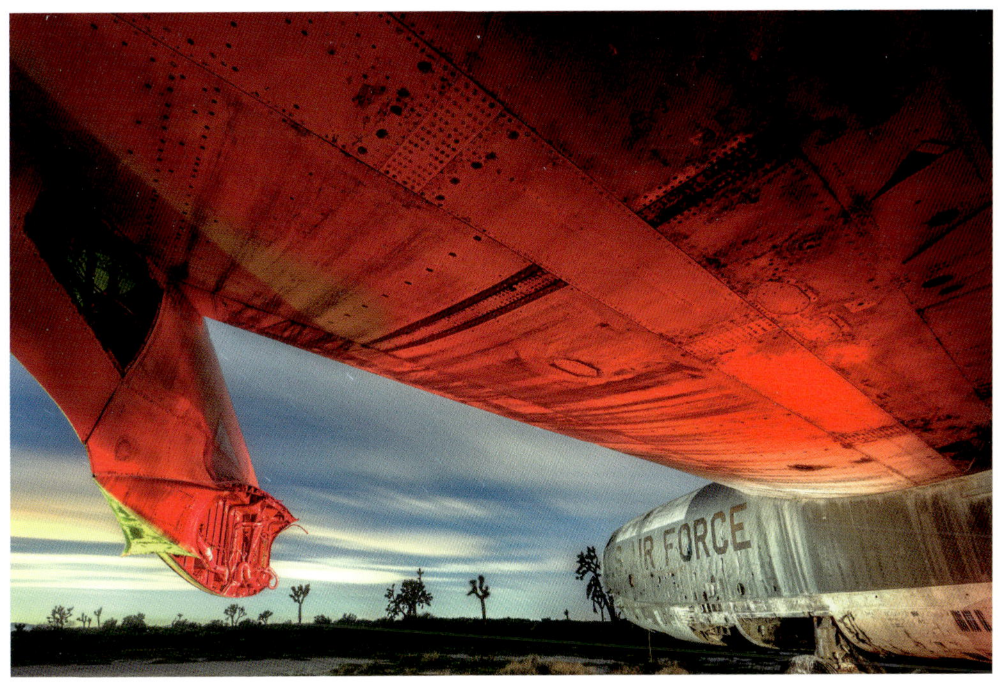

No Wind Beneath My Wing, underneath the massive wing of a Mojave warbird.
Nikon D750/Nikkor 14–24-mm f/2.8 lens. Three minutes thirty-one seconds f/8 ISO 320. March 2019.
Full moon, warm white and red light from ProtoMachines LED2.

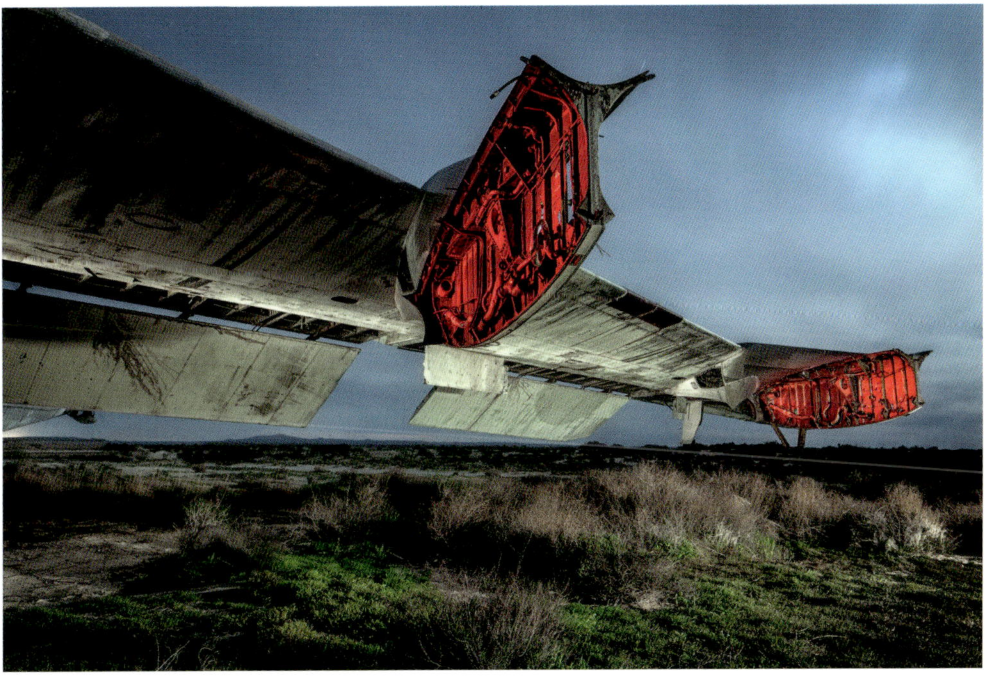

Wing of the Red Dragon, underneath the massive wing of a Mojave warbird.
Nikon D750/Nikkor 14–24-mm f/2.8 lens. Two minutes six seconds f/8 ISO 320. March 2019.
Full moon, warm white and red light from ProtoMachines LED2.

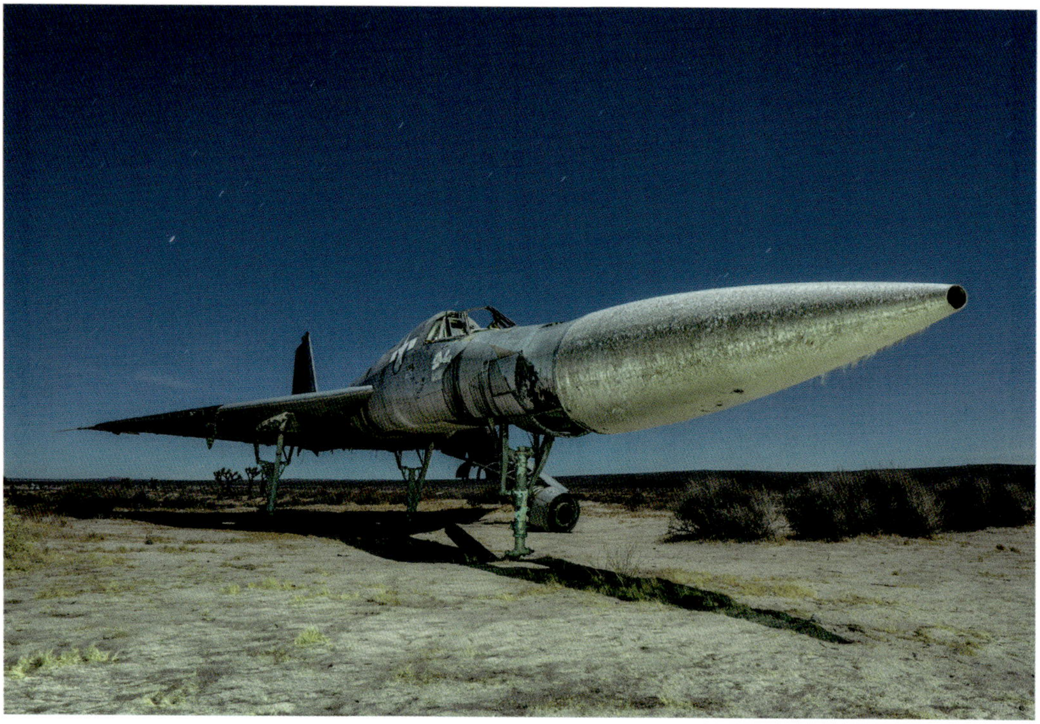

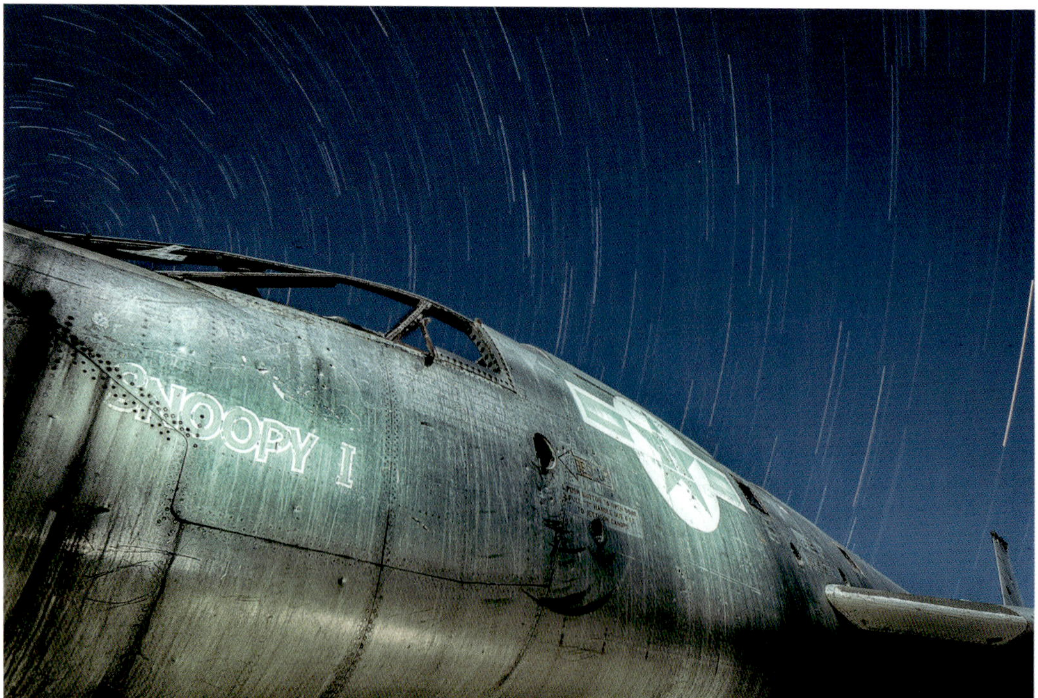

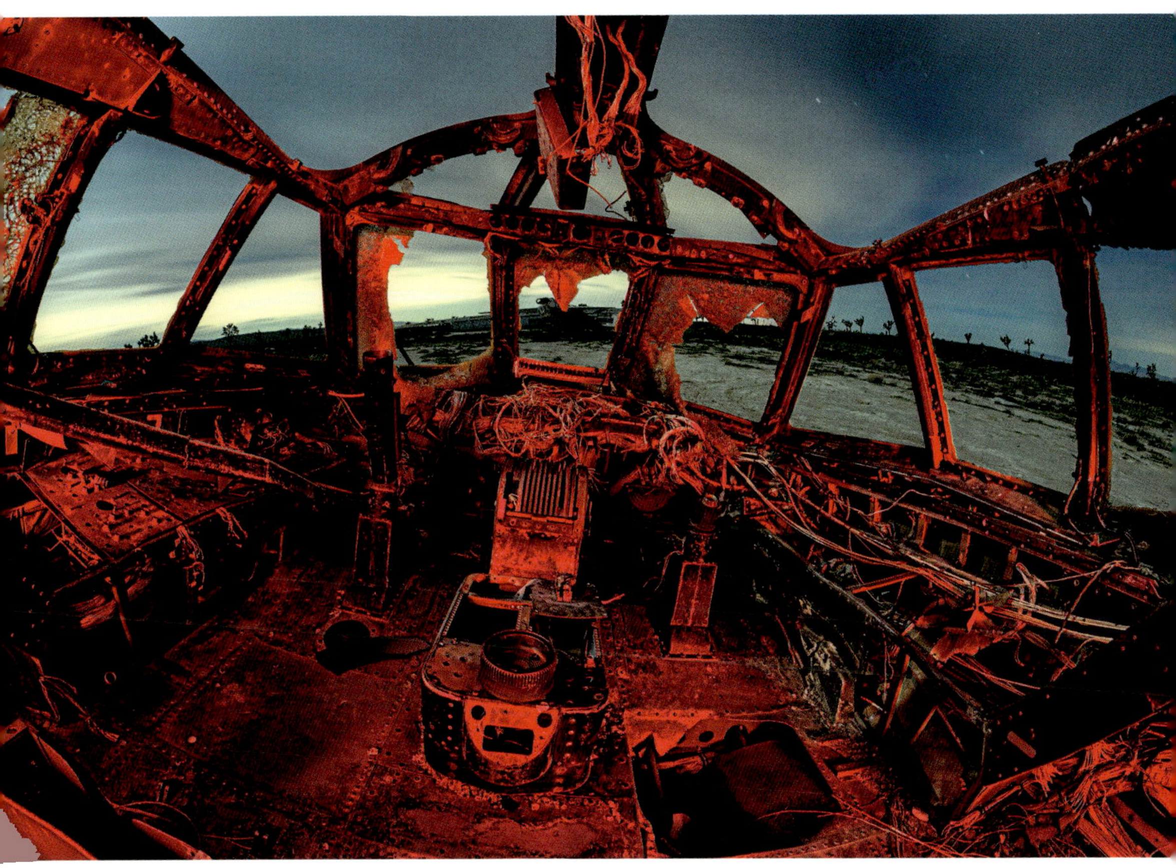

In the Event of Loss of Cabin Pressure, Masks Will Descend from the Ceiling, Mojave warbird. The red light was mostly reflected either from my hand or the back of the surprisingly tiny cockpit.
Nikon D610/Rokinon 12-mm f/2.8 fisheye lens. Two minutes f/8 ISO 200. March 2019.
Full moon, red light from ProtoMachines LED2.

Opposite page

▲ **Pinocchio**, a very long-nosed warbird in the Mojave desert.
Nikon D610/Nikkor 14–24-mm f/2.8 lens. Two minutes f/8 ISO 200. January 2018.
Full moon, warm white light from ProtoMachines LED2.

▼ **Curse You, Red Baron!**, Mojave Snoopy warbird close-up and personal.
Nikon D610/Nikkor 14–24-mm f/2.8 lens. Forty-eight-minute total exposure "stacked." Each photo two minutes f/8 ISO 200. January 2018.
Full moon, warm white and yellow light from ProtoMachines LED2.

Joe Davies Heritage Airpark

It is spring 2015. I am recovering from arthroscopic surgery due to a torn meniscus in my knee. I stopped limping a while ago and am going to physical therapy two times a week. It has been over half a year since I have done night photography. I had just been getting obsessed with it prior to the knee issues. Now I can walk all right but have limited mobility. I begin looking for something easy and flat, offering minimal chances for me to trip over rocks or cactus or uneven ground.

With thirty-seven browser tabs open, I come across Joe Davies Heritage Airpark in Palmdale. The airpark displays a collection of aircraft flown, tested, designed, produced or modified at U.S. Air Force Plant 42, all outside in a comfortable park setting. The collection of airplanes is remarkable. I grow excited, as this could be my first opportunity to photograph airplanes.

I contact the park and exchange emails with a very friendly person named Kathleen Whiteside, the facilities coordinator. She seems genuinely excited about it. It is on!

Driving up, I eat at Lee Esther's Creole and Cajun Cooking in Palmdale, the first of numerous times that would become a quasi-tradition whenever passing by the area to do night photography. I am greeted enthusiastically at the airpark by Kathleen. Fascinated with photography, she stays up quite late, sometimes watching me photograph, and is great company.

I notice I have lost that sort of "muscle memory" that night photographers develop. I have to think about the process and the settings on the intervalometer or the camera settings. But slowly, I begin to shake off the rust.

The area around the airpark has a lot of sodium vapor lights, casting an ugly orange glow on many of the airplanes, especially the ones closest to the street. I have to improvise and photograph at specific angles that block out the light. The C-46 Commando is bathed in orange light, so I aim the camera straight up at the cockpit instead. I have to photograph the F-14 Tomcat from the back. I begin photographing more of the ones that are farther back.

The 747 is a shuttle vehicle transport carrier, one of only two that ferried the space shuttles to and from destinations. And it is impossibly immense. This is farthest away from the sodium vapor lights, much better for night photography. I set up my smaller D7000 camera in just two positions, both for two-hour star trails. I then use my other camera to photograph elsewhere.

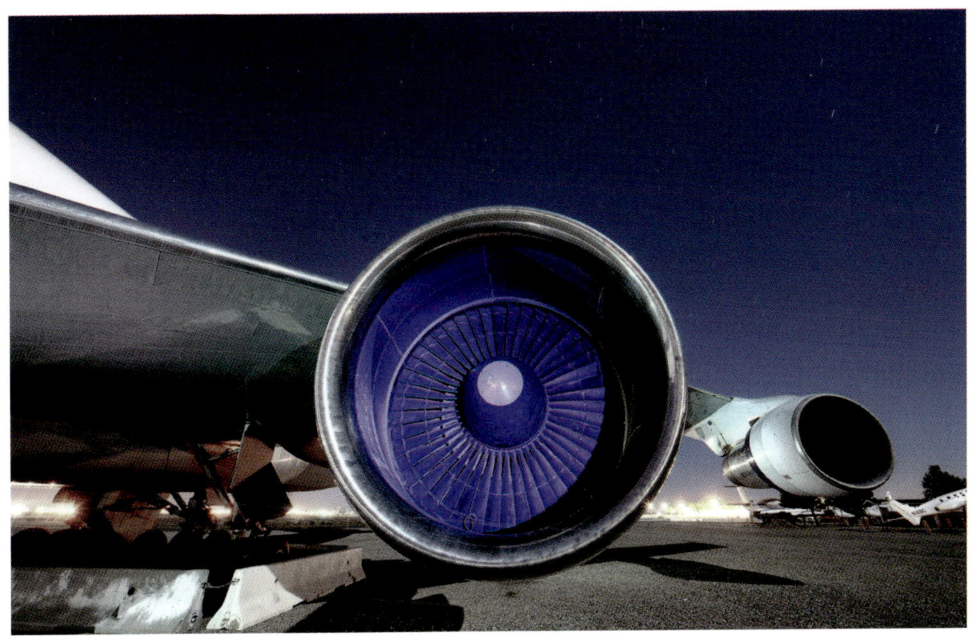

Engine of Change, Boeing 747 Tail #N911NA. Built by the Boeing Company, this shuttle vehicle transport carrier is one of two that ferried the space shuttles to and from destinations, and is on loan from NASA Armstrong, Joe Davies Heritage Airpark.
Nikon D610/Nikkor 14–24-mm f/2.8G lens. Two minutes fifty seconds f/8 ISO 200. March 2015.
Full moon, strong ambient light, warm white and purple light from ProtoMachines LED2.

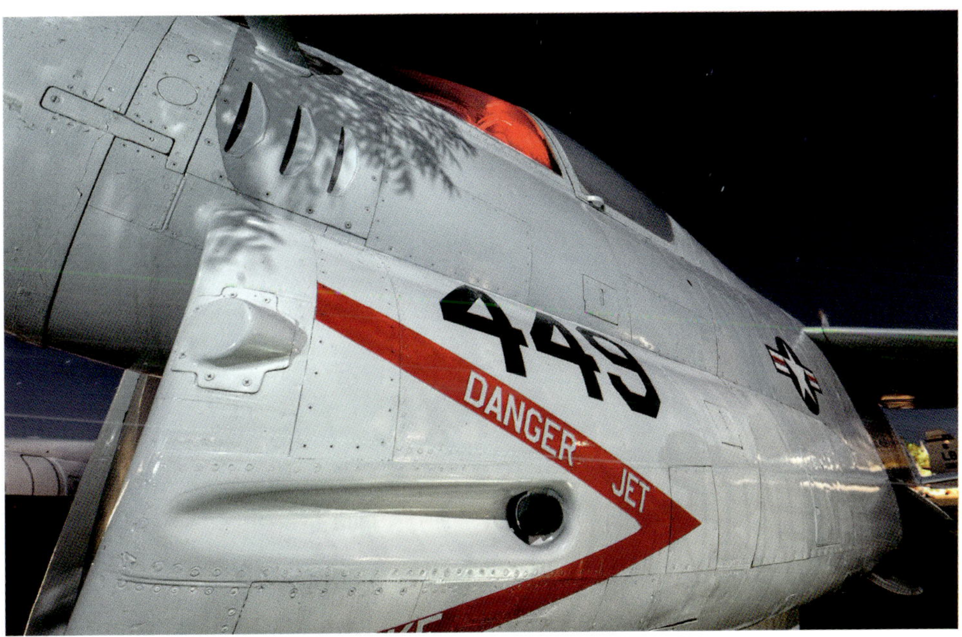

Danger Jet Intake, A-7 Corsair II BuNo. 15-4449. This aircraft was in operation from 1968 until 1987. In 1969, the plane served on both the USS *Roosevelt* and *Oriskany*. Restored at Joe Davies Heritage Airpark.
Nikon D610/Nikkor 14–24-mm f/2.8G lens. One minute fifty-seven seconds f/8 ISO 200. March 2015.
Full moon, warm white and red light from ProtoMachines LED2.

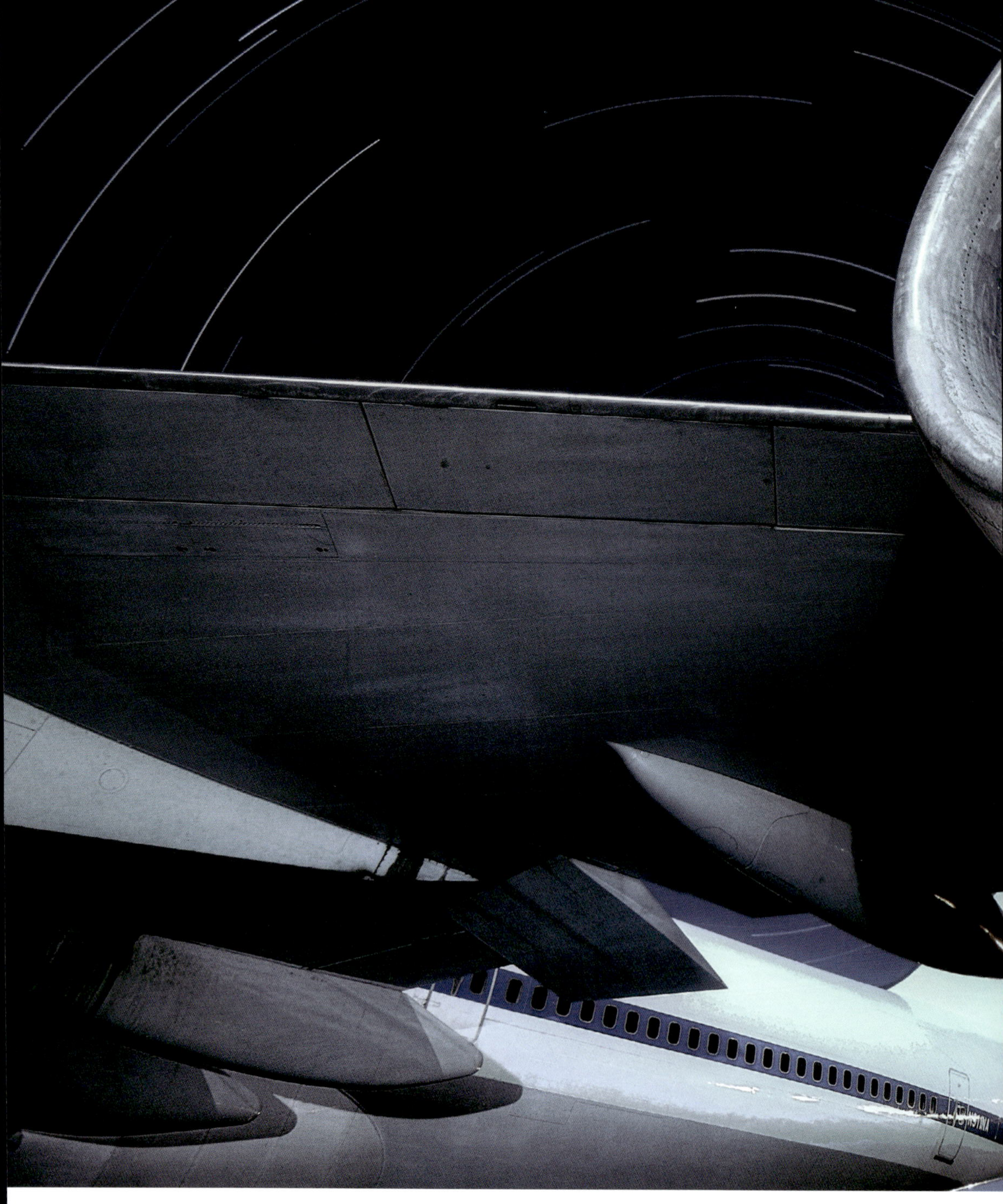

Reach for the Sky, Just Spread Your Wings, Boeing 747 Tail #N911NA shuttle vehicle transport carrier in a long exposure image showing the celestial movements for over two hours, Joe Davies Heritage Airpark.

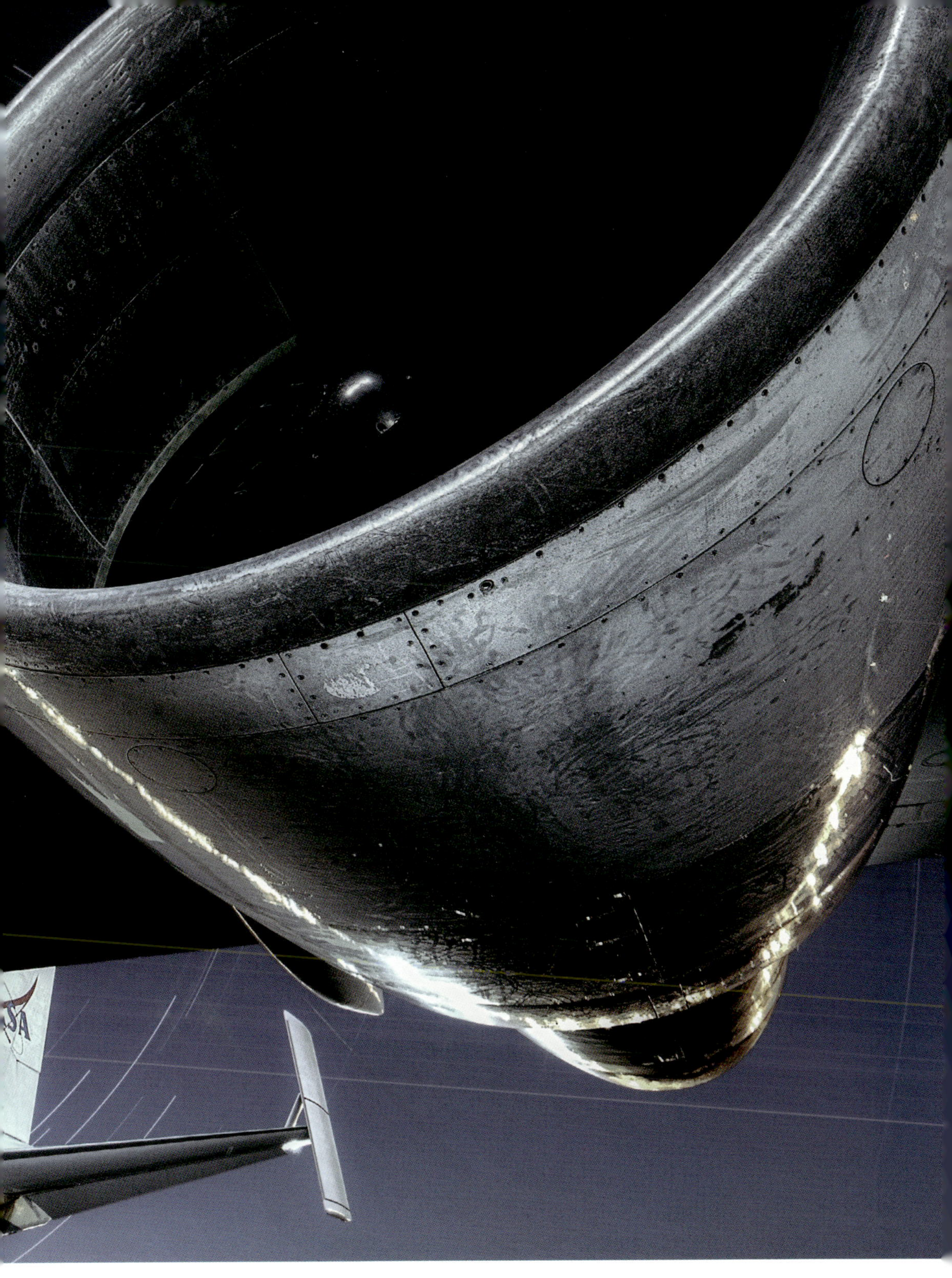

Nikon D7000/Tokina 11–16-mm f/2.8 lens. Two hours and twenty-one minutes total "stacked." Each photo was three minutes f/8 ISO 200. March 2015.
Full moon, strong ambient light, warm white light from ProtoMachines LED2.

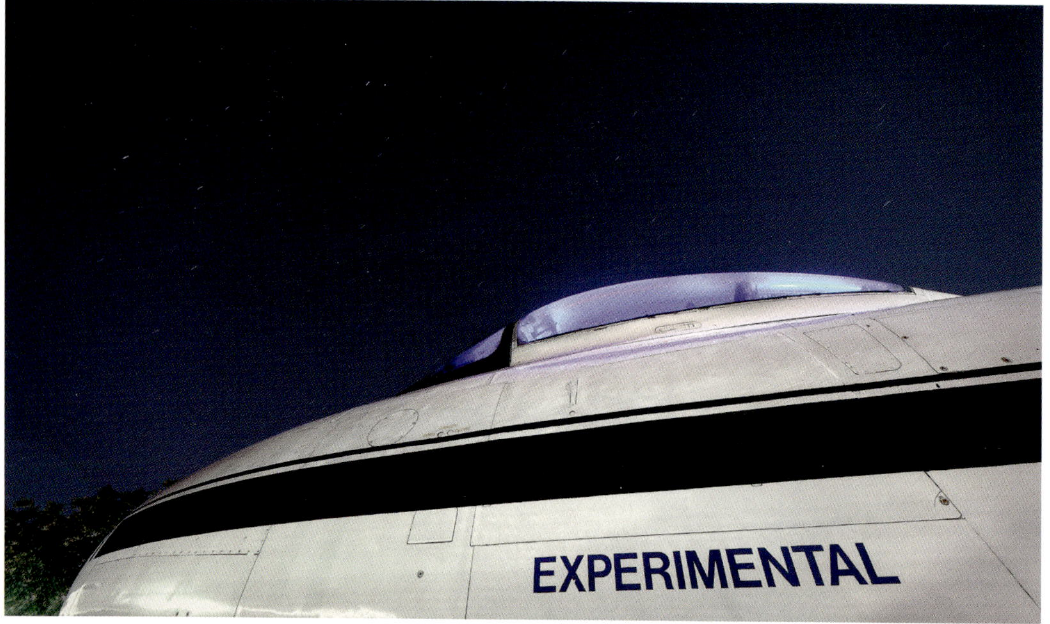

The Experimental Blues, CL-13 SABRE Mk 5 (aka F-86 Sabre) Tail # N91FS. Built by Canadair Ltd. Flew with the Royal Canadian Air Force and was then sold to TRACOR to use with pulling drones, hence "experimental" on its side. Joe Davies Heritage Airpark.
Nikon D610/Nikkor 14–24-mm f/2.8G lens. Two minutes thirty-five seconds f/8 ISO 200. March 2015.
Full moon, warm white and blue light from ProtoMachines LED2.

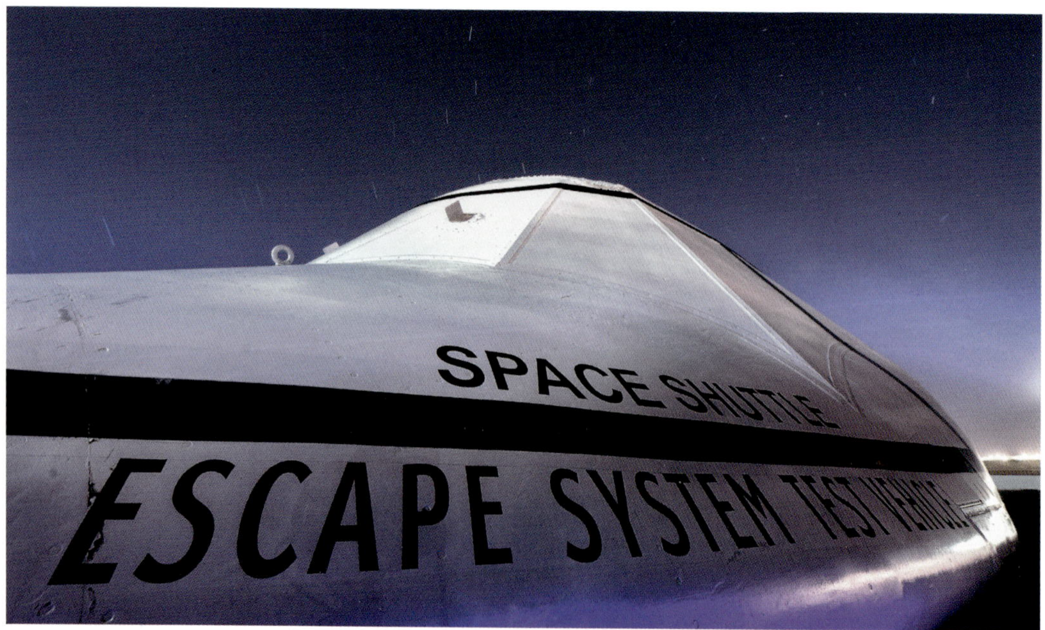

Space Shuttle Escape Pod, Space Shuttle Escape System Test Vehicle Prototype. After the Space Shuttle *Challenger* disaster, NASA grounded all fleets and then created an escape system for future flights. Joe Davies Heritage Airpark.
Nikon D610/Nikkor 14–24-mm f/2.8G lens. Ten-minute twenty-one-second exposure f/9 ISO 200. March 2015.
Full moon, strong ambient light, warm white and red light from ProtoMachines LED2.

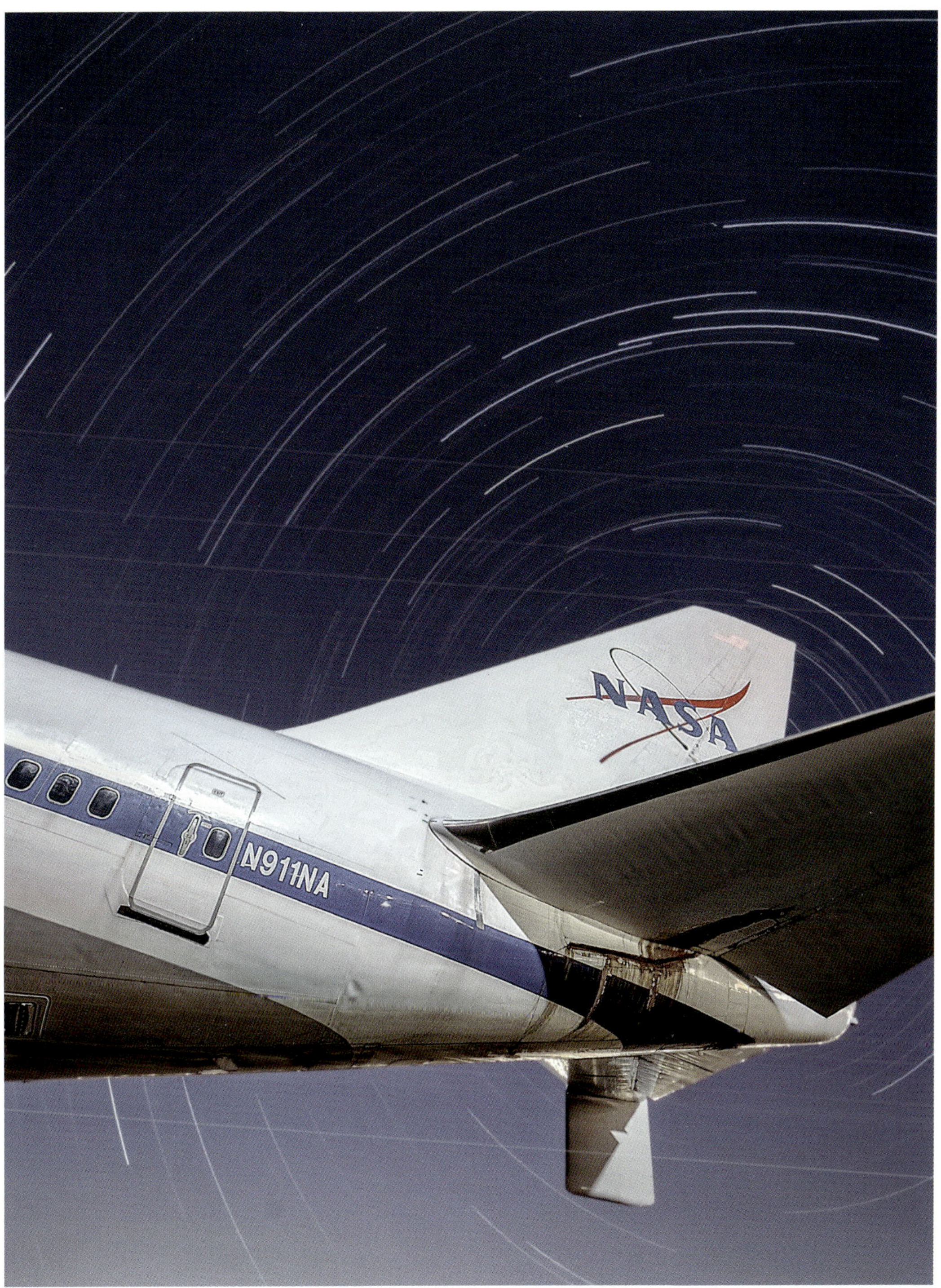

NASA Space Shuttle Carrier Tail Star Trails, Boeing 747 Tail #N911NA shuttle vehicle transport carrier in a long exposure image showing the celestial movements for almost two hours. Joe Davies Heritage Airpark.
Nikon D7000/Tokina 11–16-mm f/2.8 lens. One hour fifty-one minutes total "stacked"; each photo was three minutes exposure f/8 ISO 200. March 2015.
Full moon, strong ambient light, warm white light from ProtoMachines LED2.

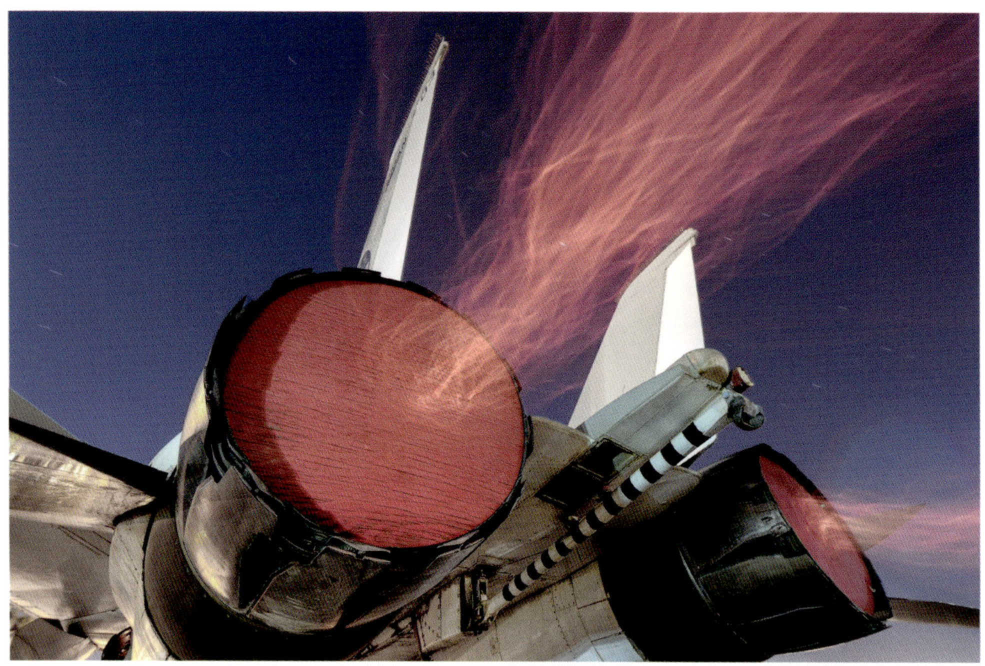

You Can't Housebreak a Tomcat, F-14 Tomcat BuNo. 16-4350. This and the other Tomcat photo was near strong streetlights and challenging to photograph. Joe Davies Heritage Airpark.
Nikon D610/Nikkor 14–24-mm f/2.8G lens. Three-minute thirty-eight-second exposure f/8 ISO 200. March 2015. Full moon, strong streetlights, warm white light from ProtoMachines LED2, red light from electroluminescent wire.

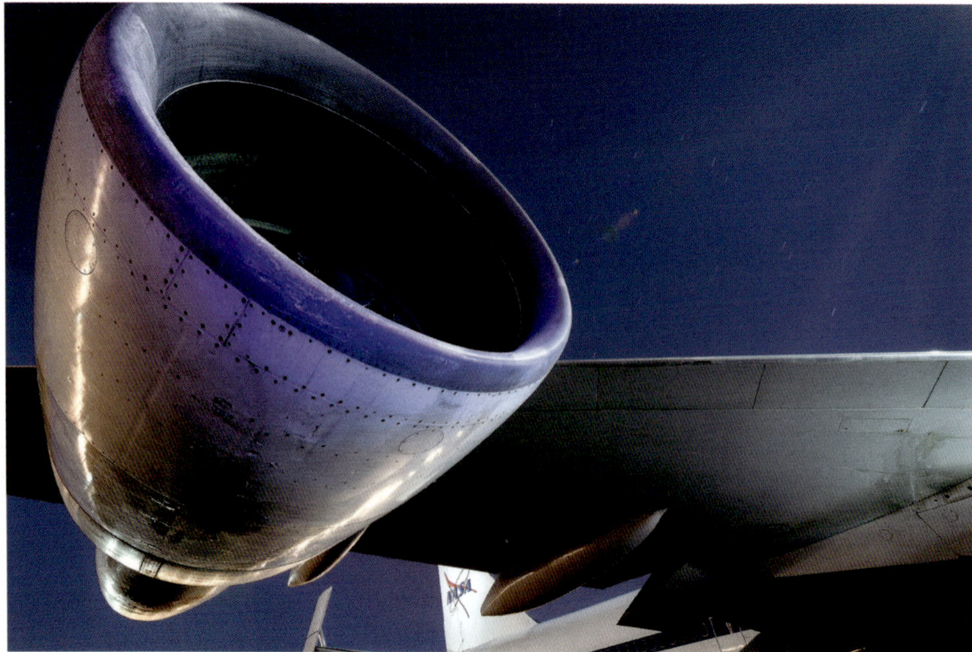

The Engine That Could, Boeing 747 Tail #N911NA shuttle vehicle transport carrier engine. Joe Davies Heritage Airpark.
Nikon D7000/Tokina 11–16-mm f/2.8 lens. Three minutes thirty-one seconds f/8 ISO 200. March 2015. Full moon, strong ambient light, warm white, yellow, red light from ProtoMachines LED2.

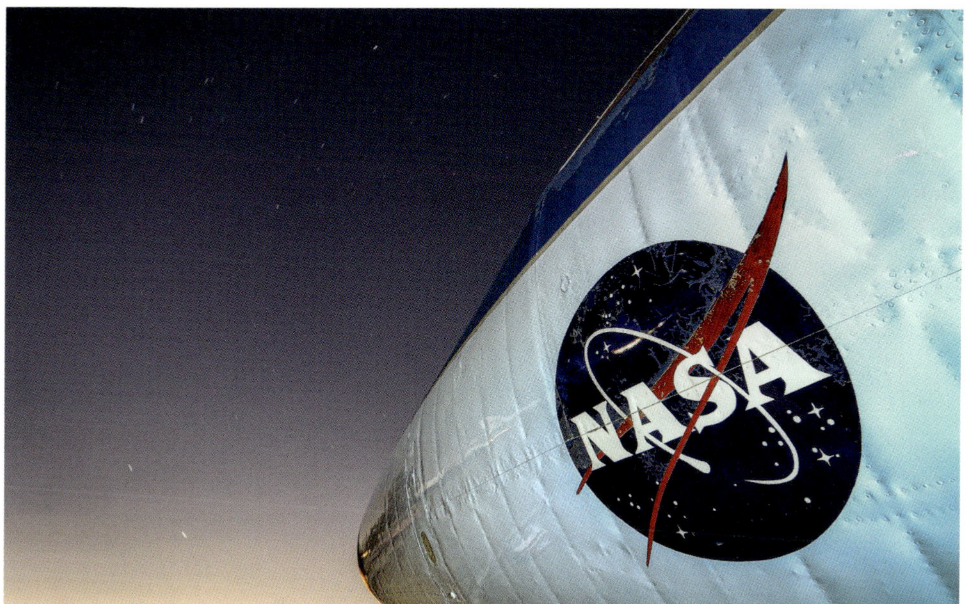

NASA Jet Star, C-140 Jet Star BuNo. N814NA. In the 1960s, this aircraft was equipped with a General Purpose Airborne Simulator. The aircraft could duplicate the flight characteristics of a wide variety of advanced aircraft and was used for supersonic transport and general aviation research. Joe Davies Heritage Airpark.
Nikon D7000/Tokina 11–16-mm f/2.8 lens. Two minutes thirteen seconds f/8 ISO 200. March 2015.
Full moon, warm white and yellow light from ProtoMachines LED2.

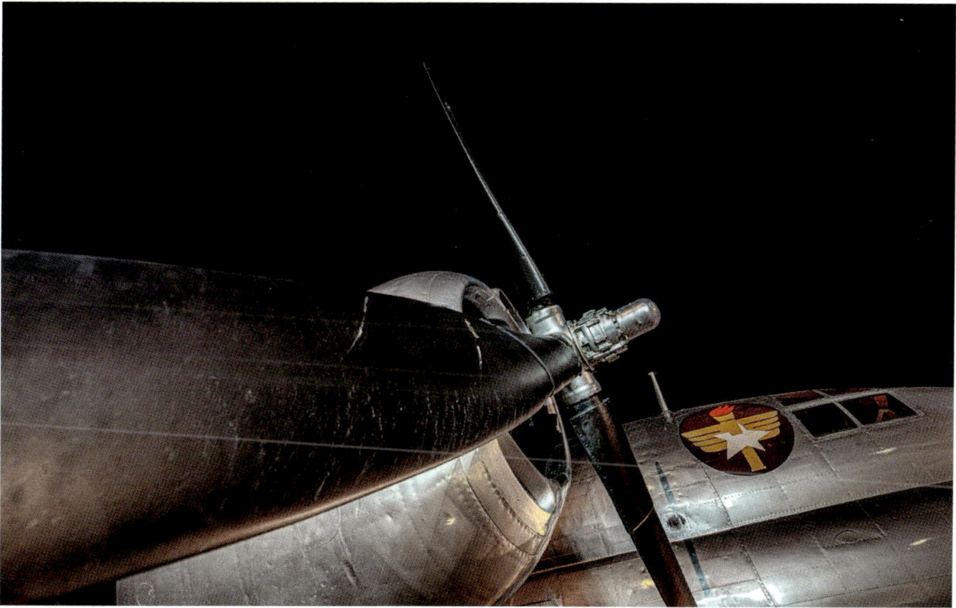

Going Commando, C-46 Commando #44-78019-A. Propeller view of a C-46 Commando. Built by Curtiss-Wright, it was used primarily as a military troop carrier and had cargo/paratroop doors. Out of 3,000-plus built for use in WWII, roughly fifty-plus are still flying as cargo transport aircraft.
Nikon D610/Nikkor 14–24-mm f/2.8G lens. Fifty-one-second exposure f/8 ISO 200. March 2015.
Full moon, warm white and red light from ProtoMachines LED2

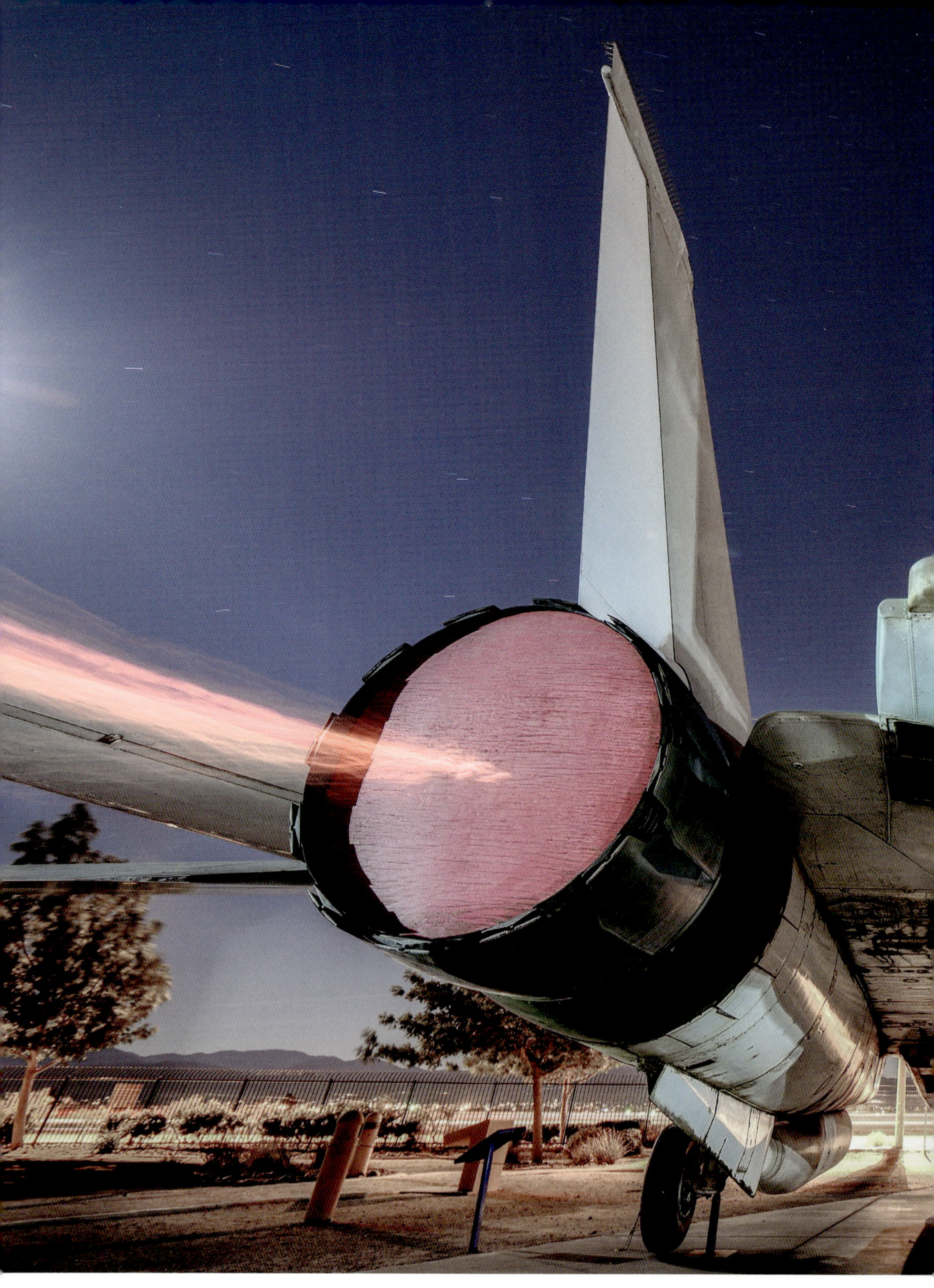

Tomcat, F-14 Tomcat BuNo. 16-4350 made famous by *Top Gun*. This aircraft is a carrier-based multi-role strike fighter and was attached to a squadron on USS *Saratoga*. Joe Davies Heritage Airpark.

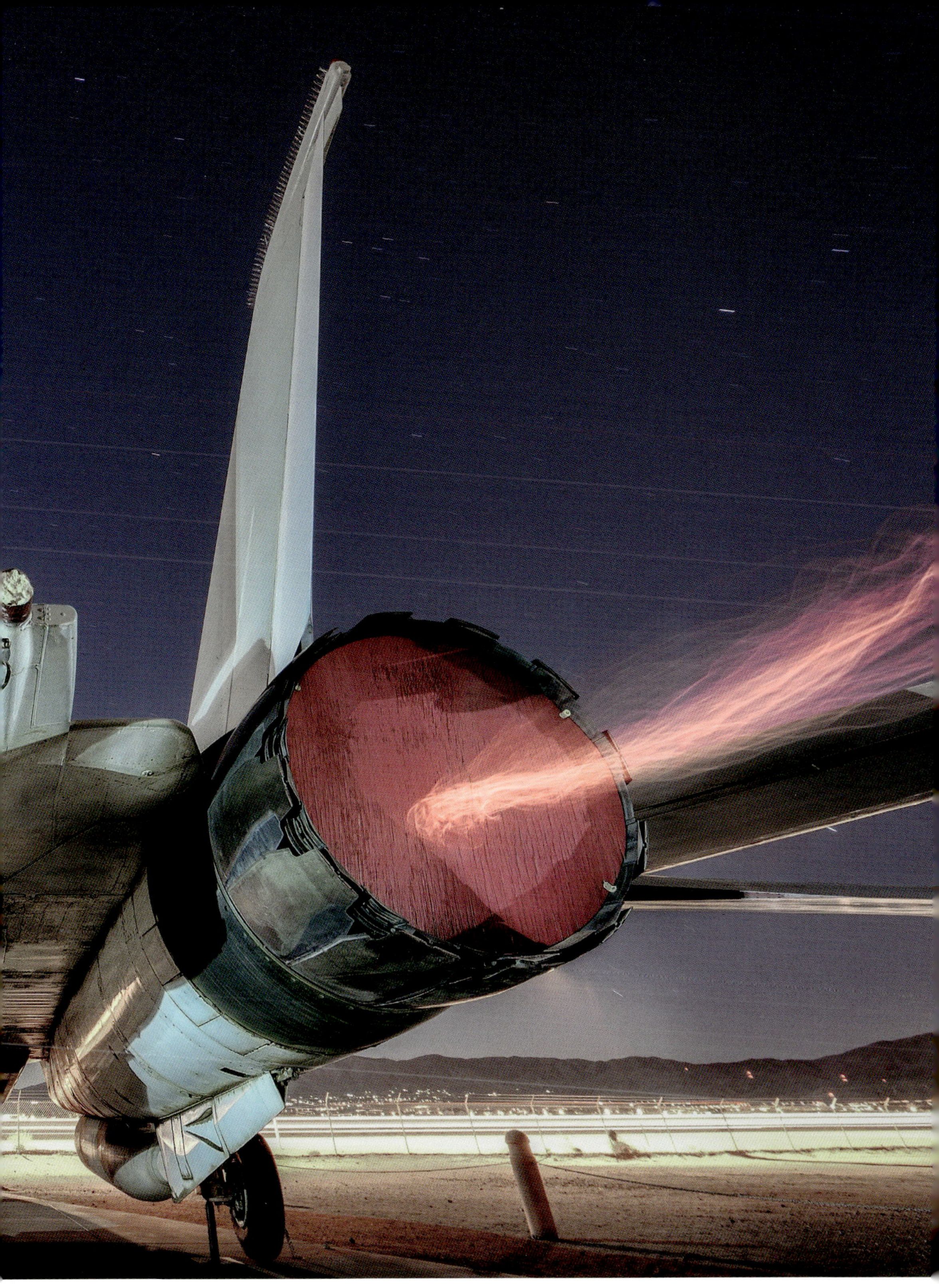

Nikon D610/Nikkor 14–24-mm f/2.8G lens. Two minutes twenty seconds f/8 ISO 200. March 2015.
Full moon, streetlights, warm white light from ProtoMachines LED2, red light from electroluminescent wire.

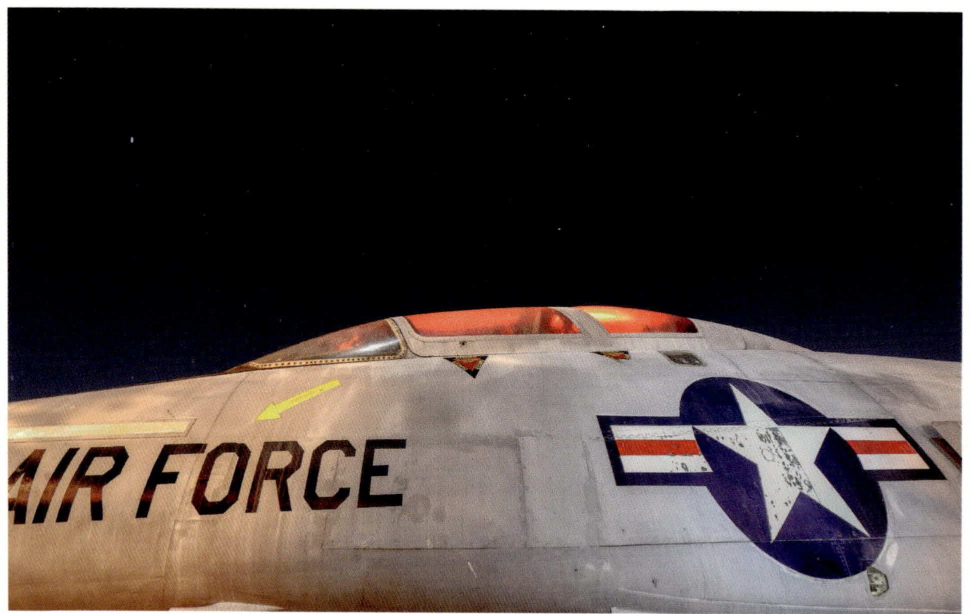

The Starfighter in Red, F-104 Starfighter BuNo. 57-0915. The Starfighter is a single-engined, supersonic interceptor aircraft originally developed by Lockheed for the United States Air Force. One of the Century Series of aircraft, it was operated by the air forces of more than a dozen nations from 1958 to 2004.
Nikon D610/Nikkor 14–24-mm f/2.8G lens. One-minute fifty-second exposure f/9 ISO 200. March 2015.
Full moon, warm white and red light from ProtoMachines LED2.

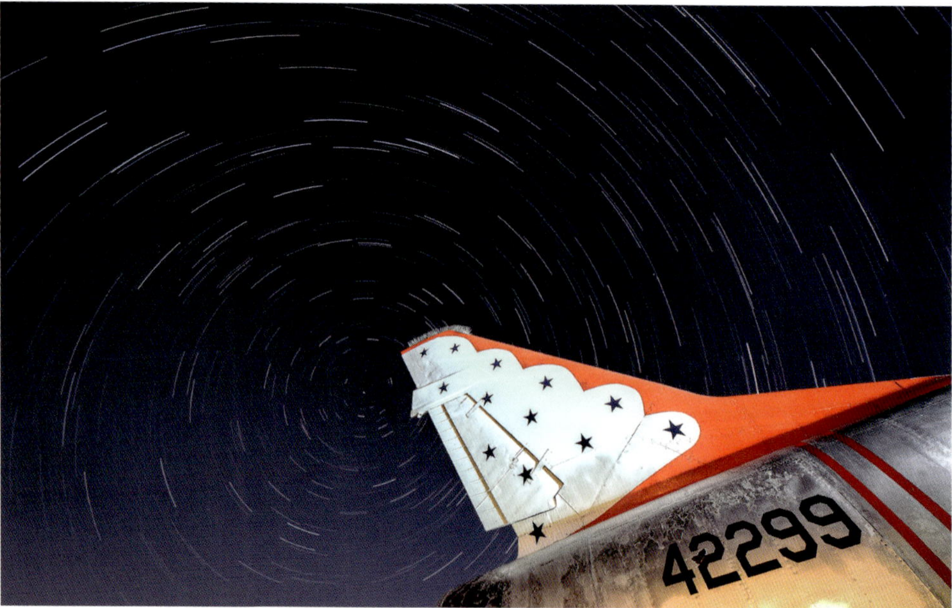

Super Sabre, F-100 Super Sabre BuNo. 54-2299 built by North American Aviation. This was the first operational aircraft capable of flying faster than 760 mph in level flight, which meant it was the first to go supersonic.
Nikon D610/Nikkor 14–24-mm f/2.8G lens. Fifty-minute total exposure "stacked." Each photo was thirty seconds f/5.6 ISO 200. March 2015.
Full moon, warm white and yellow light from ProtoMachines LED2.

2

TRAINS

HALLORAN SPRINGS

Hundreds of thousands of cars make their way from Southern California to Las Vegas on I-15. Along the way, one can stop for food or gas at EddieWorld, Peggy Sue's Diner, The Mad Greek, or the world's largest Chevron. Nevertheless, despite over 40,000 cars per day zipping past Halloran Springs, it is still possible for a business to fail. This might happen if someone owes property taxes or the site is contaminated with hazardous materials. Fortunately, that is not why the Santa Fe boxcar is glowing inside. That is caused by me illuminating the interior with some red light during the exposure.

I cannot find any information on the Santa Fe car. Nonetheless, it would seem the boxcar has been abandoned twice, once as a boxcar and later as a billboard.

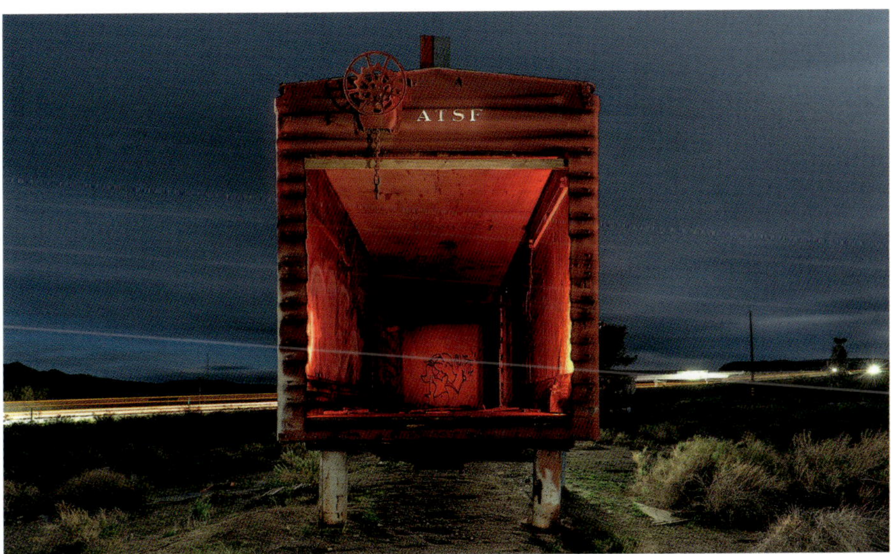

Train of Consequences, peering inside the Santa Fe Boxcar alongside busy I-15.
Nikon D750/Nikkor 14–24-mm f/2.8G lens. Five minutes seventeen seconds f/8 ISO 320. March 2019.
Full moon obscured in clouds, red and warm white light from ProtoMachines LED2.

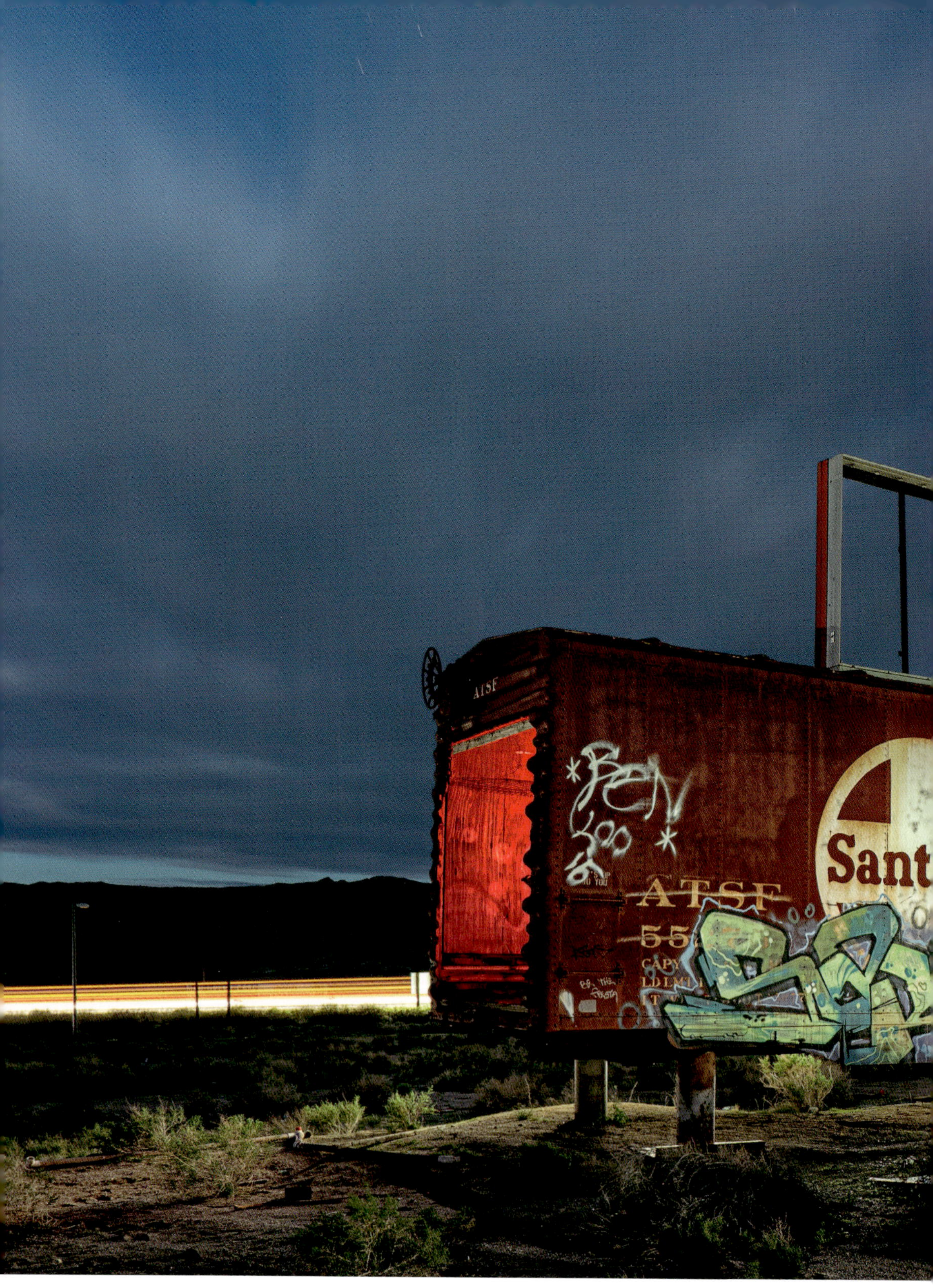

Dear, Dear, Dear Santa Fe, Santa Fe boxcar looks out upon Interstate 15, with many motorists streaking toward Las Vegas from Los Angeles on a cloudy evening.

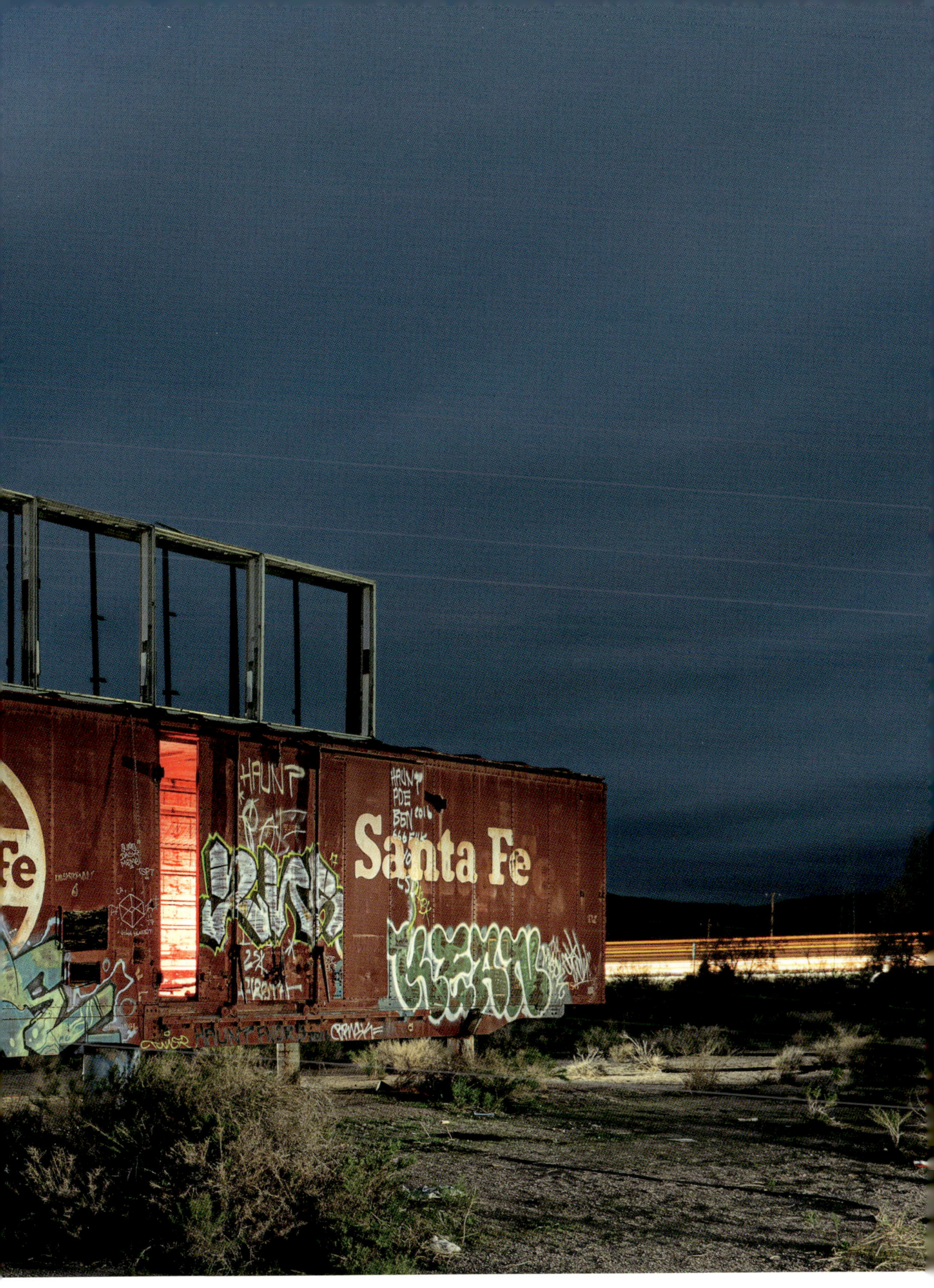

Nikon D750/Nikkor 14–24-mm f/2.8G lens. Five minutes seventeen seconds f/8 ISO 320. March 2019. Full moon obscured in clouds, red and warm white light from ProtoMachines LED2.

Mojave Trains

Sometimes, you find trains in the Mojave Desert, and sometimes you are asked not to tell anyone where they are. Tucked away among beautiful desert mountains are numerous trains: a Southern Pacific mail car; a 1920s dinner car, which had an air conditioning unit with an ice system; an old wooden Southern Pacific caboose made in the 1910s.

As a small child, one of the first words I liked to say was "choo choo train." I loved trains so much as a four year old that my grandmother used to take me to the railyard in Skokie, Illinois, to watch the trains come in. Although I really do not know very much about trains, I still love them, and having the opportunity to photograph them at night is a special treat.

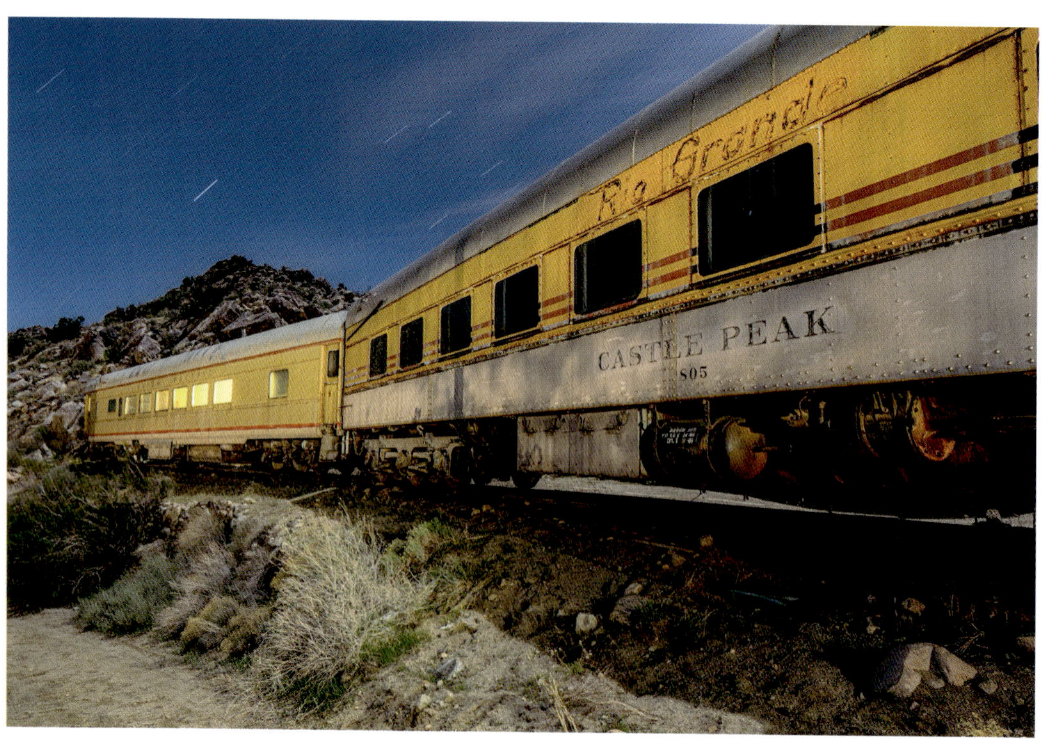

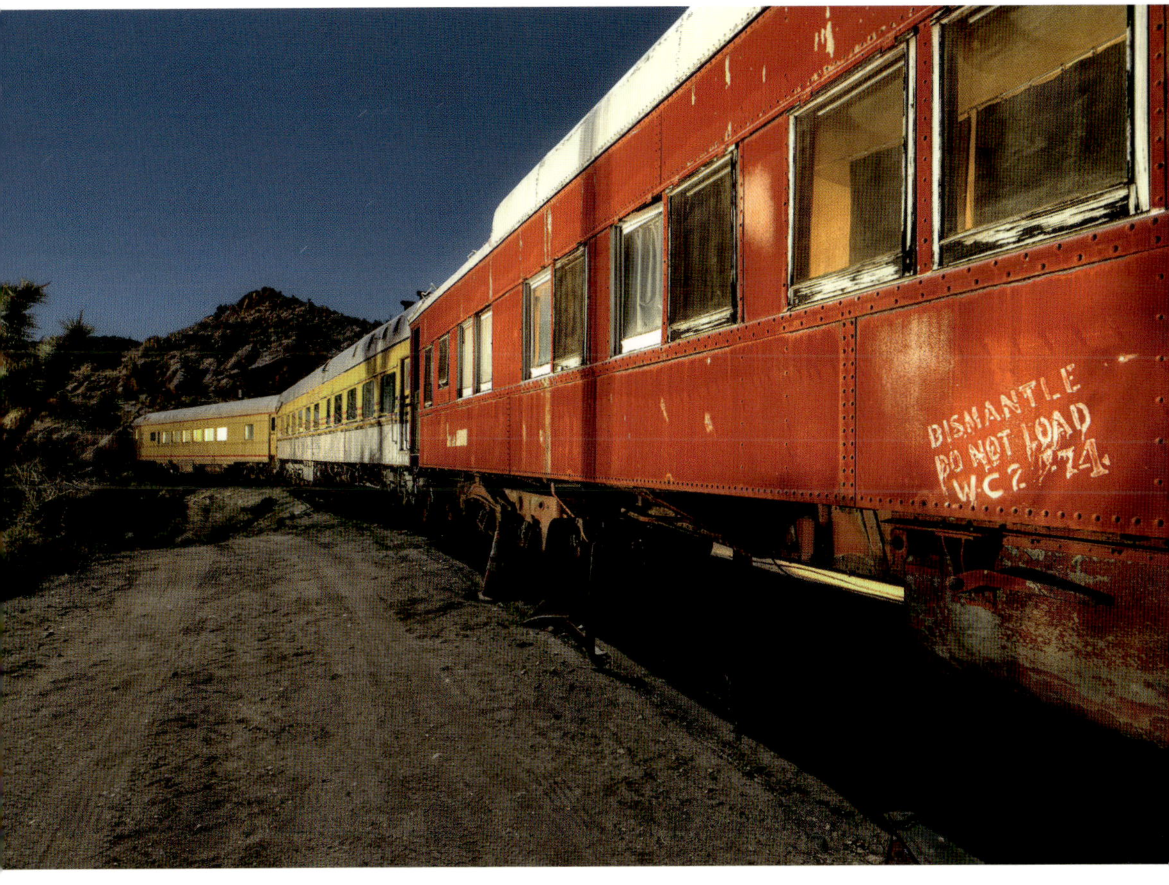

Dismantle Do Not Load, Pullman coach, Mojave Desert.
Pentax K-1/15–30-mm f/2.8 lens. Three minutes f/8 ISO 200. March 2020.
Full moon, warm white light from ProtoMachines LED2.

◀ **Last Stop of the Rio Grande**, Rio Grande dinner car, which had an air conditioning unit with an ice system. Built by American Car and Foundry for The Denver and Rio Grande Western Railroad in 1927. Mojave Desert.
Pentax K-1/15–30-mm f/2.8 lens. Nine minutes total exposure "stacked." Each photo three minutes f/8 ISO 200. f/8 ISO 200. March 2020.
Full moon, warm white light from ProtoMachines LED2.

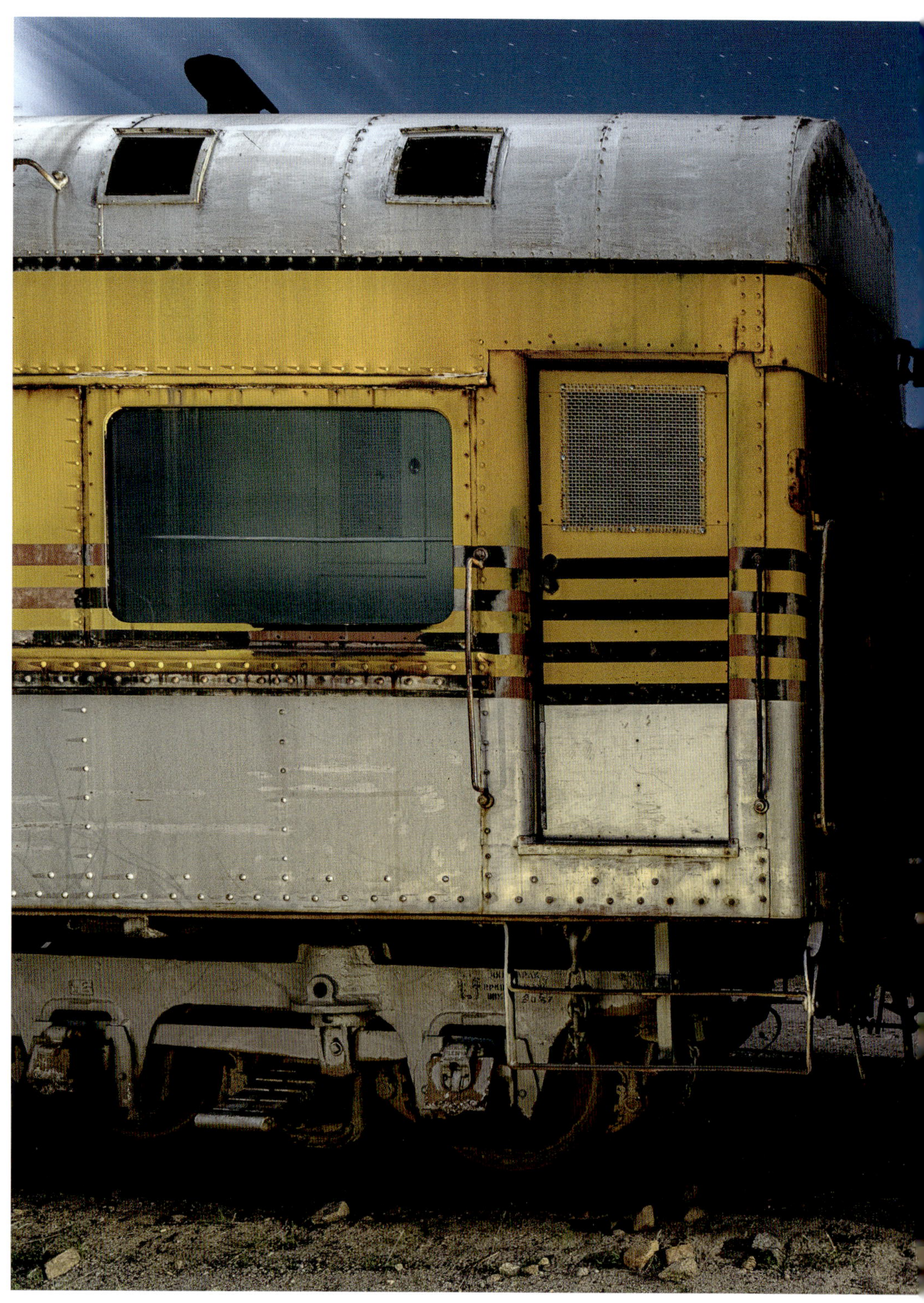

The Joining, dinner car and Pullman coach, Mojave Desert.

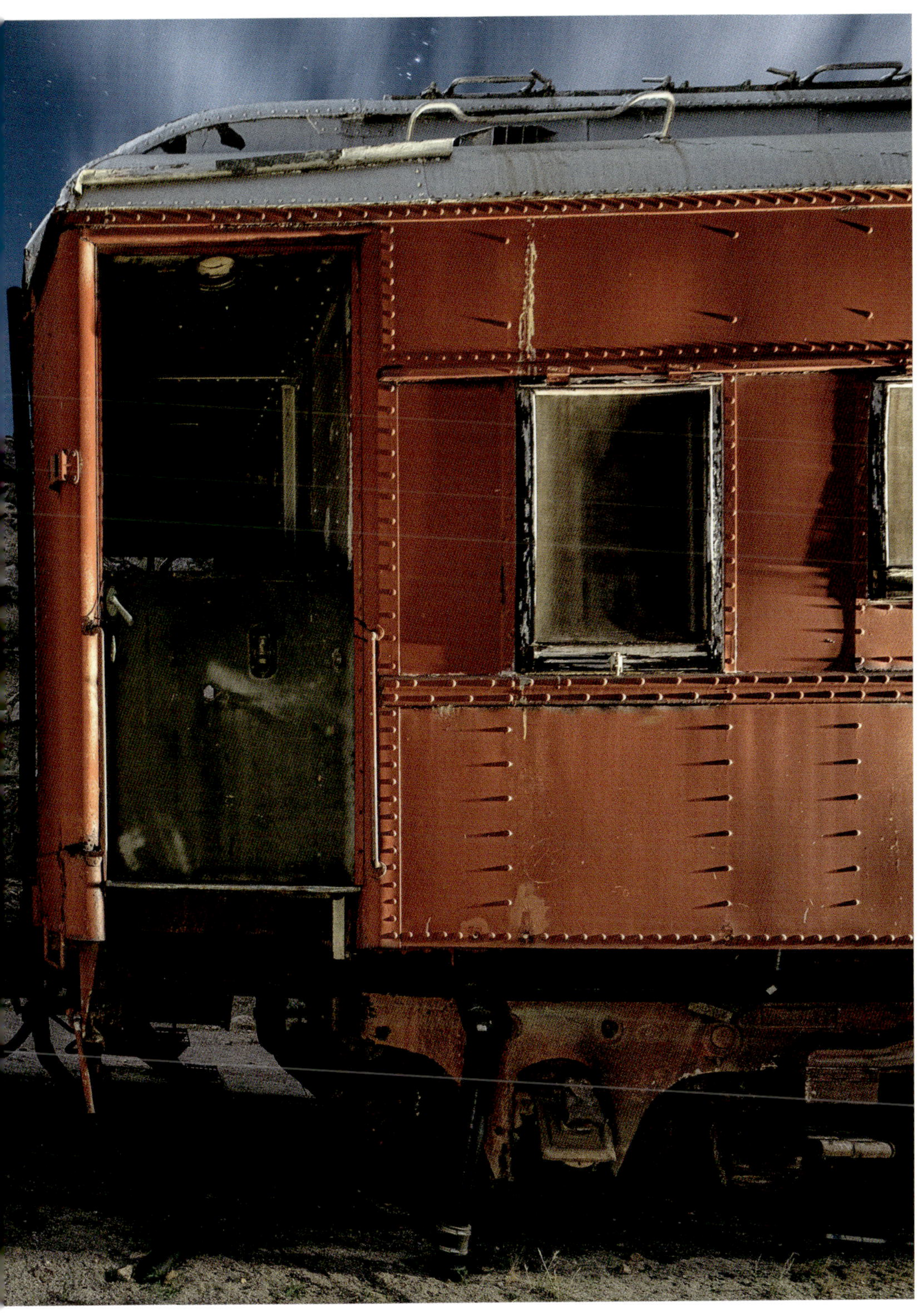

Pentax K-1/15–30-mm f/2.8 lens. Thirty-nine seconds f/7.1 ISO 800. March 2020.
Full moon, warm white light from ProtoMachines LED2.

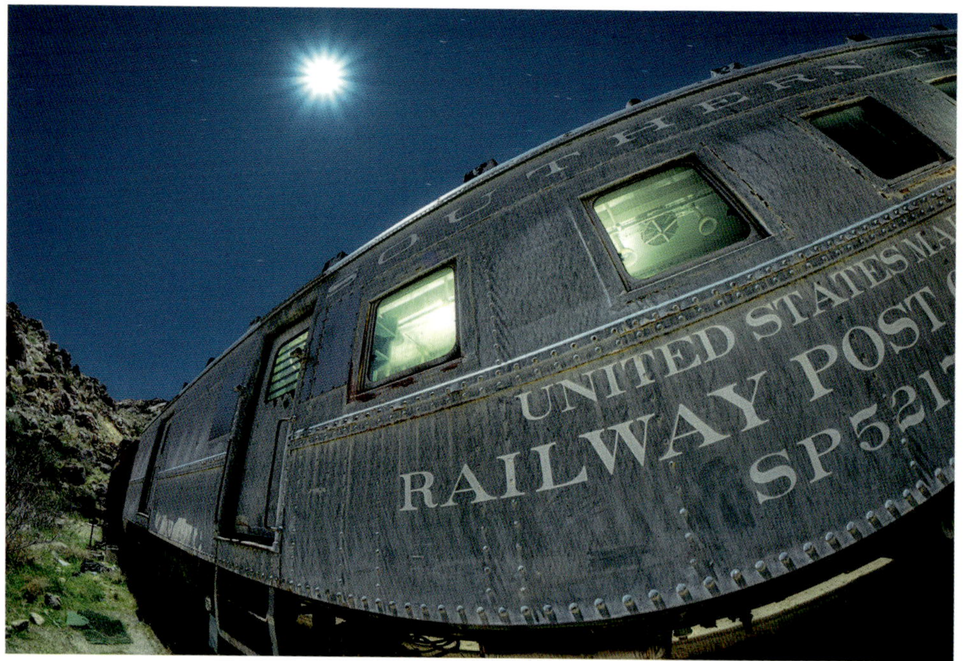

Southern Pacific Moon, 1914 mail car train once used by the U.S. Post Office. This car had two bunk beds inside. Mojave Desert.
Nikon D750/Rokinon 12-mm f/2.8 fisheye lens. Two minutes thirty-one seconds f.8 ISO 320. March 2020. Full moon, warm white and green light from ProtoMachines LED2.

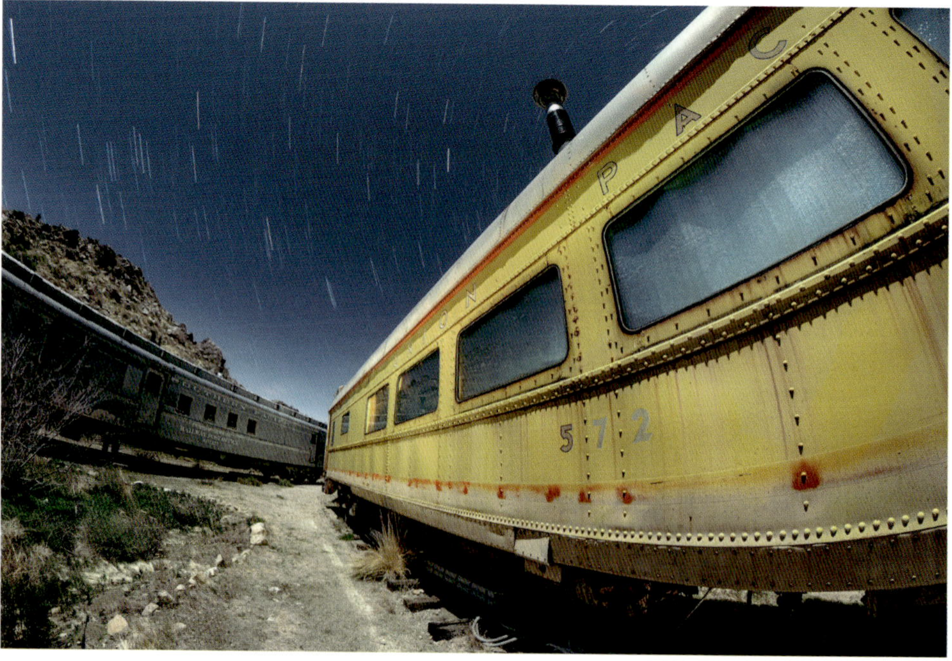

Coming Around the Bend, Southern Pacific mail car (left) and a 1920s dinner car, Mojave Desert.
Nikon D750/Rokinon 12-mm f/2.8 fisheye lens. Twenty-one minutes total exposure “stacked”; each photo three minutes f/8 ISO 200. f/8 ISO 320. March 2020.

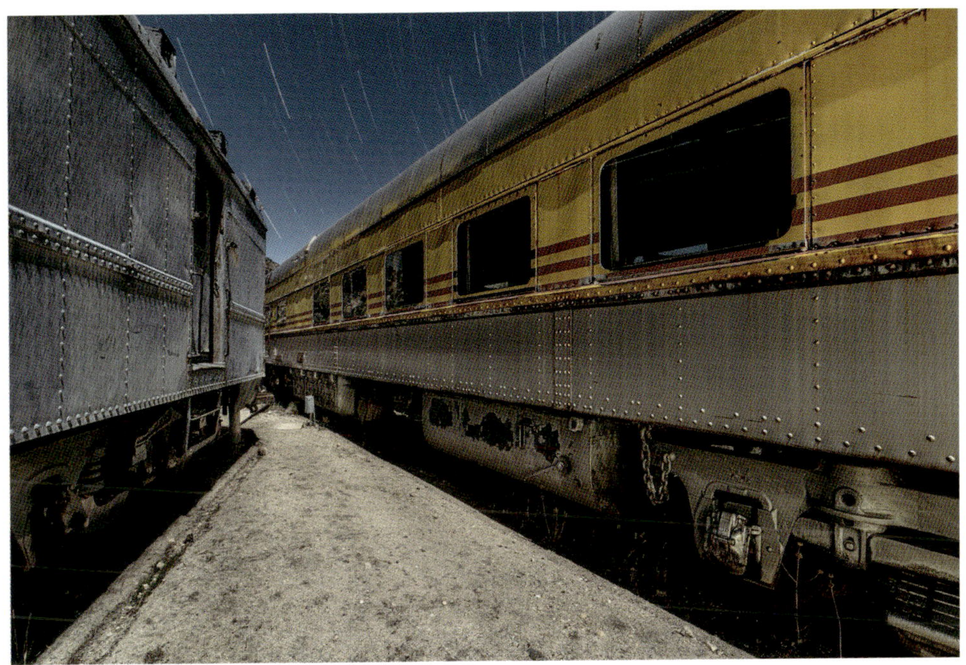

Angling for More, Southern Pacific mail car (left) and a 1920s dinner car, Mojave Desert. Pentax K-1/15–30-mm f/2.8 lens. Three minutes f/8 ISO 200. March 2020. Full moon, warm white light from ProtoMachines LED2.

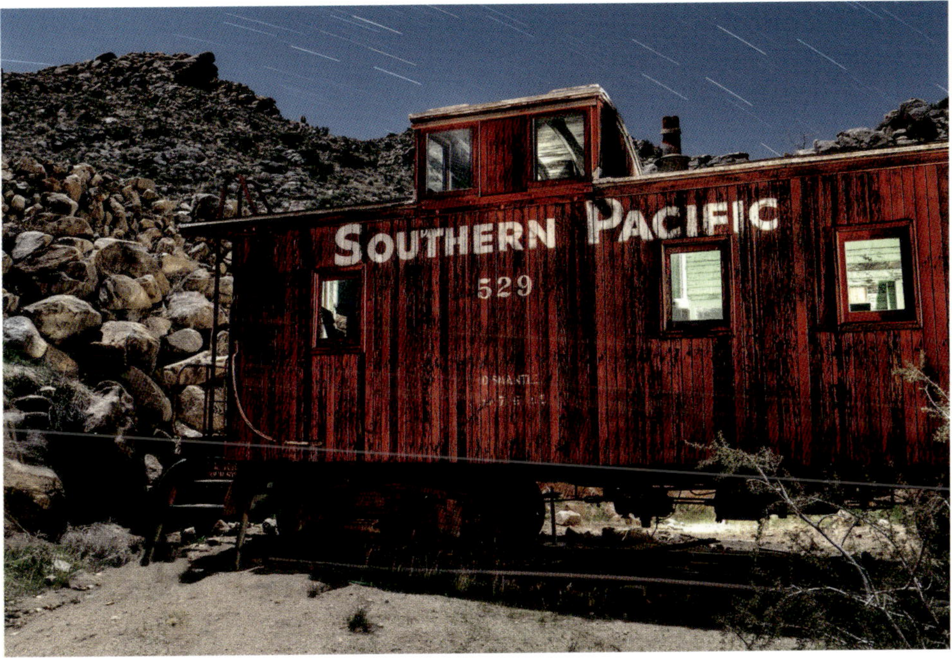

The Red Caboose of the Mojave, wooden Southern Pacific caboose made in the 1910s. Many of these were in service for over fifty years. Pentax K-1/15–30-mm f/2.8 lens. Fifteen minutes total exposure "stacked." Each photo three minutes f/7.1 ISO 200. March 2020.
Full moon, warm white light from ProtoMachines LED2.

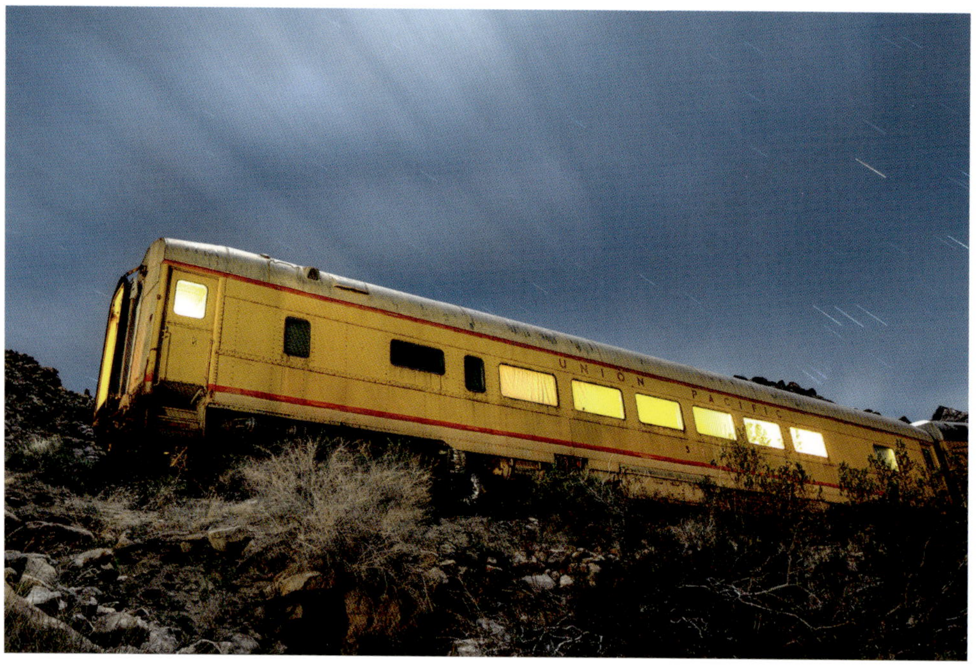

Midnight Dinner Train, 1920s dinner car, Mojave Desert.
Pentax K-1/15–30-mm f/2.8 lens. Nine minutes total exposure "stacked." Each photo three minutes f/8 ISO 200. March 2020.
Full moon, warm white light from ProtoMachines LED2.

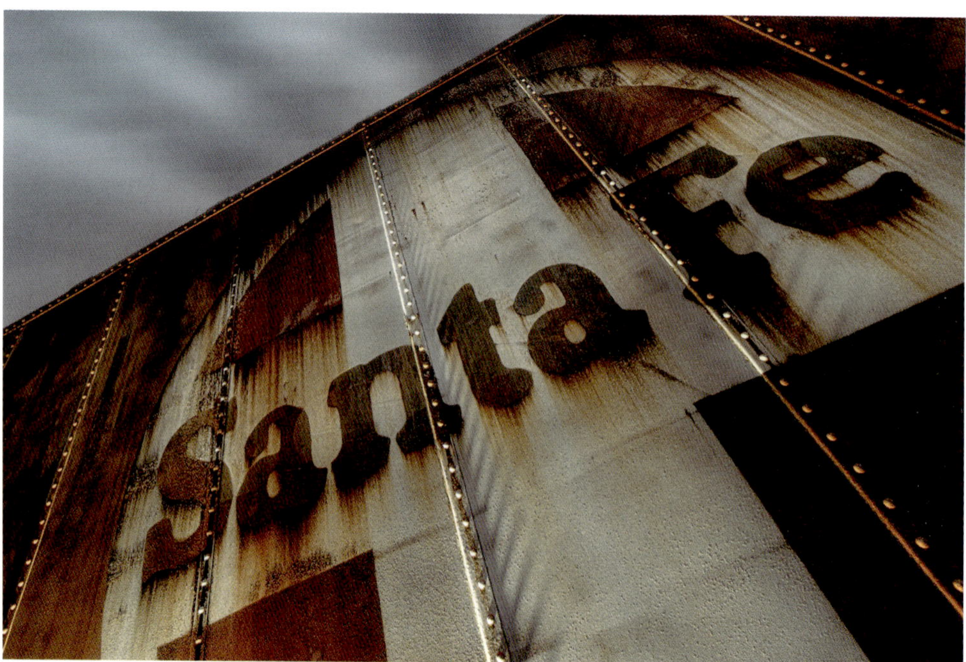

Santa Fe, Santa Fe, Santa Fe boxcar, Mojave Desert.
Pentax K-1/15–30-mm f/2.8 lens. Thirty seconds f/8 ISO 800. March 2020.
Full moon obscured by clouds, warm white and yellow light from ProtoMachines LED2.

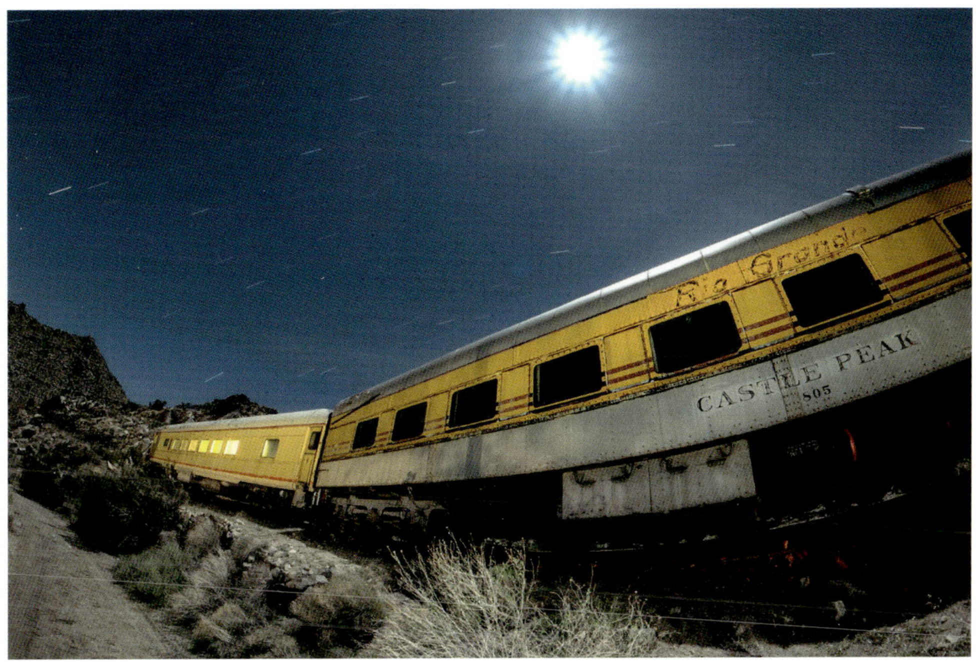

The Bend of the Rio Grande, 1920s Rio Grande dinner car, Mojave Desert.
Pentax K-1/15–30-mm f/2.8 lens. Twelve minutes total exposure "stacked." Each photo three minutes f/8 ISO 320. March 2020.
Full moon, warm white light from ProtoMachines LED2.

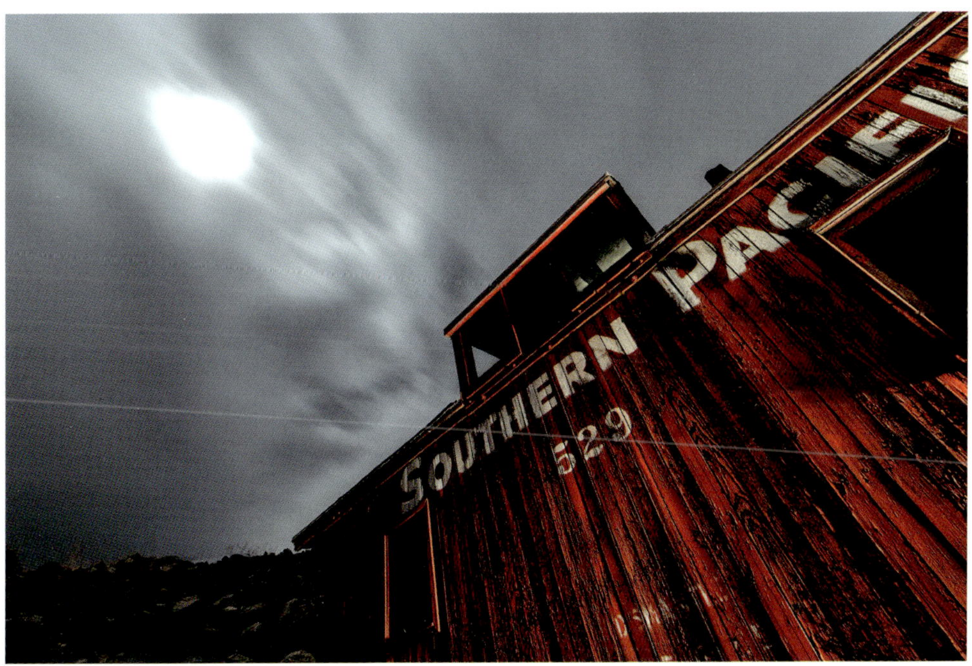

Southern Pacific Moon, wooden Southern Pacific caboose, Mojave Desert.
Pentax K-1/15–30-mm f/2.8 lens. Twenty seconds f/7.1 ISO 800. March 2020.
Full moon obscured by clouds, warm white light from ProtoMachines LED2.

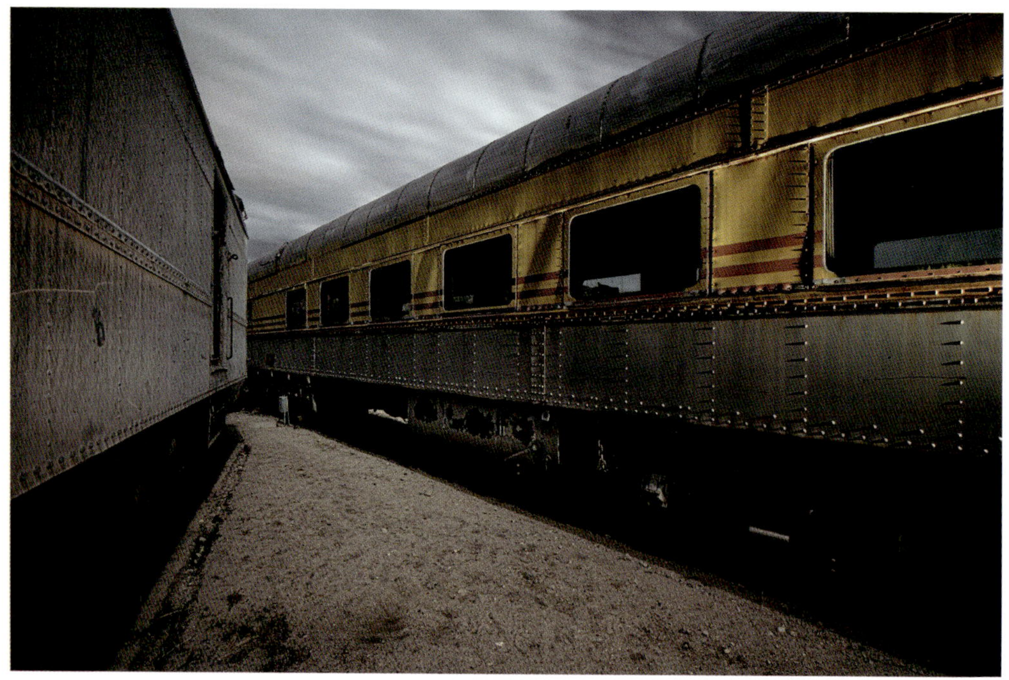

The Combining, Southern Pacific mail car (left) and a 1920s dinner car, Mojave Desert.
Pentax K-1/15–30-mm f/2.8 lens. Twenty-five seconds f/7.1 ISO 800. March 2020.
Full moon, warm white light from ProtoMachines LED2.

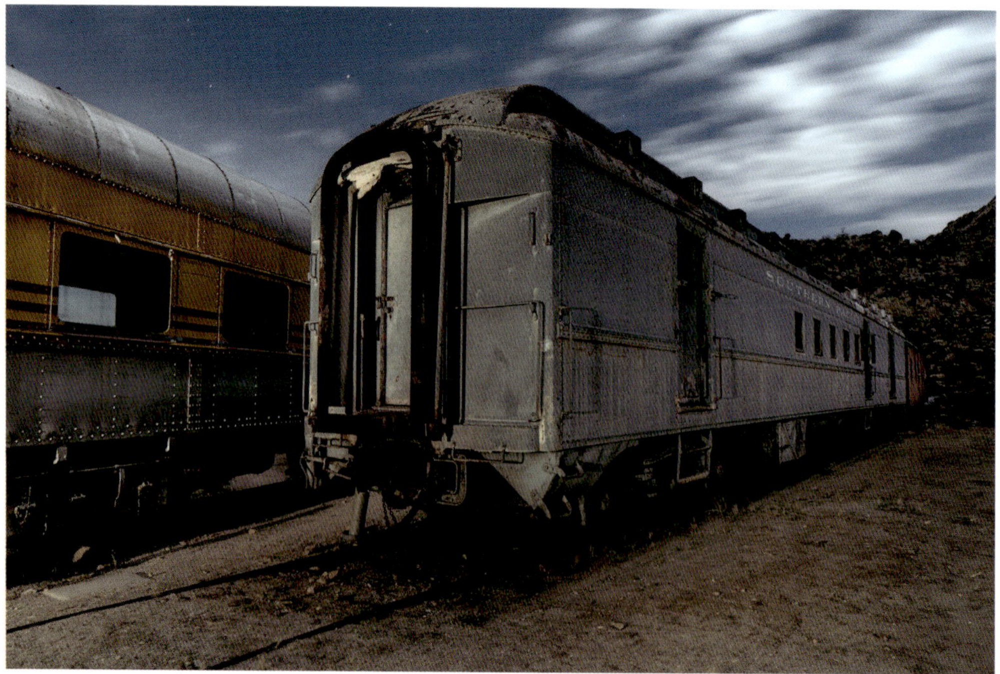

You've Got Mail, Southern Pacific mail car, Mojave Desert.
Pentax K-1/15–30-mm f/2.8 lens. Thirty seconds f/8 ISO 800. March 2020.
Full moon obscured by clouds, warm white light from ProtoMachines LED2.

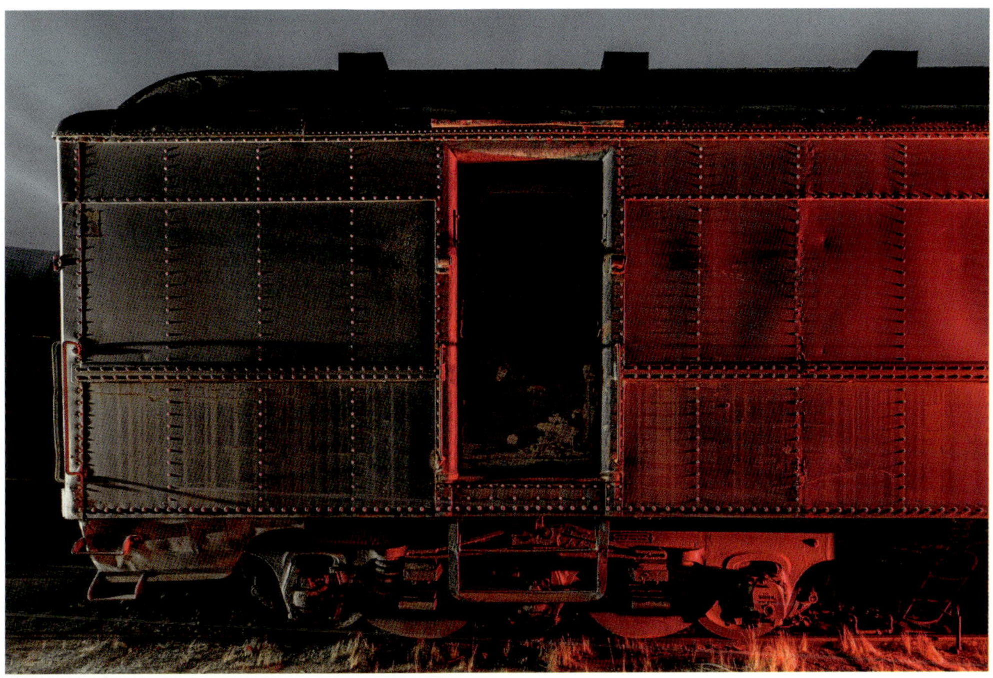

Red Car Blues, Southern Pacific mail car door, Mojave Desert.
Pentax K-1/15–30-mm f/2.8 lens. Thirty seconds f/8 ISO 800. March 2020.
Full moon obscured by clouds, warm white and red light from ProtoMachines LED2.

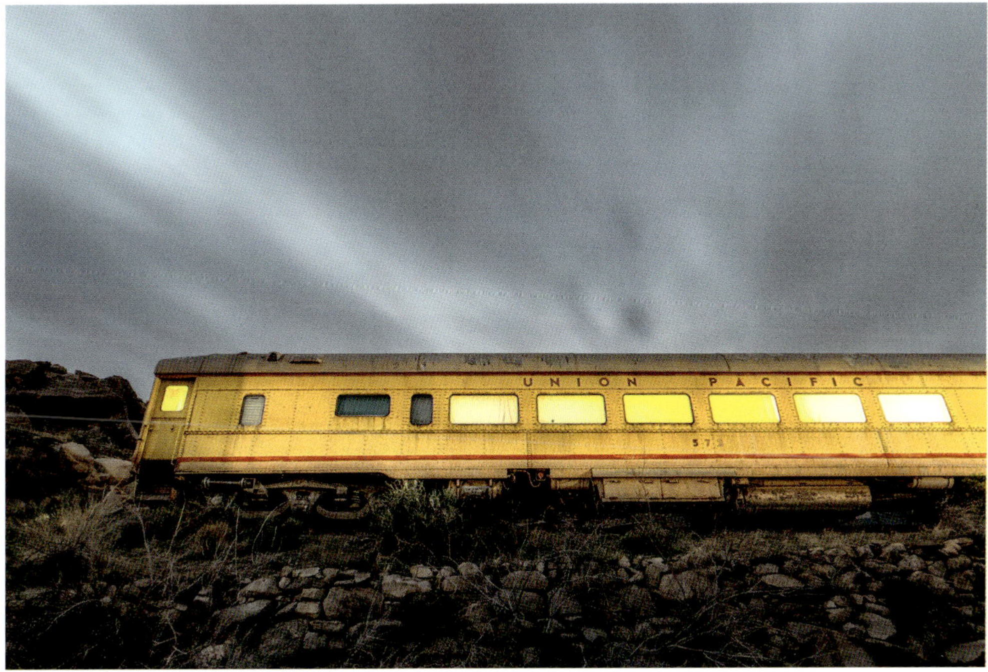

The Grey Thickening, looking up at a 1920s dinner car and the very cloudy sky.
Pentax K-1/15–30-mm f/2.8 lens. Forty seconds f/7.1 ISO 800. March 2020.
Full moon obscured by clouds, warm white light from ProtoMachines LED2.

Laws Railroad Museum and Historic Site

The mighty oil-burning steam locomotive Baldwin Engine 9 was built in 1909 for the Nevada–California–Oregon Railway, one of the early Western narrow gauge runs. When this run ceased operating, Southern Pacific purchased the engine in the 1920s and kept it running, sometimes intermittently, becoming one of the last narrow-gauge steam locomotives running in the west. The "Slim Princess," as it was nicknamed, continued heaving away into the 1950s, finally stopping when an ICC inspector declared its boiler shot. A 50-ton diesel locomotive dragged all 40 tons of Southern Pacific 9 to Laws while someone lit a fire in the smokestack to replicate a still-working steam engine. The tracks around Laws and Keeler were torn up, leaving the "Slim Princess" to rust away at the Laws Depot.

The story for the Southern Pacific 9 gets better, though. Several years later, not wanting to leave the engine to neglect, several people purchased not only the engine but the entire historic Laws Depot. In February 1964, those old-timers formed the Bishop Museum and Historical Society.

Laws got some good fortune a short while later when Steve McQueen filmed *Nevada Smith*. Their film crews built Western-replica hollow buildings. Volunteers completed the rest, turning them into real buildings, one serving as the office. Laws Railroad Museum and Historic Site was born on the site of the former railroad station.

The photo of the "Slim Princess" brings back a lot of fun memories. We photographed as a group effort, with my friend Lance Keimig running back and forth while brandishing a Coast LED flashlight, illuminating the amazing steam engine while we stood by our tripods, completely amused. The blue light on the interior is from a Luxli Viola LED panel that someone placed there.

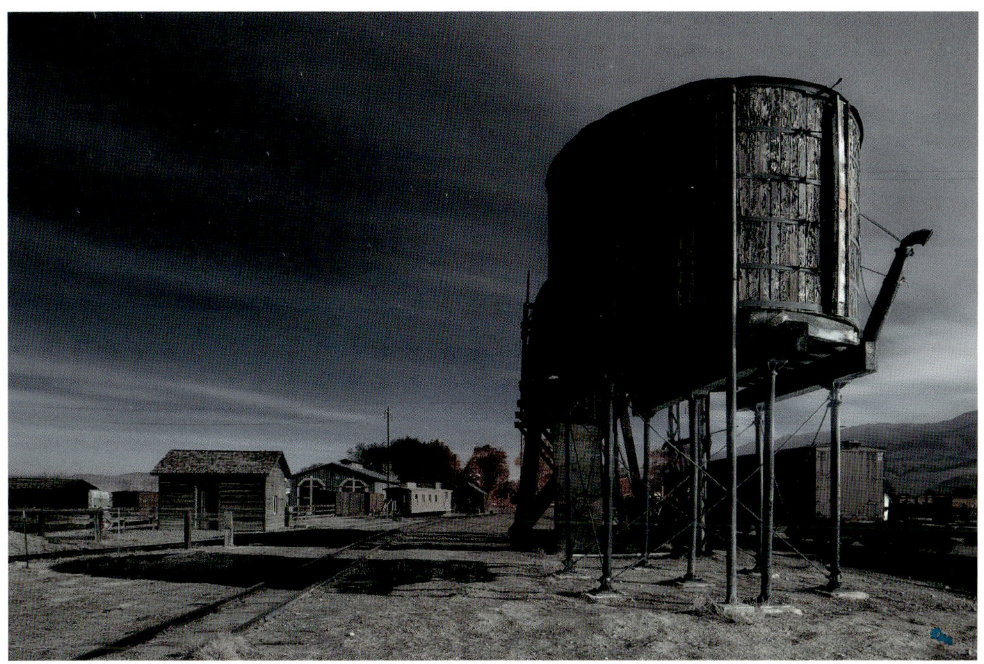

Tanks for the Memories, an old water tank from yesteryear at the Laws Museum, Bishop.
Nikon D610/Nikkor 14–24-mm f/2.8G lens. Two minutes f/8 ISO 200. November 2017.
Full moon, warm white light from ProtoMachines LED2.

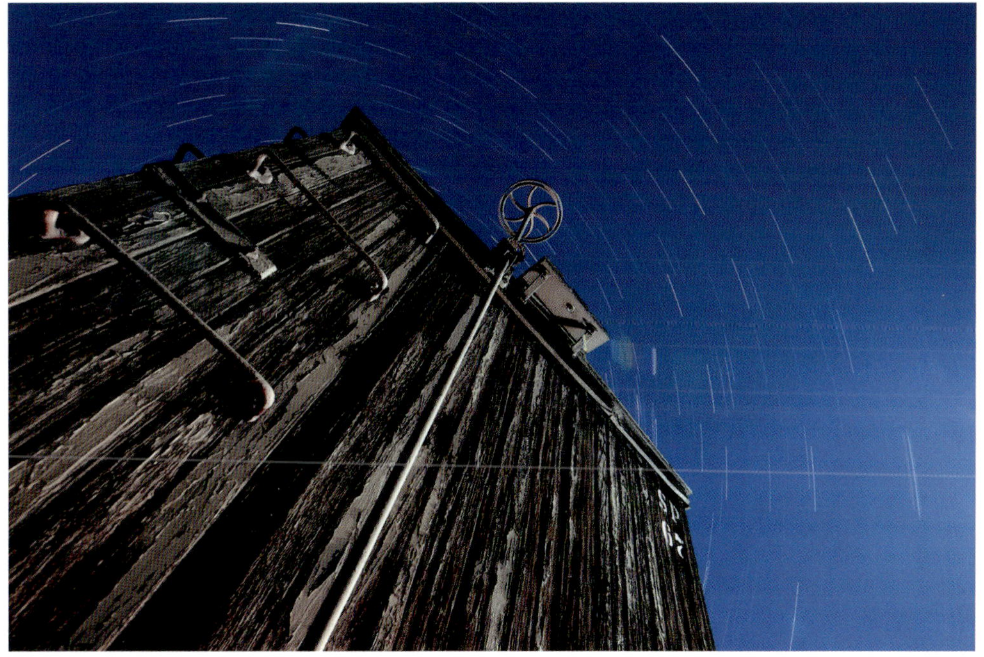

Boxcar Blues, an old wooden Southern Pacific 67 boxcar, Laws Museum, Bishop.
Nikon D610/Nikkor 14–24-mm f/2.8G lens. Thirty minutes total "stacked"; each photo three minutes f/8 ISO 200. November 2017.
Full moon, warm white light from ProtoMachines LED2.

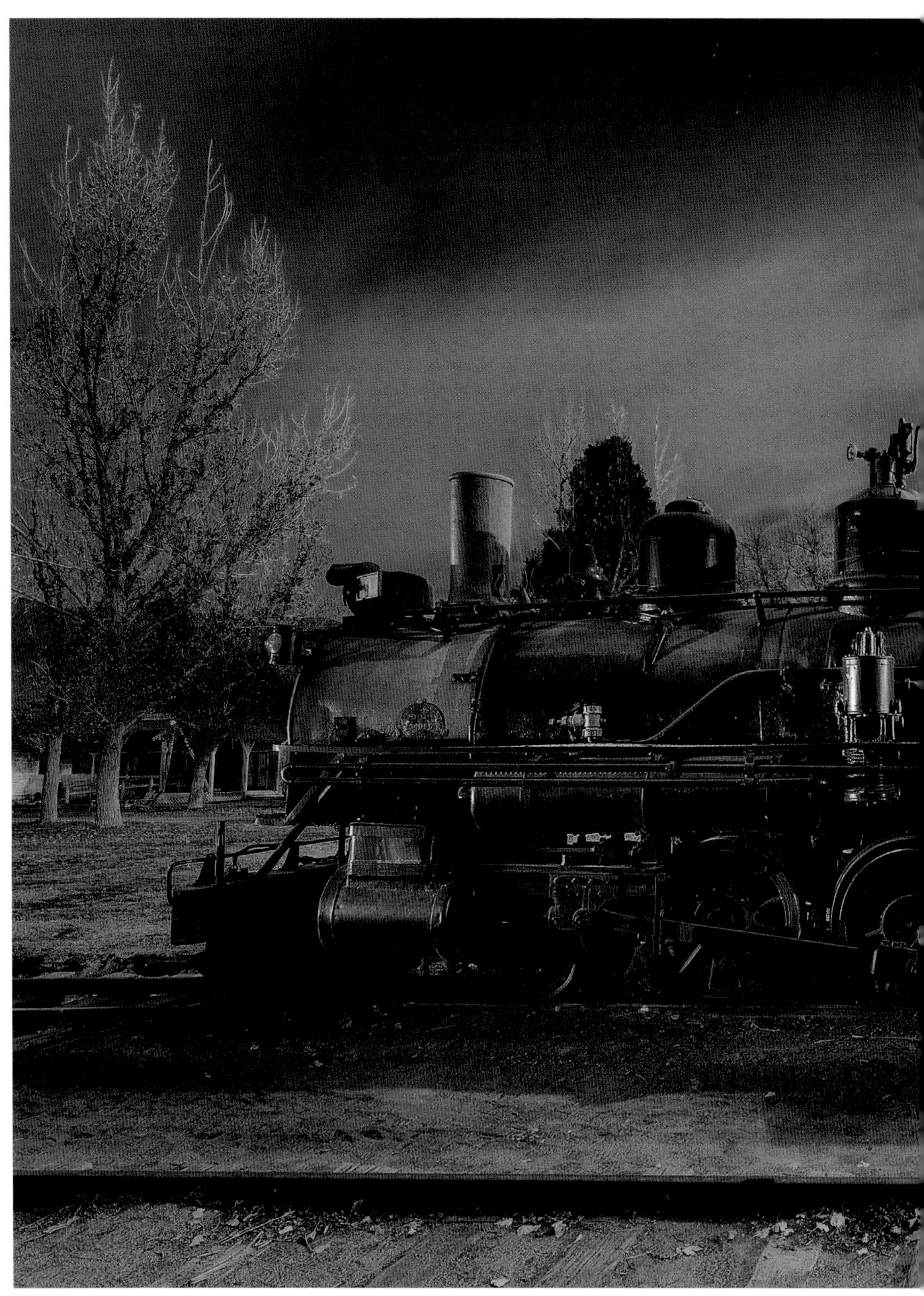

Locomotive Breath, the mighty Baldwin Engine 9 was built in 1909 for the Nevada–California–Oregon Railway and continued running until the 1950s. Laws Museum, Bishop.

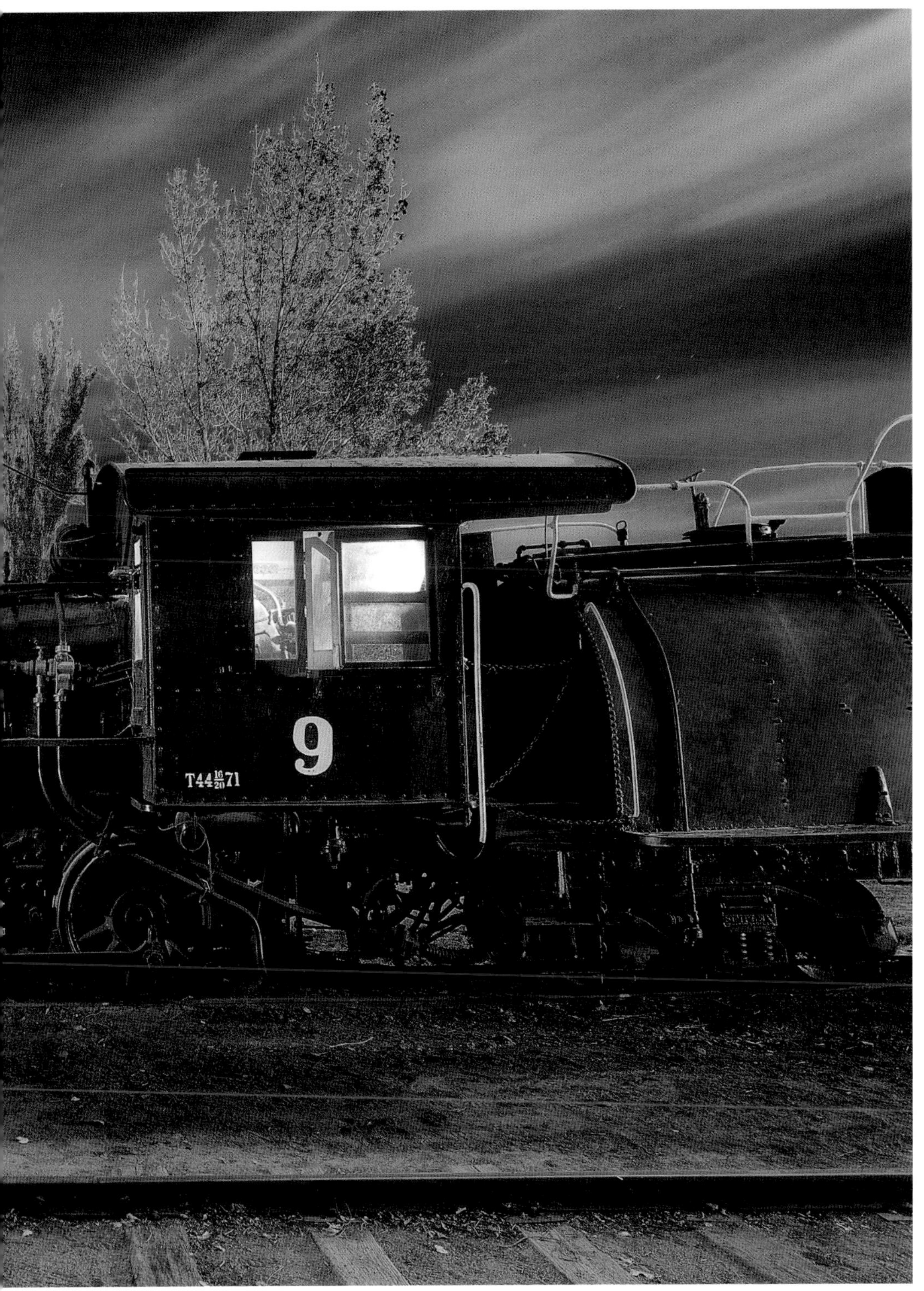

Nikon D610/Nikkor 14–24-mm f/2.8G lens. Thirty seconds f/7.1 ISO 500. November 2017.
Full moon, warm white light from Coast LED flashlight, bright blue light from a Luxli Viola LED panel placed inside.
Group effort with Lance Keimig providing the lighting of the locomotive.

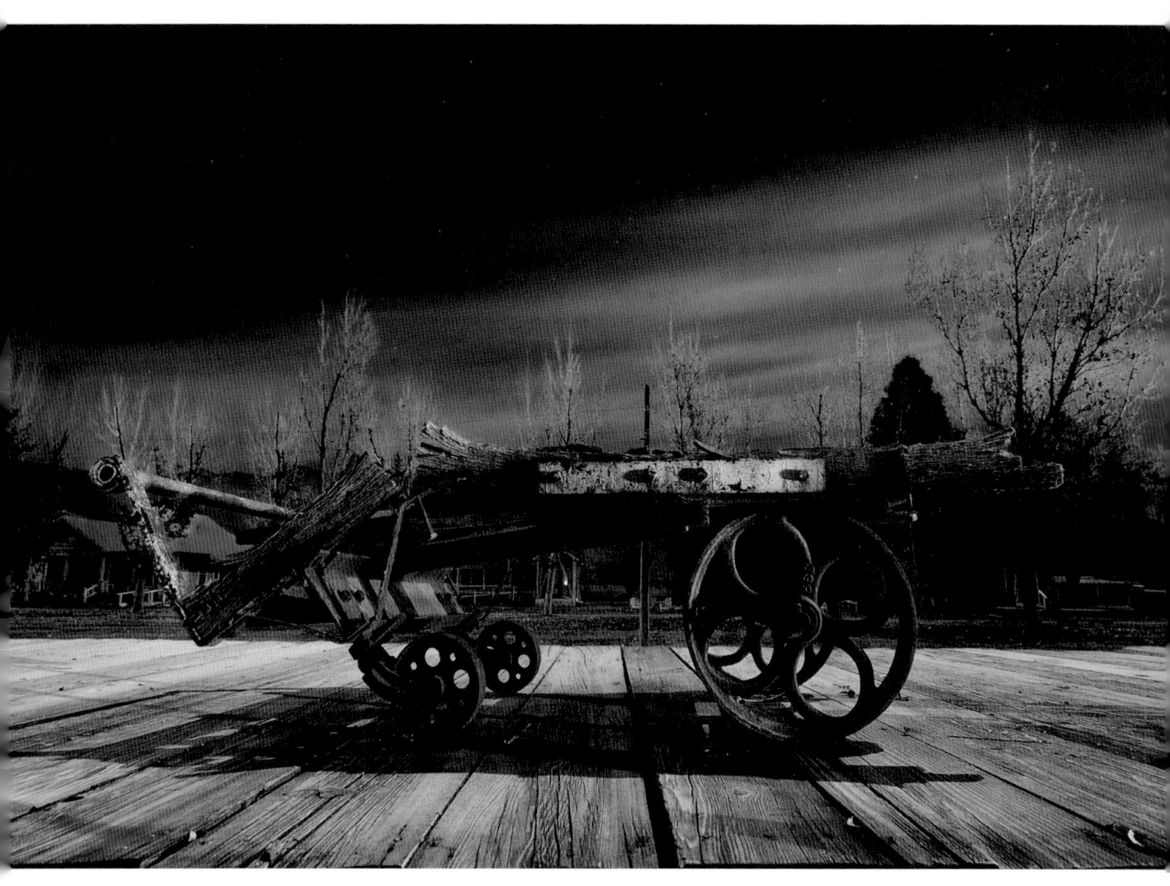

Kneeling Before the Night, a vintage railway depot baggage cart. I kept saying that I was packing it in for the night. Then I would walk 20 feet and take a photo of something else: "Just one more!"
Nikon D610/Nikkor 14–24-mm f/2.8G lens. Thirty seconds f/7.1 ISO 500. November 2017.
Full moon, warm white light from ProtoMachines LED2.

Salton Sea Trains

I feel like you can find almost any derelict item near the Salton Sea. These are abandoned locomotives north of Calipatria, along a Southern Pacific line near what used to be a drop-off area for farm workers in the early 1900s. A water tower and several other structures, including some areas for washing items, are still standing.

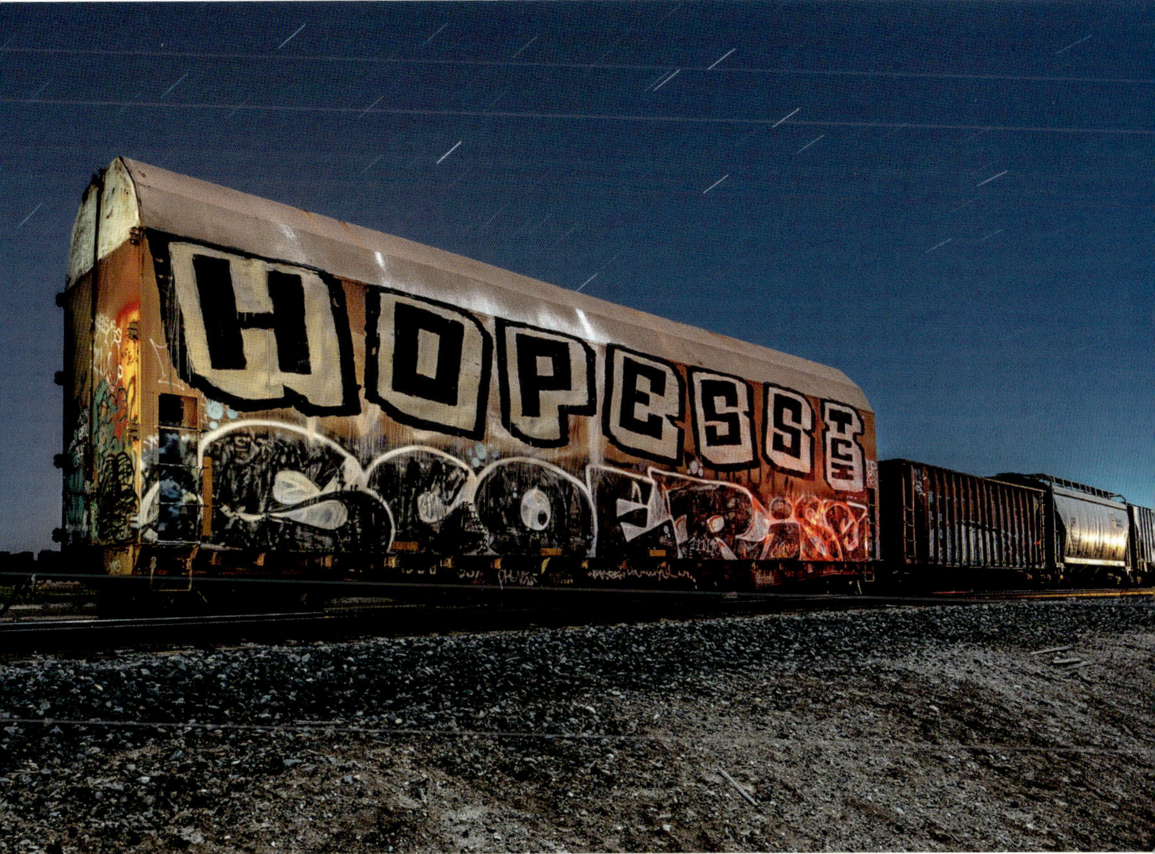

Hopess, watching the stars arc overhead near Salton Sea.
Nikon D750/Nikkor 14–24-mm f/2.8G lens. Eight minutes total "stacked"; each photo two minutes f/8 ISO 400. March 2019.
Full moon, warm white light from ProtoMachines LED2.

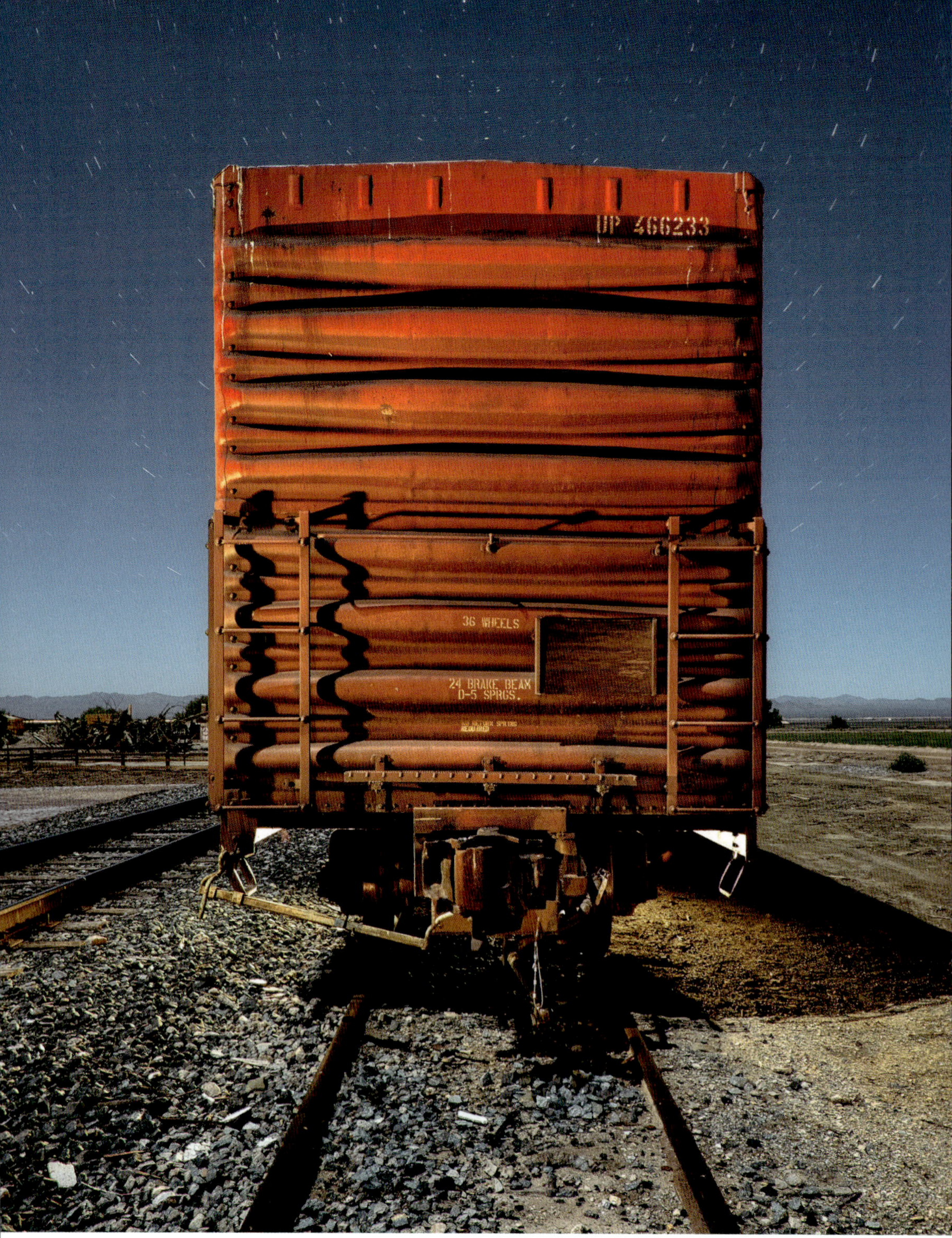

Boxcar Heading North, facing north as stars swirl above. Near Salton Sea.
Nikon D750/Nikkor 14–24-mm f/2.8G lens. Eight minutes total "stacked"; each photo two minutes f/8 ISO 400. March 2019.
Full moon, warm white light from ProtoMachines LED2.

METRA Pullman Cars

On a cool March evening, Mike and I drive up to the road leading to the clothing-optional resort tucked away in the Sonoran Desert just north of the border of Mexico. On this evening, we will eventually photograph trains at three separate sites, a supreme privilege.

We park our car on a dirt pull-out and walk up, following the defunct train tracks in the dark. We make our way over the trestle, taking care not to walk on rotten planks of wood. Not long after, the bilevel Metra passenger cars come into view, a nearly full moon illuminating them beautifully. It is an odd sight, sitting out here in the desert.

In a most suspicious activity, the cars were moved and derailed in 2015, damaging both the spur and the main line. The cars were also heavily damaged from paint and people smashing things. Disappointed at all the damage, we nevertheless set about photographing the Metras, both the interior and exterior.

The Pullman cars appear to have come all the way from Chicago. How did they get here? Rumors include that the trains were to be sold to Mexico, while others believe it was for a tourist line that went bust.

Most night photographers relish a chance to photograph abandoned trains.

Earl Scheib, more colorful than Metra intended. Sonoran Desert.
Nikon D750/Nikkor 14–24-mm f/2.8G lens. Three minutes fifty-seven seconds f/8 ISO 400. March 2019.
Full moon, warm white light from ProtoMachines LED2.

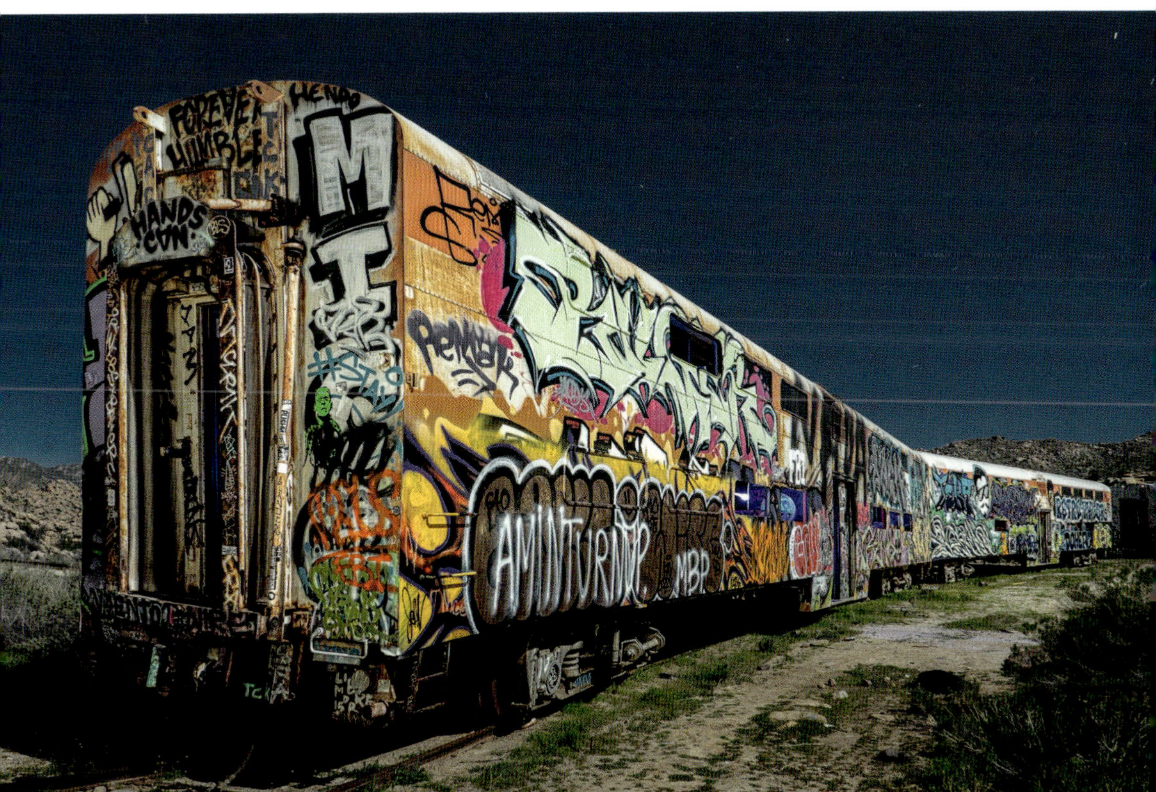

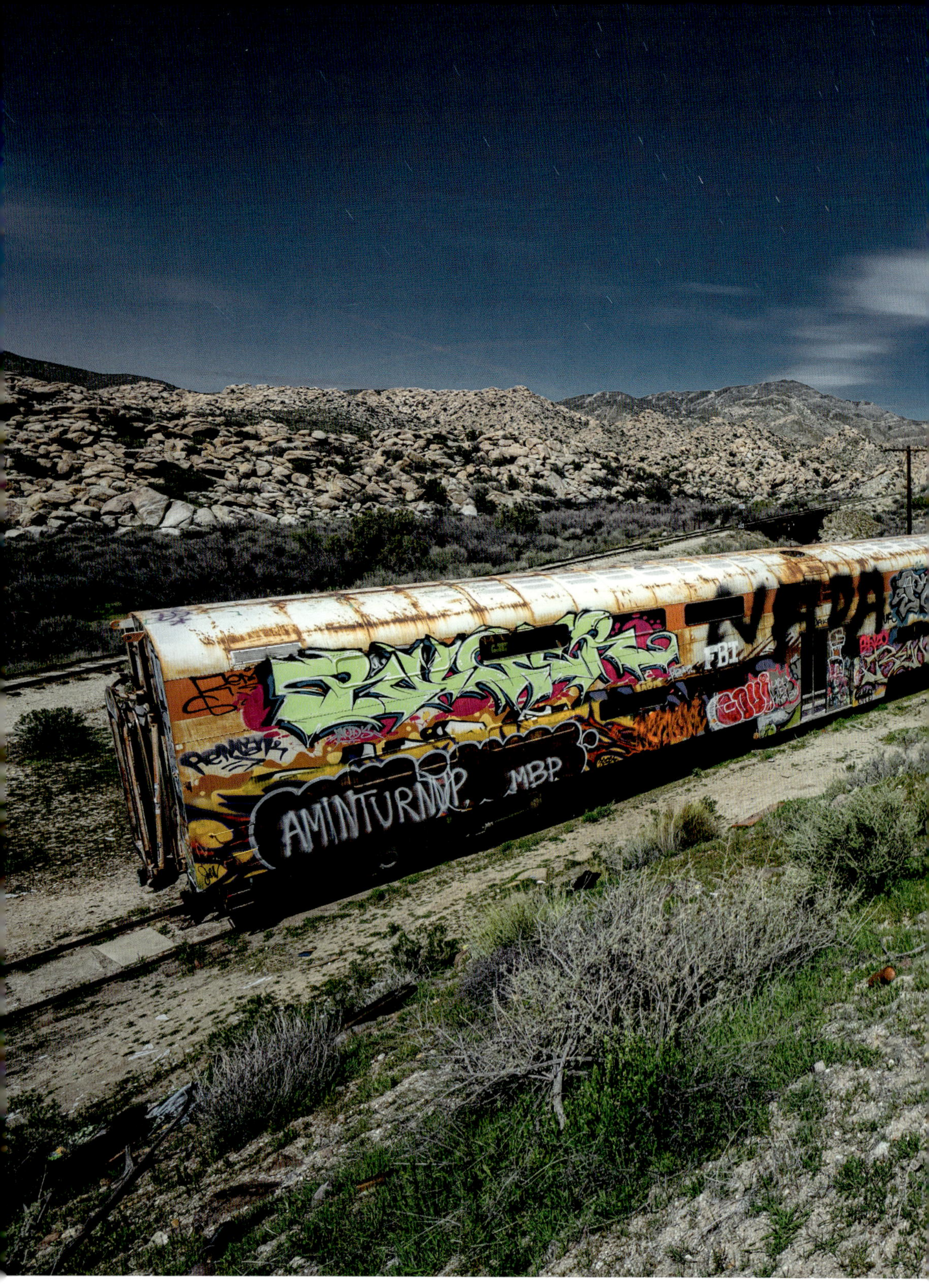

Nada Train, abandoned Metra Pullman cars near the border of Mexico, a long way from Chicago. Sonoran Desert.

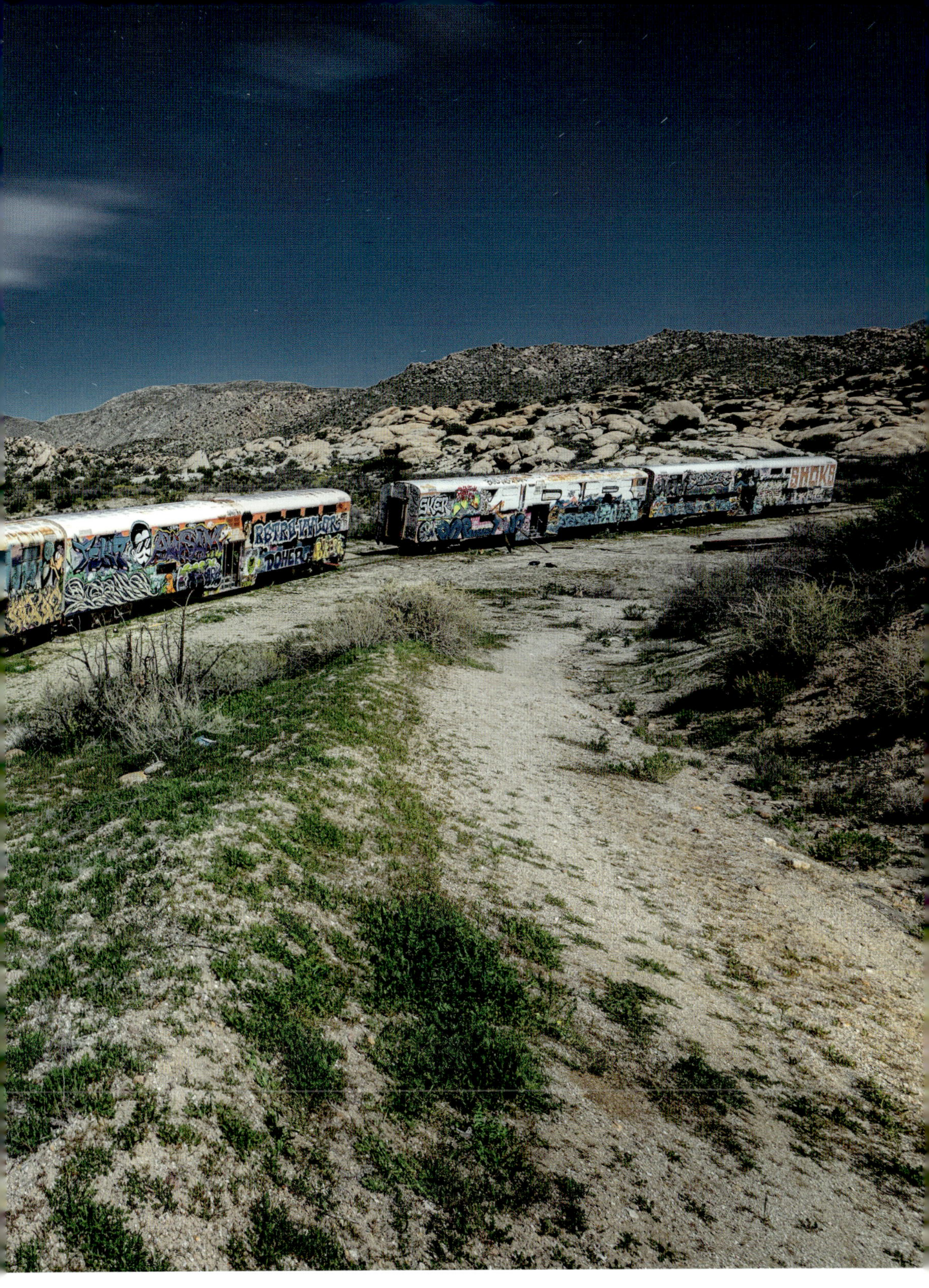

Nikon D750/Nikkor 14–24-mm f/2.8G lens. Two minutes thirty-one seconds f/8 ISO 200. March 2019. Full moon, warm white light from ProtoMachines LED2.

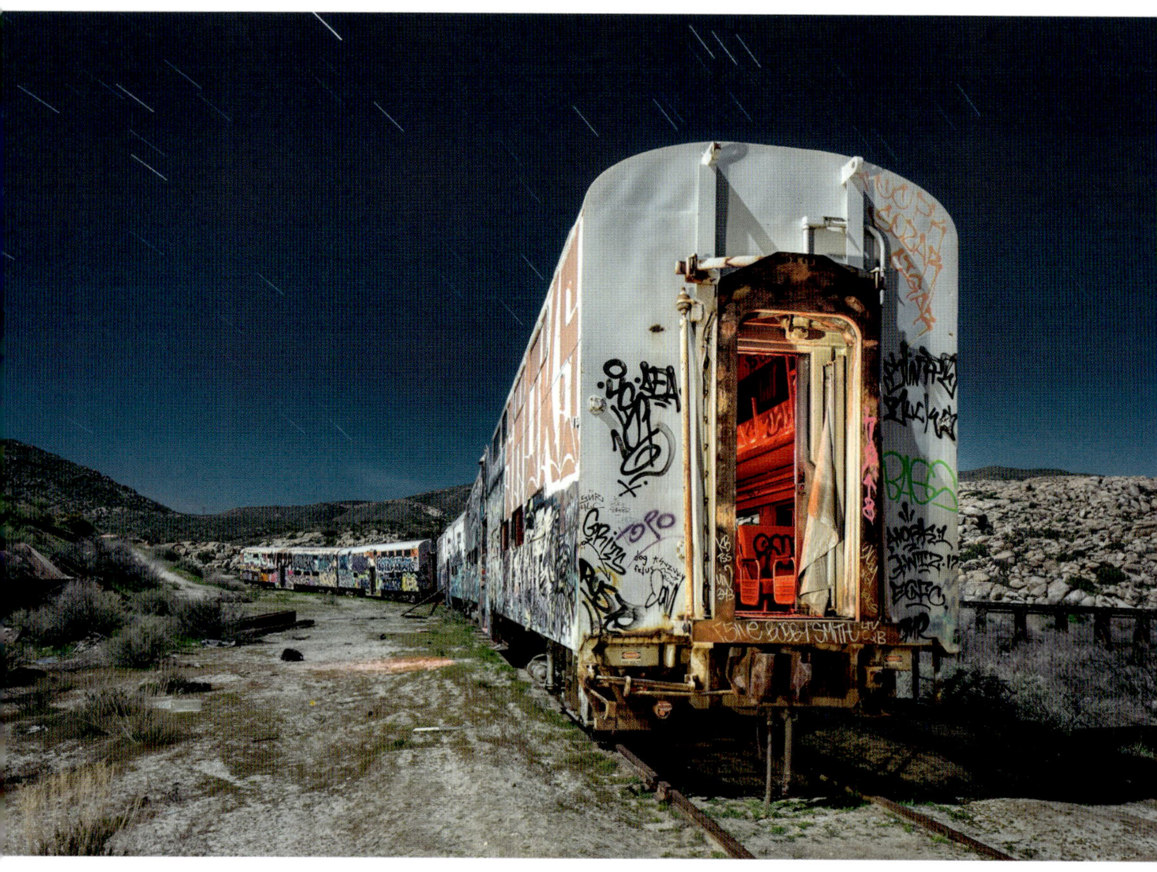

The Devil's Train, looking southwest as the stars drift over the Metra trains in the Sonoran Desert. Nikon D750/Nikkor 14–24-mm f/2.8G lens. Three minutes f/8 ISO 400. March 2019. Full moon, warm white and red light from ProtoMachines LED2.

▶ **Frankenpus Rides Again**, interior of one of the Metra trains near the border of Mexico. Sonoran Desert. Nikon D610/Rokinon 12-mm f/2.8 fisheye lens. One minute thirty-eight seconds f/8 ISO 200. March 2019. Green and blue light from ProtoMachines LED2.

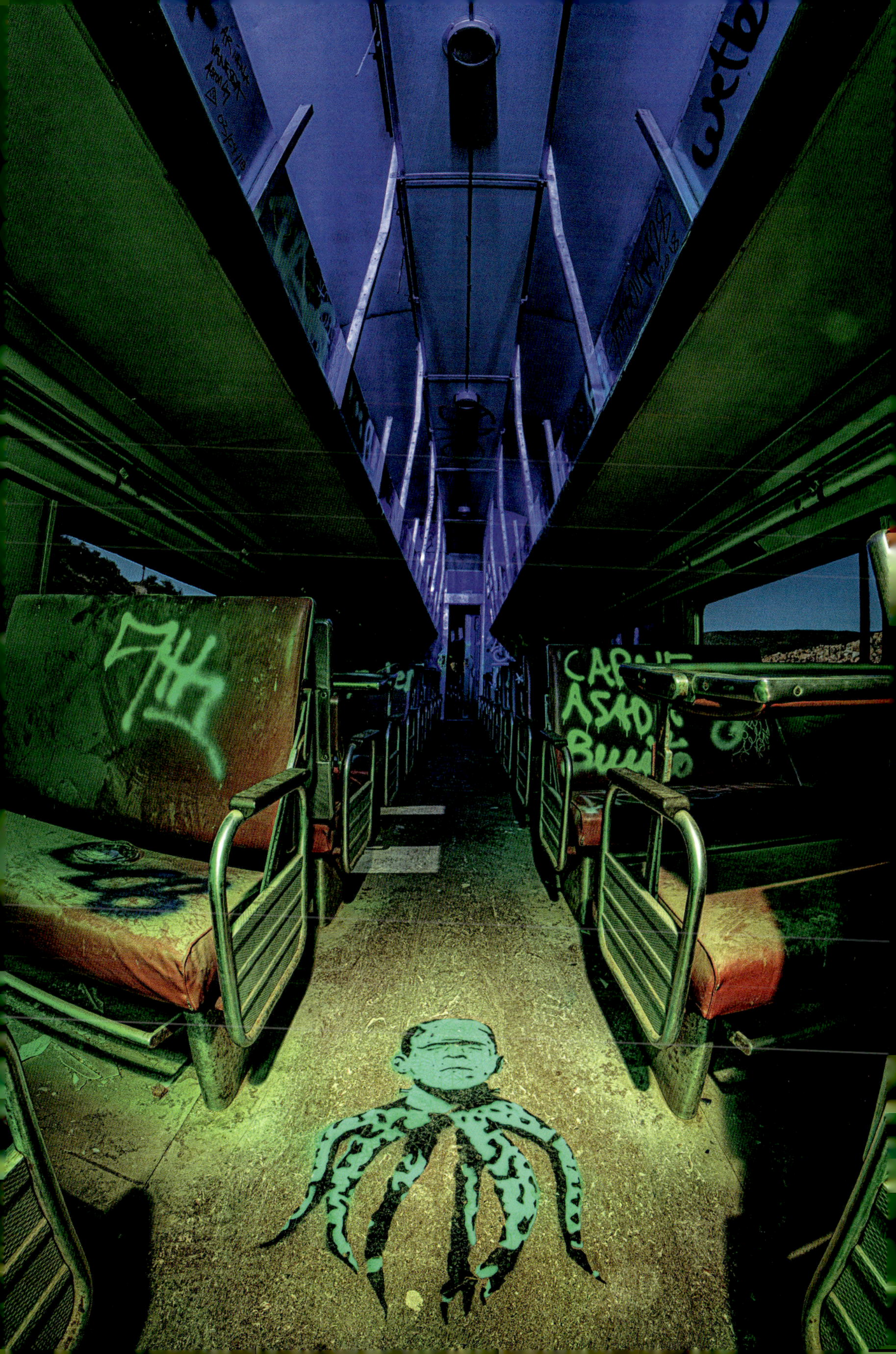

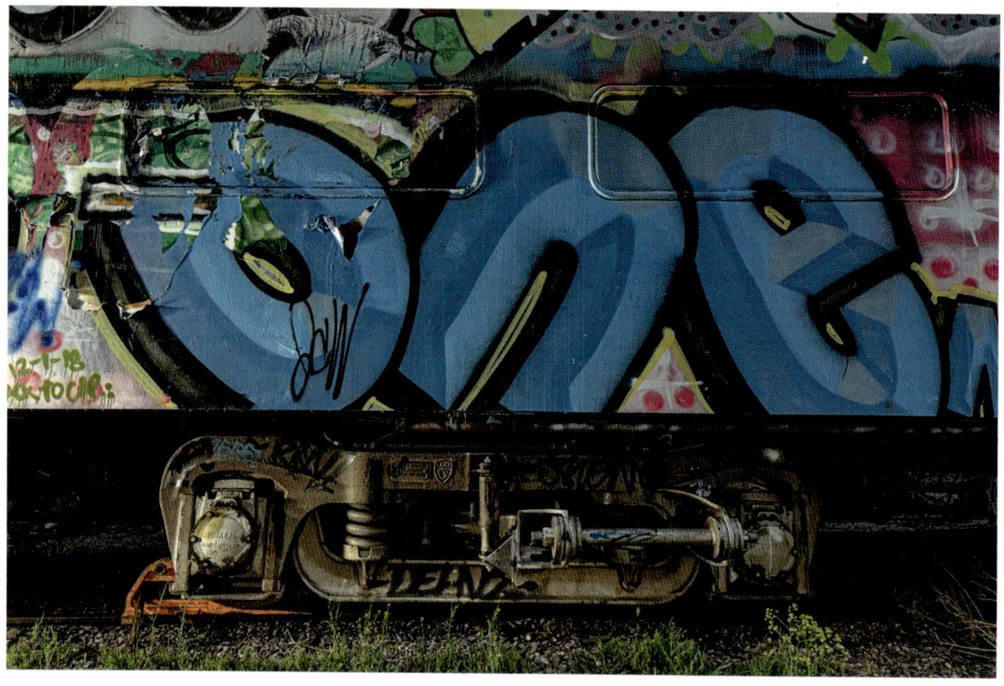

One, details of one of the abandoned Metra trains. Sonoran Desert.
Nikon D750/Nikkor 14–24-mm f/2.8G lens. One minute ten seconds f/8 ISO 200. March 2019.
Full moon, warm white light from ProtoMachines LED2.

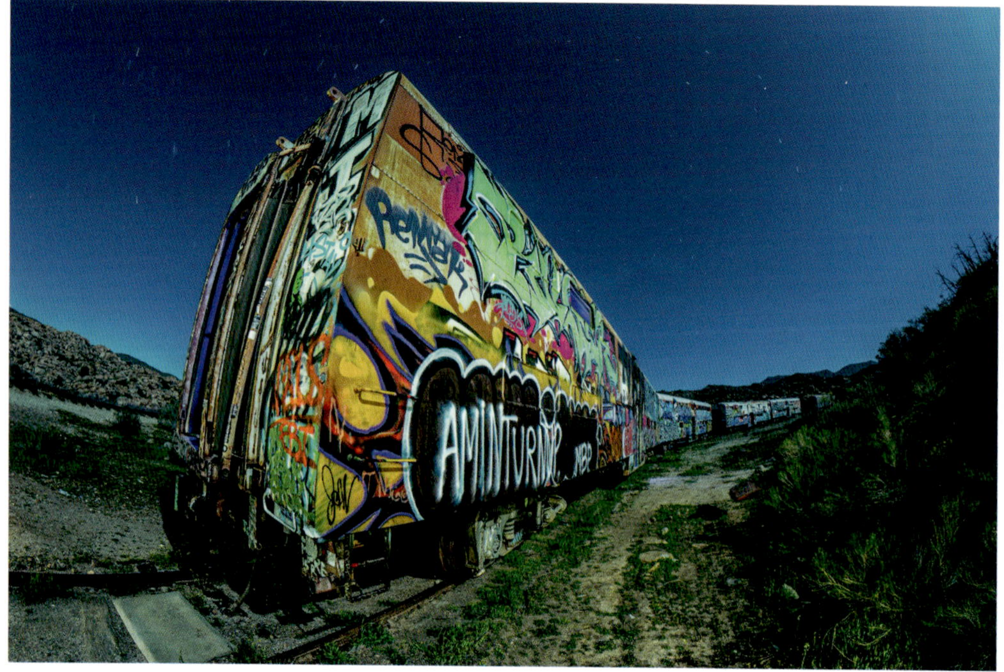

Driver 8, fisheye view of the end of the Metra trains. Sonoran Desert.
Nikon D610/Rokinon 12-mm f/2.8 fisheye lens. Four minutes nine seconds f/8 ISO 200. March 2019.
Full moon, warm white and blue light from ProtoMachines LED2.

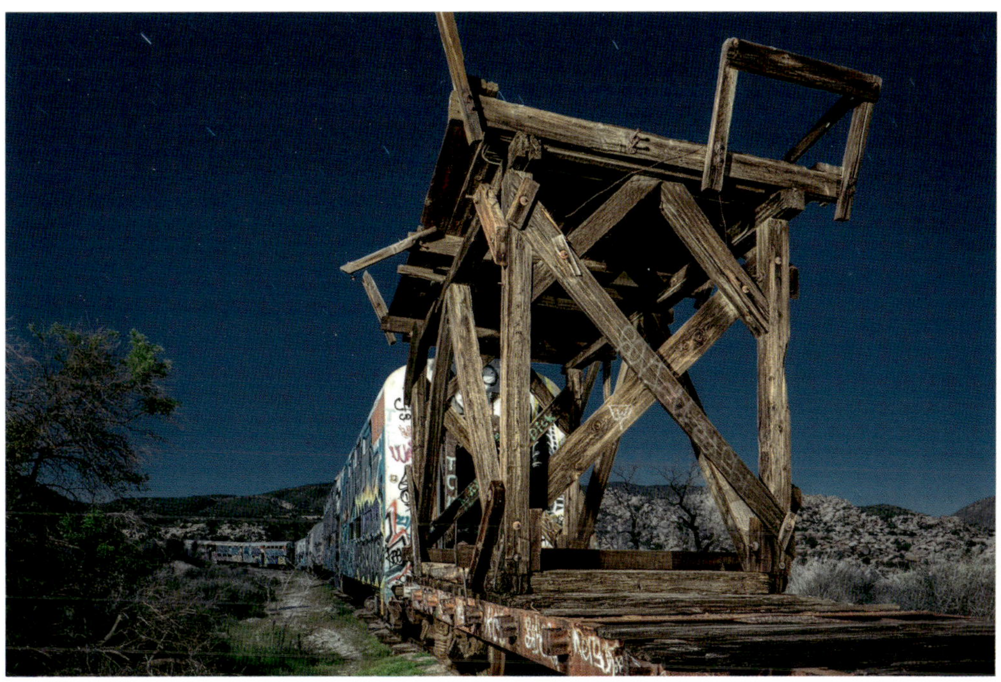

All the World's a Stage, wooden platform near the tail end of the Metra trains. Sonoran Desert.
Nikon D750/Nikkor 14–24-mm f/2.8G lens. Two minutes twenty-seven seconds f/8 ISO 400. March 2019.
Full moon, warm white light from ProtoMachines LED2.

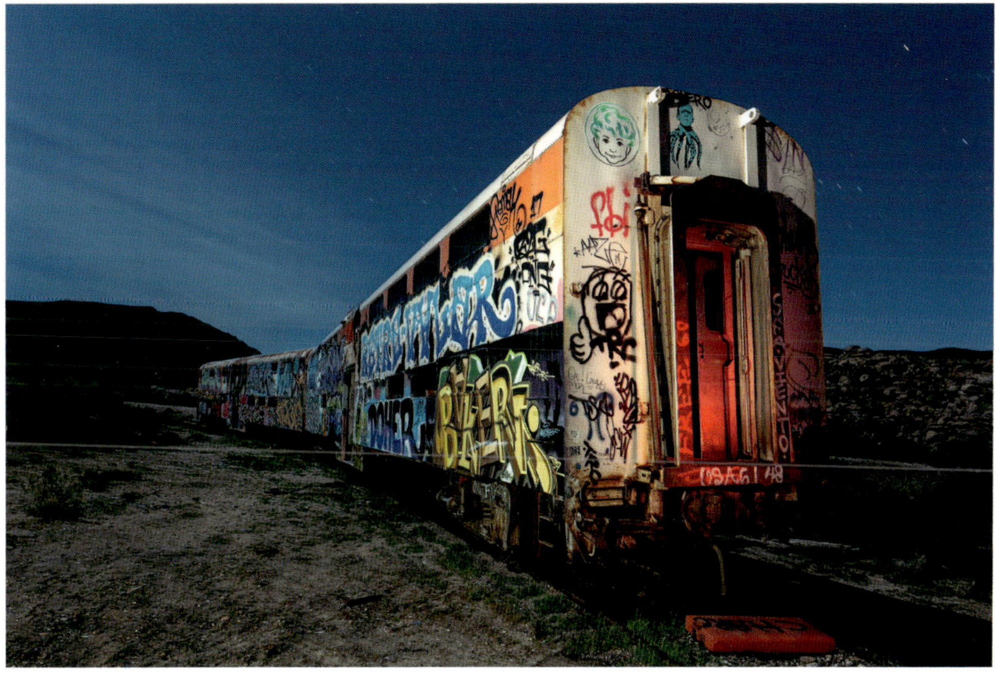

Painted Lady, Metra cars on an unused portion of railroad tracks in the Sonoran Desert.
Nikon D750/Nikkor 14–24-mm f/2.8G lens. One minute forty-four seconds f/8 ISO 200. March 2019.
Full moon, warm white and red light from ProtoMachines LED2.

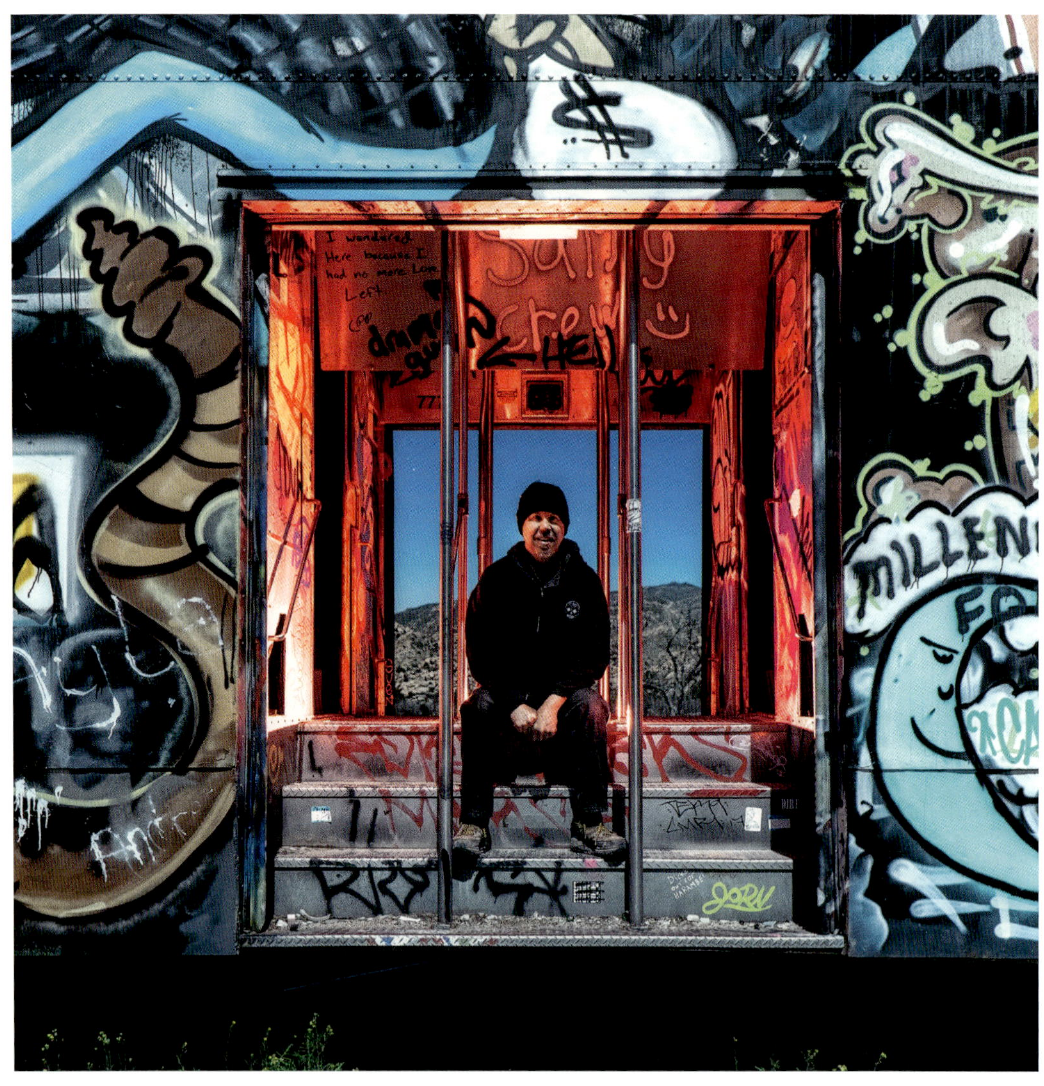

Last Ride to the Border, I managed to sit reasonably still on a Metra car for thirteen seconds. Sonoran Desert. Nikon D750/Nikkor 14–24-mm f/2.8G lens. Thirteen seconds f/8 ISO 1000. March 2019. Full moon, warm white and red light from ProtoMachines LED2.

Wooden Trains

The Impossible Train—an evocative title for a train line. Determined men wanted trains to barrel through the precipitous Carrizo Gorge mountain area despite engineers declaring it "impossible." And indeed, throughout construction, the project was beset by calamity after calamity. Railroad entrepreneurs John D. and Adolph Spreckels teamed up with Edward H. Harriman, persevering through financial depression, all Mexican laborers leaving the job to join the revolution in Mexico, World War I siphoning off railroad money, floods sweeping steam engines into mud, a worldwide flu pandemic, death, rock slides, and more.

Somehow, the project was finished on November 15, 1919. Spreckels drove in a golden spike inscribed "Spike driven, by John D. Spreckels, President." On the other side of the spike, it said, "Last spike driven, San Diego & Arizona Railway, in Carriso Gorge—November 15, 1919." By December 1, the first trains completed the almost 148-mile journey from El Centro to San Diego. By May, Mother Nature decided to put the "Impossible" back into "Impossible Train," sending rocks and dirt tumbling into a tunnel. Throughout the years, there was more disaster, including flash floods, fires, mountain slides, and World War II, and with it, passenger lines finally came to an end in January 1951, marking the end of an era.

One depot for handling passengers for the San Diego & Arizona Eastern Railroad's Desert Line was built in 1919 at Jacumba Hot Springs (a place so close to the border of Mexico that my friend's mobile phone sent him alerts about his service provider's roaming policies). This depot handled the passengers in 1951. For now, the former depot serves as a yard for abandoned railway cars and is on private property.

After photographing the Metras during our "Night of Trains," we walk back down the railway tracks and drive to photograph wooden trains at the old depot. These cars appear to be about 100 years old and seem to serve as occasional homes, with old mattresses, stoves, and even a Yerba Mate found inside. No one else is around, so we photograph in peace.

Will the "Impossible Railroad" ever carry passengers? Baja Railroads and Robert Smith, who lives in the old stationmaster's house, hope to resuscitate a passenger line again, but have made little progress so far.

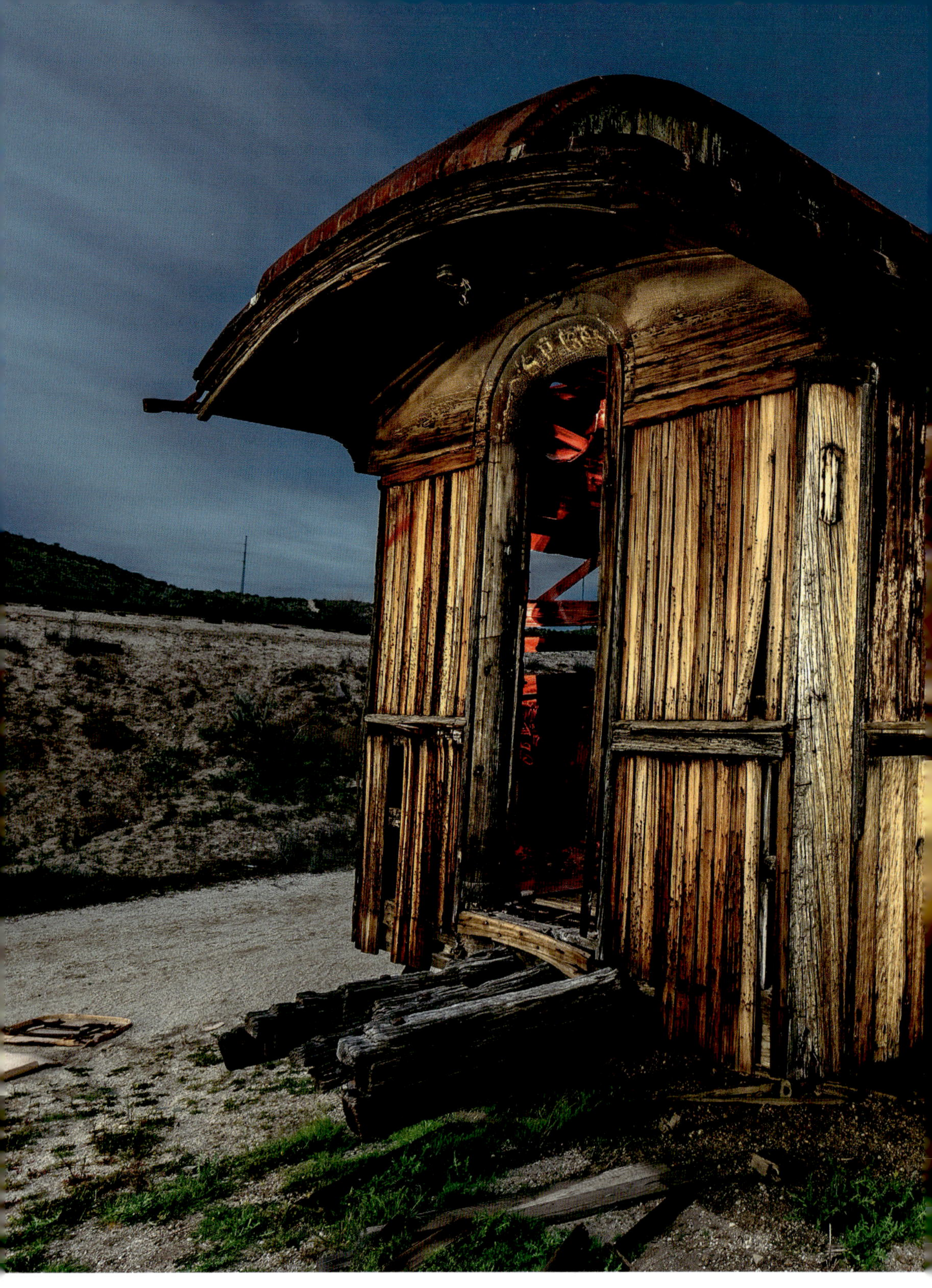

All Aboard for Dreamland, wooden passenger train at the site of the former depot for San Diego & Arizona Eastern Railroad's Desert Line in Jacumba Hot Springs.

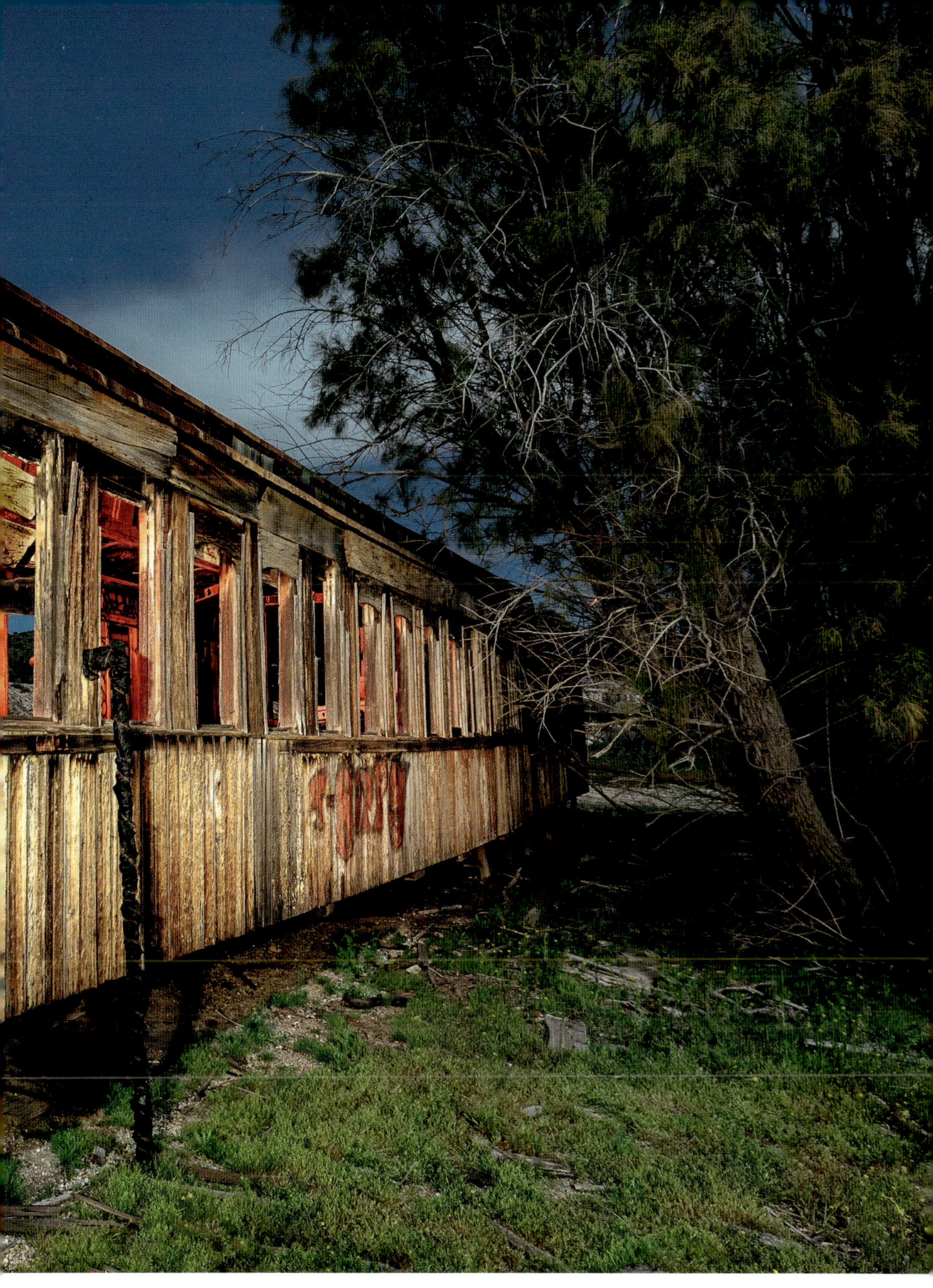

Nikon D750/Nikkor 14–24-mm f/2.8G lens. Two minutes thirty-two seconds f/8 ISO 400. March 2019. Full moon, warm white and red light from ProtoMachines LED2.

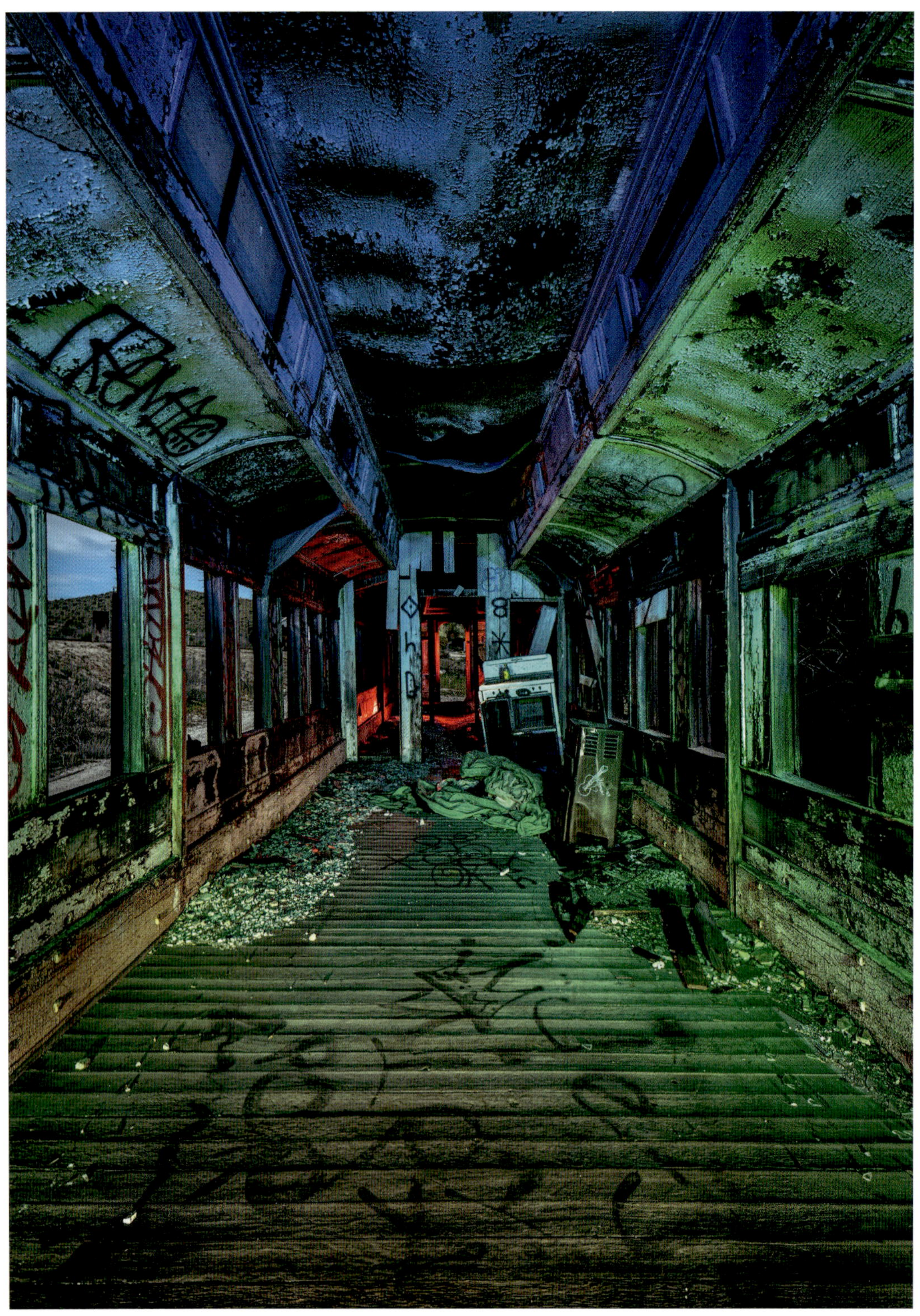

Blue Night Express, wooden passenger car and perhaps someone's temporary home. Jacumba Hot Springs. Nikon D750/Nikkor 14–24-mm f/2.8G lens. Two minutes twenty-two seconds f/8 ISO 400. March 2019. Full moon, warm white, blue, and green light from ProtoMachines LED2.

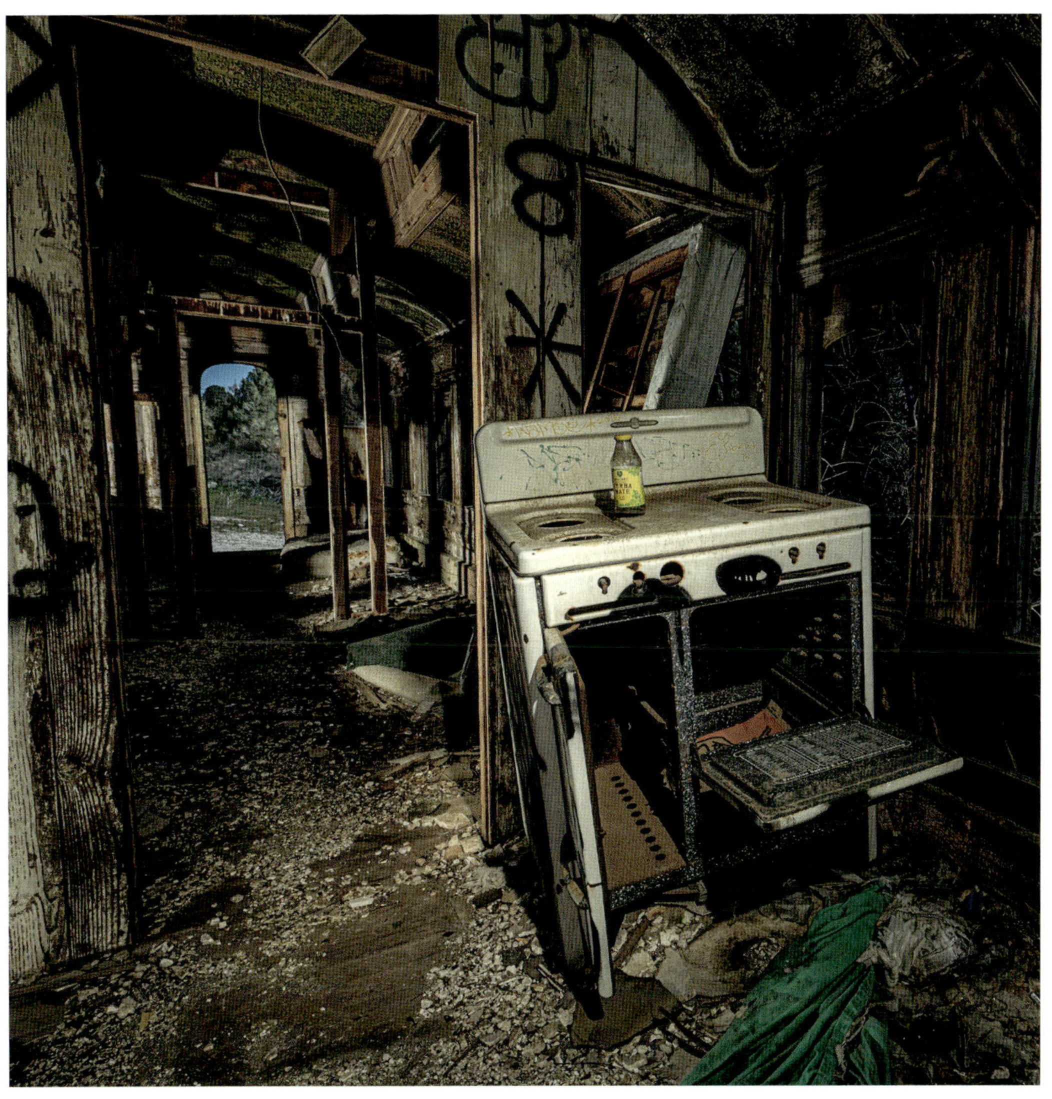

Yerba Mate Express, wooden passenger car near the border of Mexico. Jacumba Hot Springs.
Nikon D750/Nikkor 14–24-mm f/2.8G lens. One minute fifty-three seconds f/8 ISO 400. March 2019.
Full moon, warm white from ProtoMachines LED2.

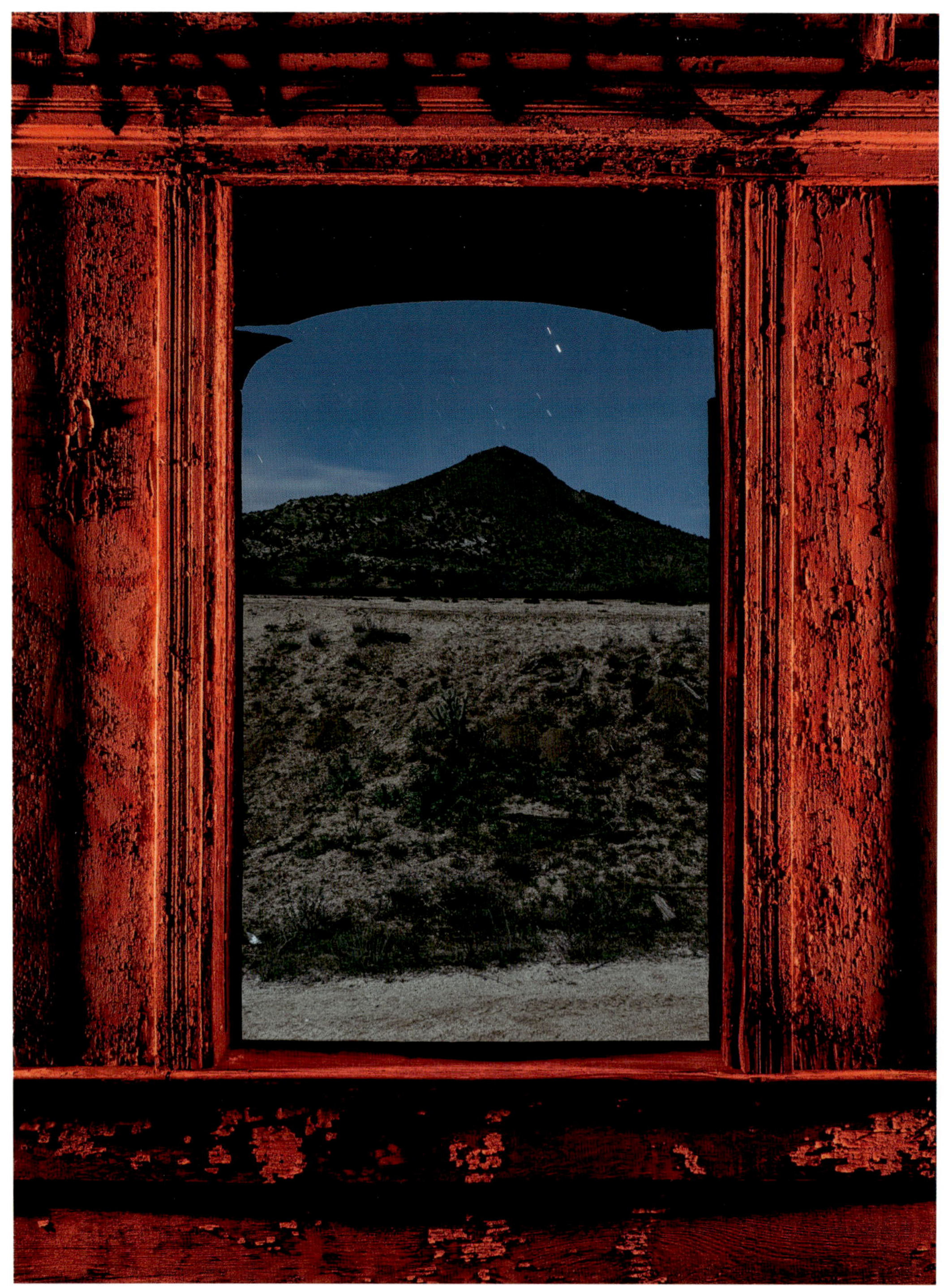

The View from the Mexico Express, a view from the train, almost looking like a picture frame hung inside the passenger car. Nikon D750/Nikkor 14–24-mm f/2.8G lens. Two minutes f/8 ISO 400. I photographed this twice, focusing first on the window frame, then on the exterior scene, then blending them together later ("focus stacking"). March 2019. Full moon, red light from ProtoMachines LED2.

Locomotives near Hwy 8

The Idaho Northern and Pacific 4501 locomotive was built in 1966. However, today, it and two other locomotives and a bent flatcar rest near the Mexico border along the San Diego and Arizona Eastern Railway. There is not a lot of information on how they got here. A post on trainorder.com states that these locomotives were not secured, causing the units to smash into at least one flatcar, destroying the car as well as the three locomotives. After that, they were moved to Coyote Wells, where they now bake beneath the hot Sonoran sun. The yellow flatcar has an S-shaped bend from this accident, plainly visible, looking like a photographer went mad with the Liquify Tool in Photoshop.

Mike and I arrive well after 1 a.m. We have already photographed Metras and wooden passenger cars. By this time, it is cold and breezy. The clouds are beautiful, blowing quickly by. Most night photographers prefer completely clear skies—not me; I love the texture and sense of motion clouds provide, and love to incorporate them into my compositions by using them to frame the subject matter. We photograph here with the sound of cars and trucks whizzing by in the distance.

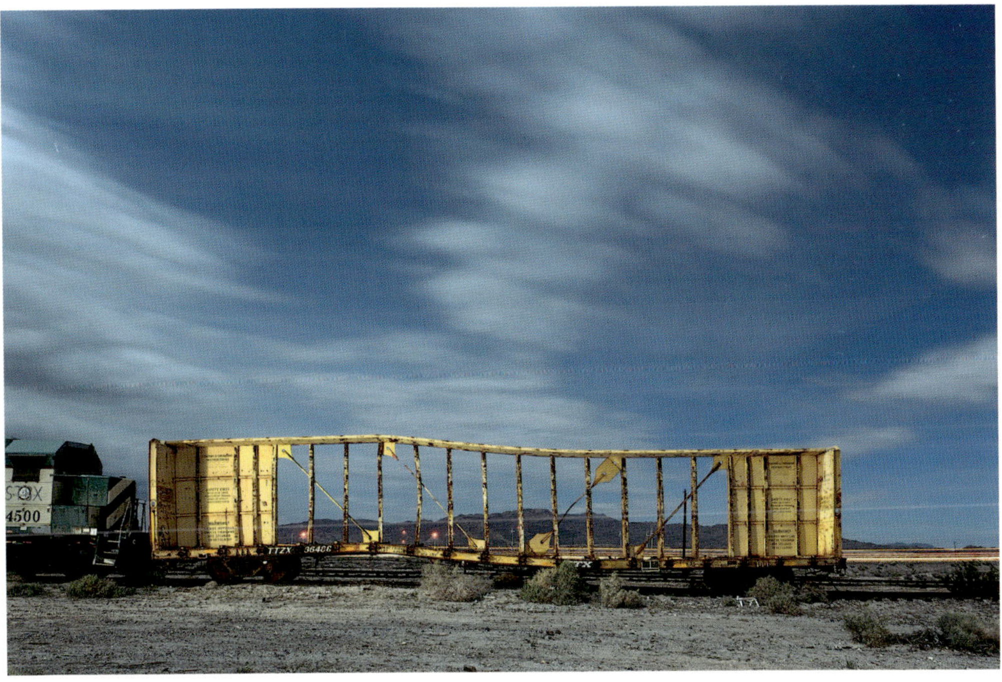

South Bend, an S-shaped flatcar, bent from an apparent accident. Sonoran Desert. Nikon D750/Nikkor 14–24-mm f/2.8G lens. Six minutes f/8 ISO 320. March 2019. Full moon, warm white light from ProtoMachines LED2.

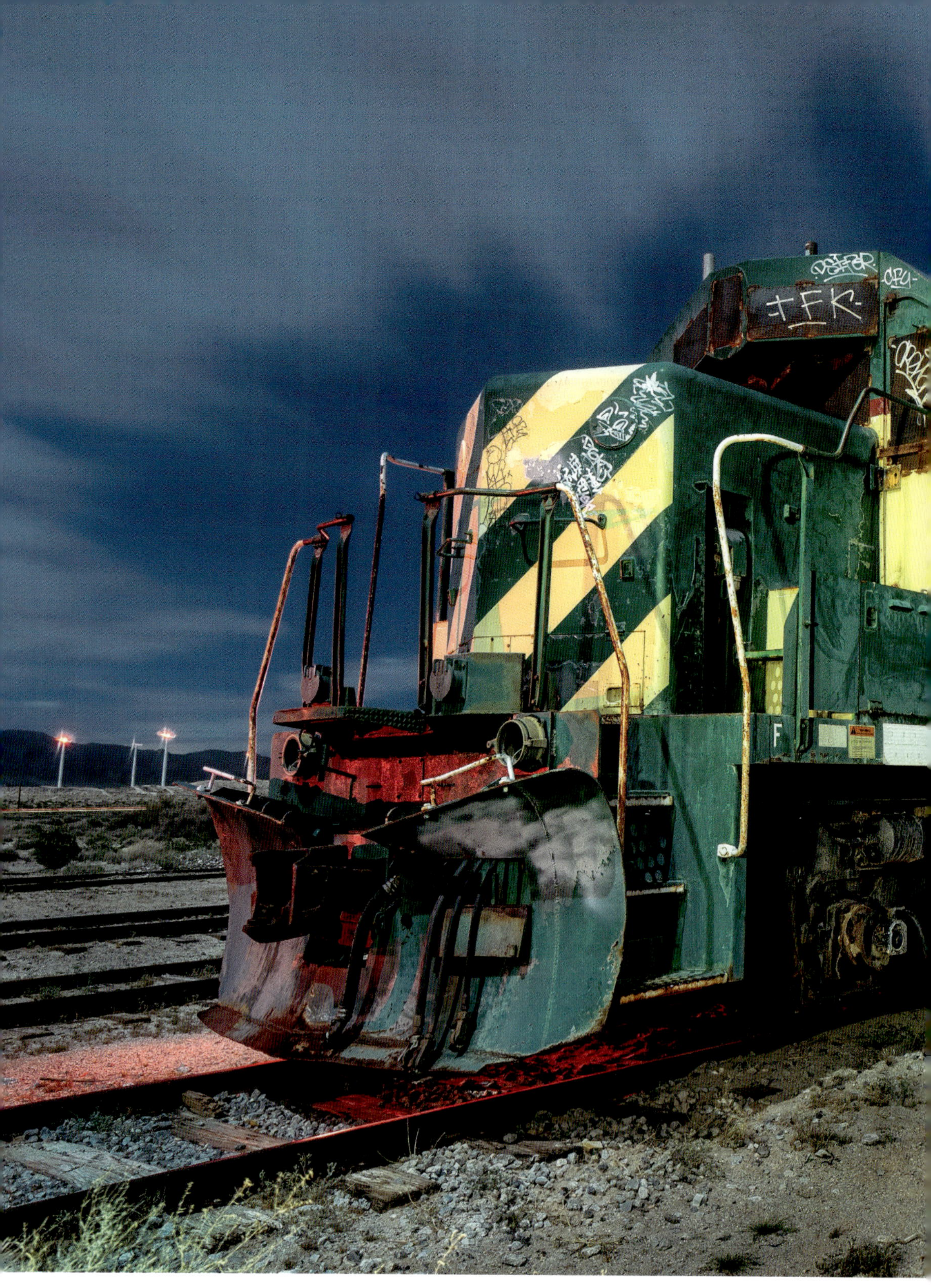

The Idaho Northern and Pacific 4501 locomotive, built in 1966, and now abandoned near the border of Mexico. Sonoran Desert.

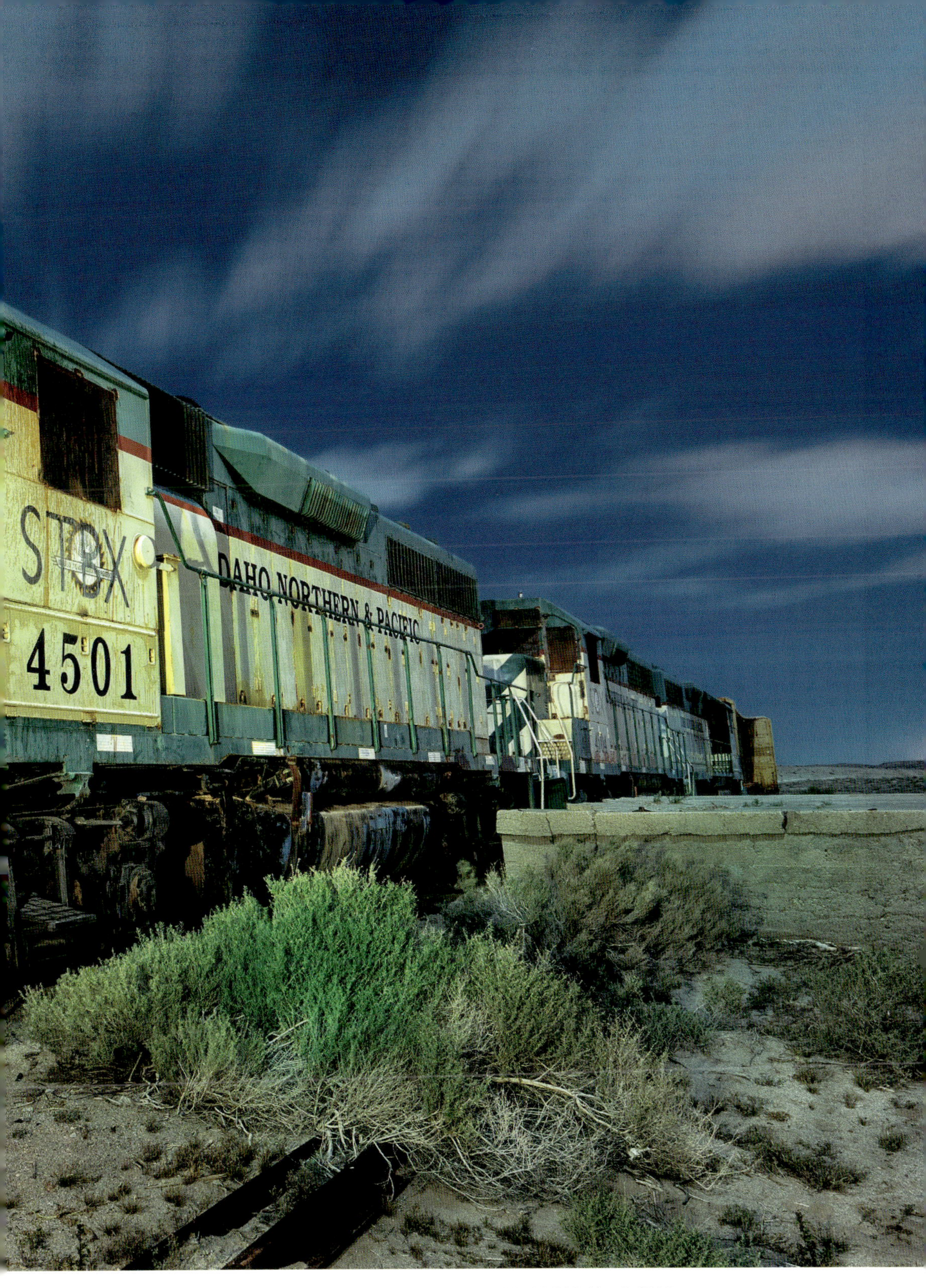

Nikon D750/Nikkor 14–24-mm f/2.8G lens. Two minutes f/8 ISO 320. March 2019.
Full moon, warm white light from ProtoMachines LED2.

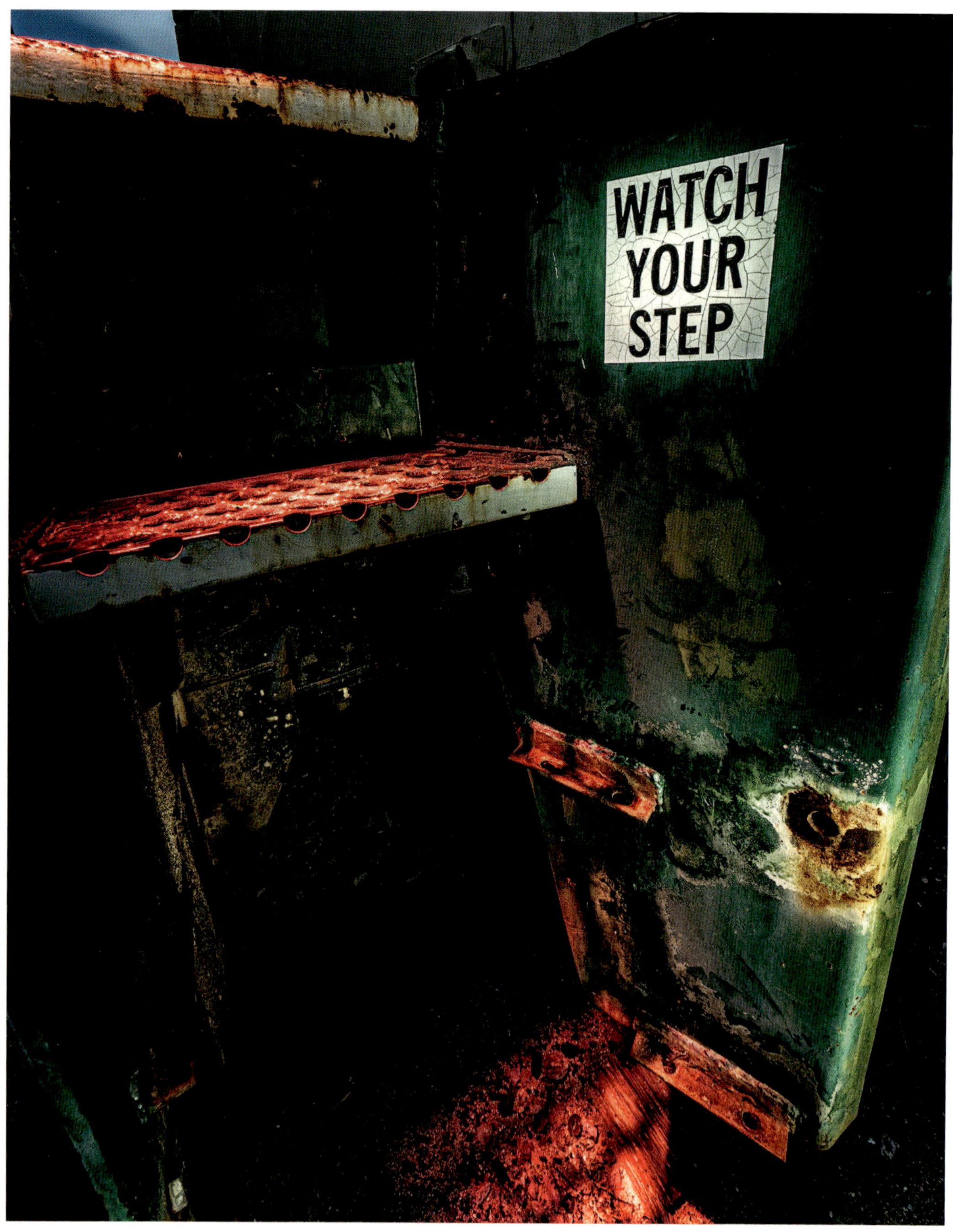

Watch Your Step, rusted steps from one of the locomotives near the border of Mexico. Sonoran Desert.
Nikon D750/Nikkor 14–24-mm f/2.8G lens. One minute five seconds f/8 ISO 320. March 2019.
Full moon, warm white and red light from ProtoMachines LED2.

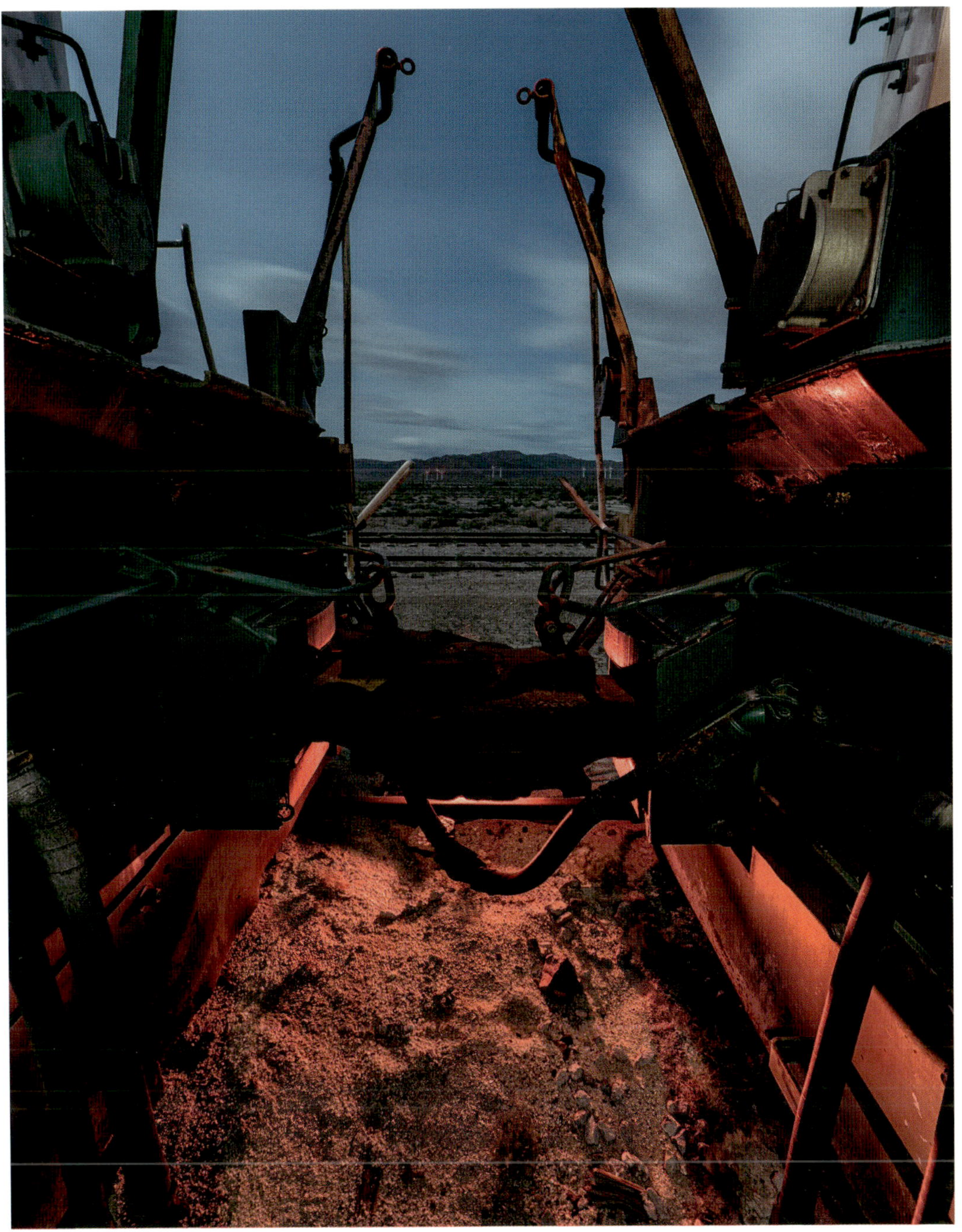

Idaho Hook-Up, locomotive couplings, and in the distance, numerous windmills. Sonoran Desert. Nikon D750/Nikkor 14–24-mm f/2.8G lens. Five minutes thirteen seconds f/8 ISO 320. March 2019. Full moon, red light from ProtoMachines LED2.

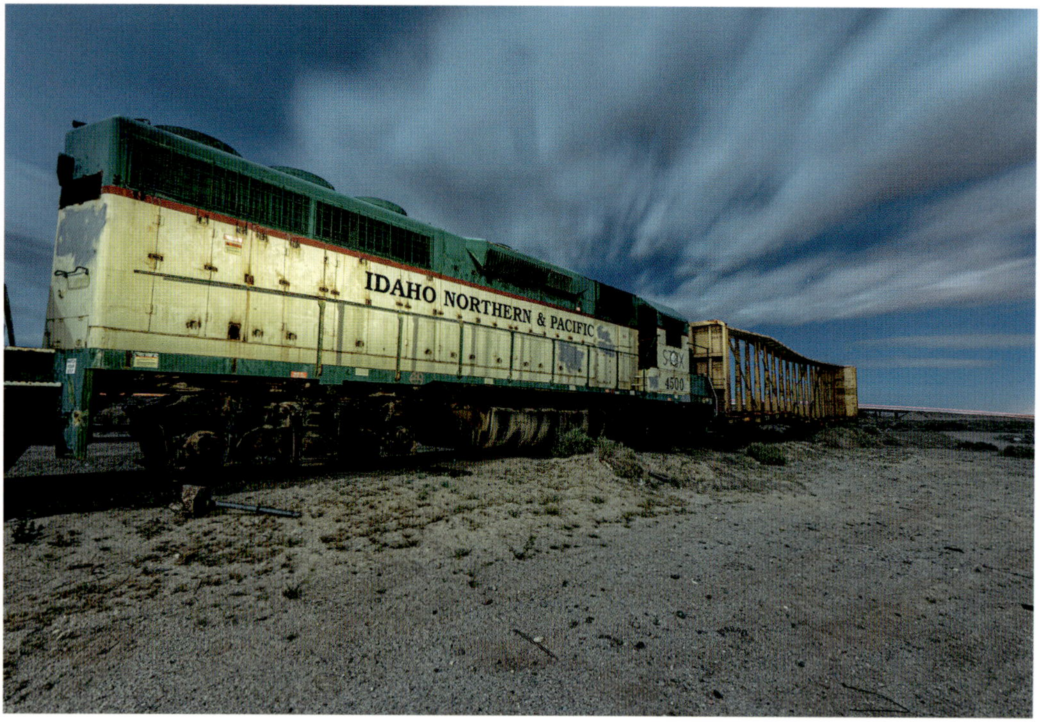
IDAHO NORTHERN & PACIFIC
4500

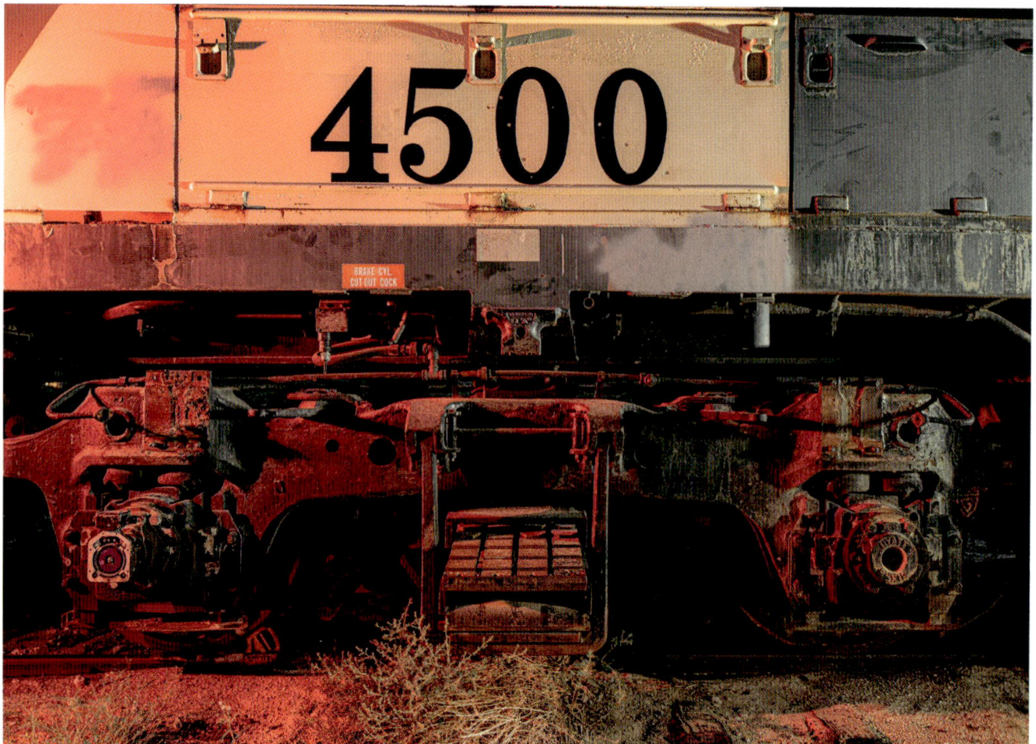
4500
BRAKE CYL.
CUT OUT COCK

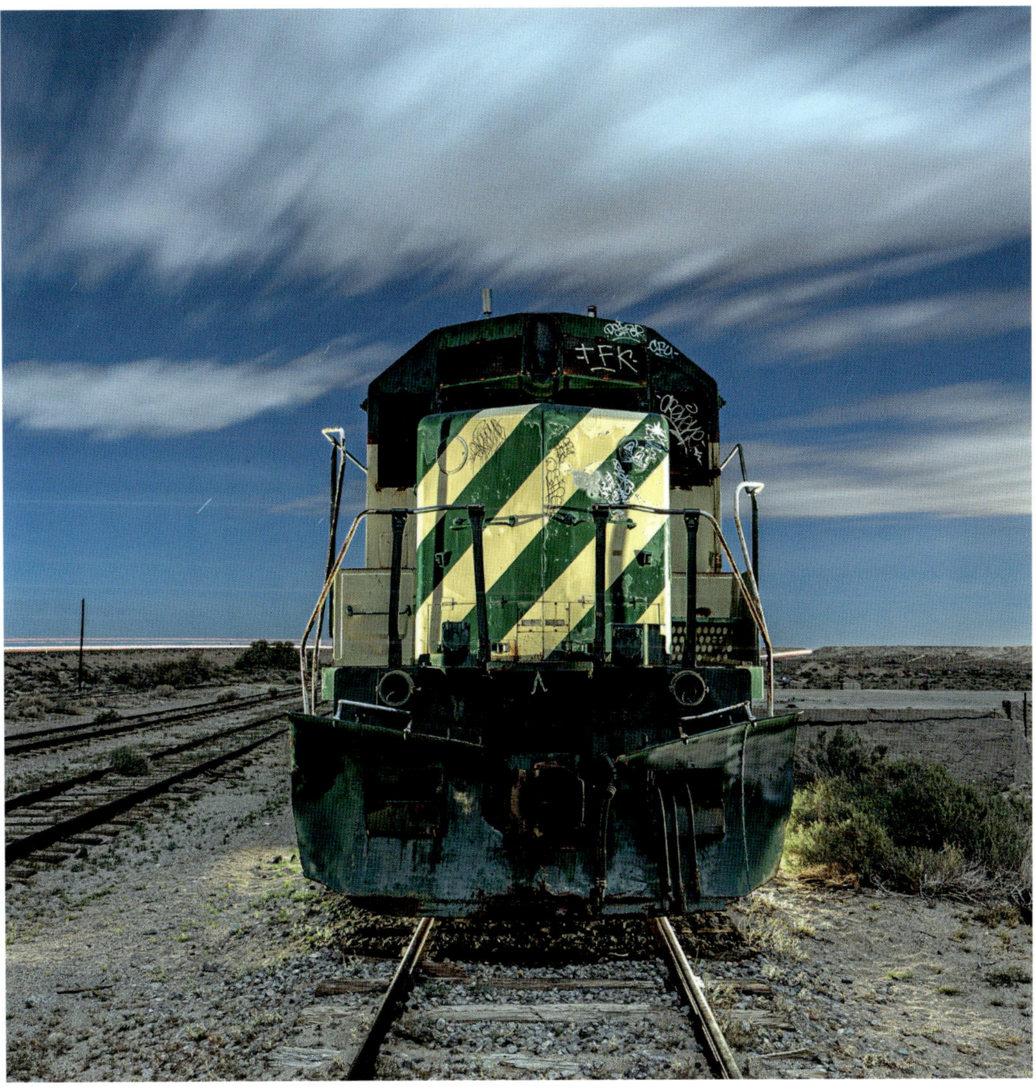

Loco Moco, front view, Idaho Northern and Pacific 4501 locomotive. Sonoran Desert.
Nikon D750/Nikkor 14–24-mm f/2.8G lens. Two minutes f/8 ISO 320. March 2019.
Full moon, red and warm white light from ProtoMachines LED2.

Opposite Page

▲ **It was a Left to Idaho**, locomotives left abandoned in the Sonoran Desert.
Nikon D750/Nikkor 14–24-mm f/2.8G lens. Two minutes f/8 ISO 320. March 2019.
Full moon, warm white light from ProtoMachines LED2.

▼ **Cut-Out Cock**, locomotive wheels. Sonoran Desert.
Nikon D750/Nikkor 14–24-mm f/2.8G lens. One minute forty-one seconds f/8 ISO 320. March 2019.
Full moon, warm white and red light from ProtoMachines LED2.

Southern California Railway Museum

I meet my friends Ron, Dave and Ivan at the museum, and we head nearby for a Hawaiian fish meal. We have not photographed together in over fifteen months. The museum grounds are considerably brighter than we anticipated. It is, after all, in the middle of Perris, CA. There are also quite a few lights on the premises. Nevertheless, the museum has many incredible train cars and locomotives, and we enjoy a beautiful night of photography.

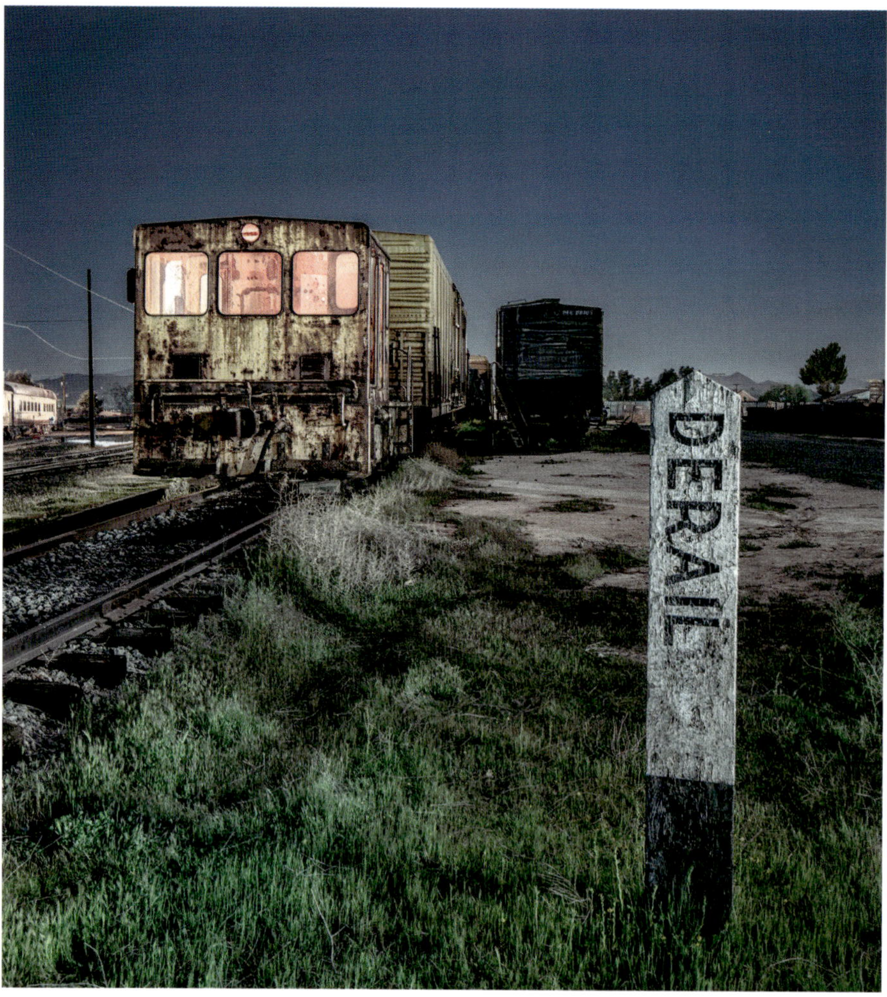

Derail, vintage railcar with faded words saying “Trona” painted on its side, Southern California Railway Museum.
Pentax K-1/15-30mm f/2.8 lens. NInety-four seconds f/8 ISO 200. March 2021.
Full moon, strong ambient light, warm white and red light from ProtoMachines LED2.

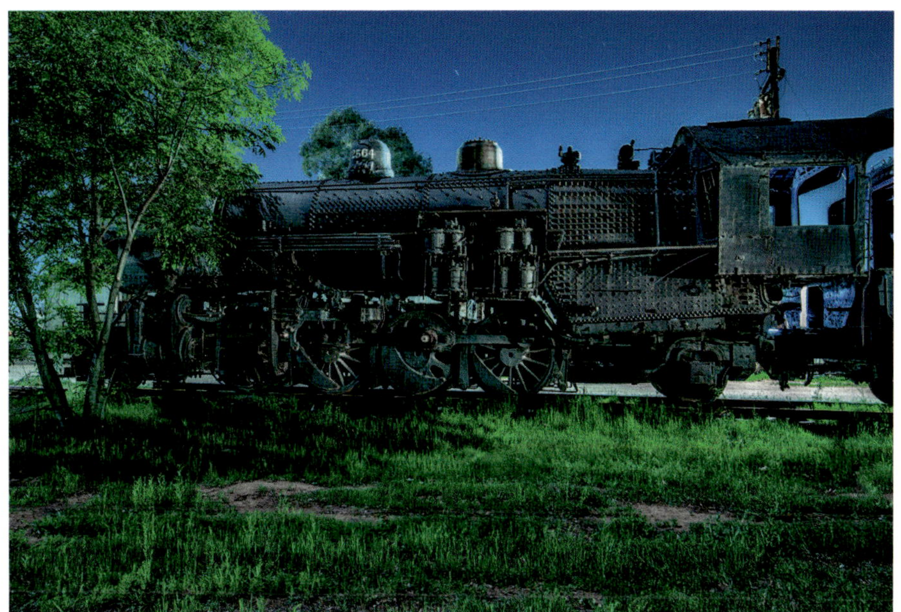

Large and In Charge, 1921 Union Pacific Steam Engine 2564, Southern California Railway Museum. This behemoth was built in 1921 and weighs 300,000 lbs./136,077.71 kg. This "Mikado"-type coal-burning steam locomotive was originally built for UP subsidiary Los Angeles & Salt Lake Railroad.
Pentax K-1/15-30mm f/2.8 lens. 104 seconds f/8 ISO 200. March 2021.
Full moon, strong ambient light, warm white light from ProtoMachines LED2.

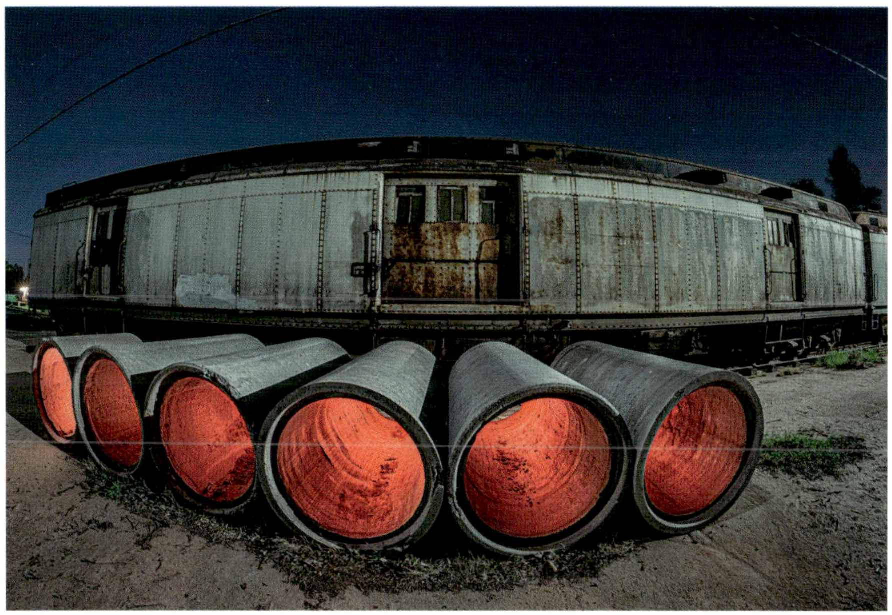

Horse Car Red, rusty vintage horse car, Southern California Railway Museum. I actually laughed out loud when I first peered into the viewfinder while composing the photo. The cement pipes looked like teeth. I made them look even weirder by light painting the inside of the cement pipes red.
Nikon D750/Rokinon 12mm f/2.8 fisheye lens. One minute f/8 ISO 200. March 2021.
Full moon, strong ambient light, warm white and red light from ProtoMachines LED2.

3

AUTOMOBILES

Cars Buried in Mojave Sand

Tim, Steve, Dave, and I are rumbling down an endless dark dirt road, many miles from the closest town. We are well-prepared with radios, water supplies, and more. We are venturing to a remote part of the Mojave Desert. There will be no cell signal and no humans there. Or so we think.

To our surprise, we see a car lit up by our headlights. It is resting in a position that is clearly not good, completely perpendicular to the road and half off. A young couple are standing forlornly to one side, stranded, waving their hands for us to stop. They had attempted to turn around, not realizing how soft the side of the road was. Now, the front of their car is considerably lower, its front wheels deep in sand and dirt. They are hoping for a ride back to town.

"You're lucky that we saw you. No one drives down this road. Especially at night." They nod, saying that they had been there for hours, and we were the first people they had seen.

We tell them that we are doing some night photography, and that we will return this way in a few hours. They look a little concerned, but we assure them we will come back this way. They tell us that they have a trunk full of water, food, and sleeping bags and will be okay for a while.

We rattle on further into the night. Finally, we stop, gather our camera backpacks and tripods, and set off even deeper into the dark desert. There are no trails. We walk across the desert floor for twenty minutes. Odd dark shapes emerge. Numerous cars are jammed into the sand at odd, awkward angles, some sideways, others upside down, and some simply buried up to the door handles.

The moon rises higher in the sky as we photograph this odd place. It is one of the quietest places I have been. I could spend several nights photographing here, but feel fortunate to be here right now.

And yes, on the way back, I give the young couple a ride back to the closest town.

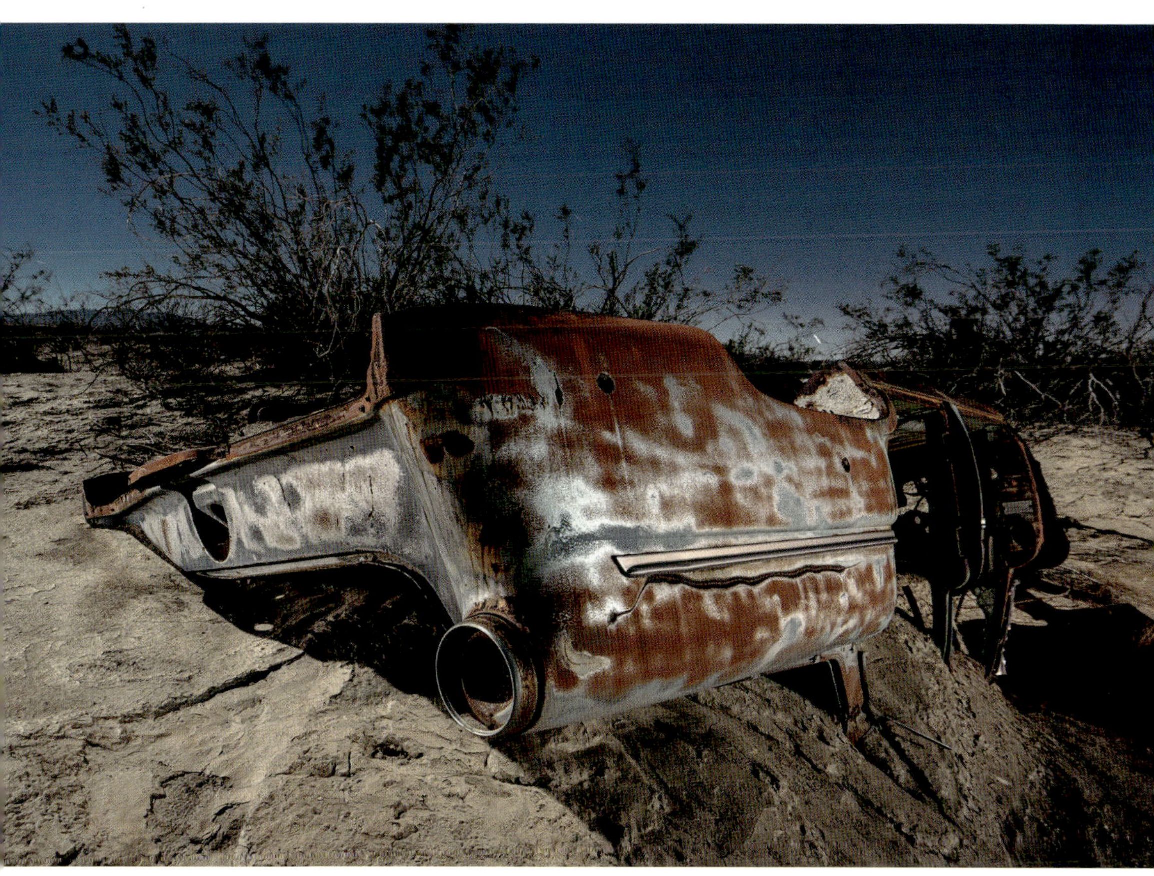

Stuck on You, upside down among the creosote. Mojave Desert.
Nikon D610/14–24-mm f/2.8G lens. Three-minute twenty-second exposure f/8 ISO 200. March 2016.
Full moon, warm white light from ProtoMachines LED2.

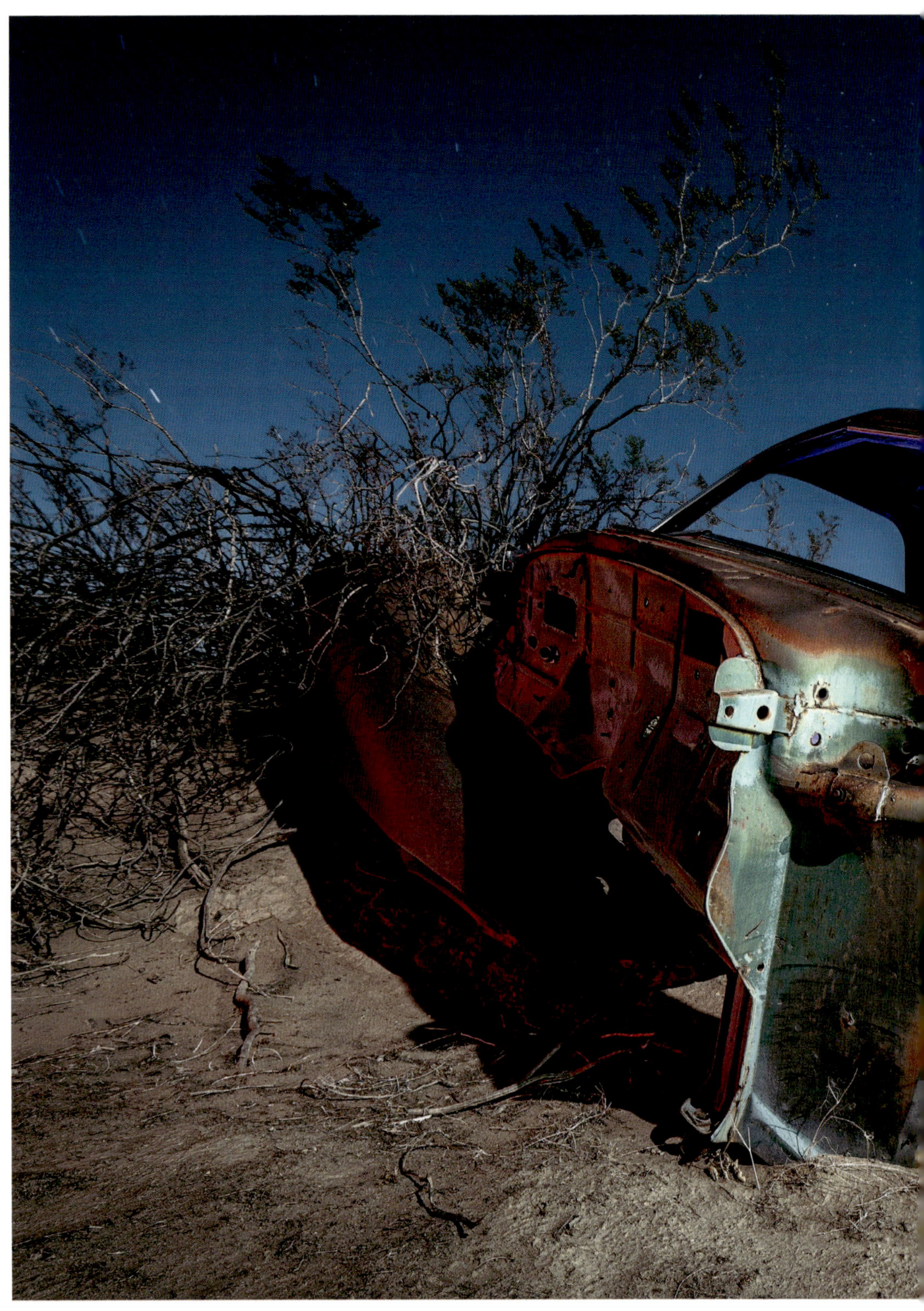

Spring is Coming, one from a mysterious collection of half-buried old cars in the Mojave Desert.

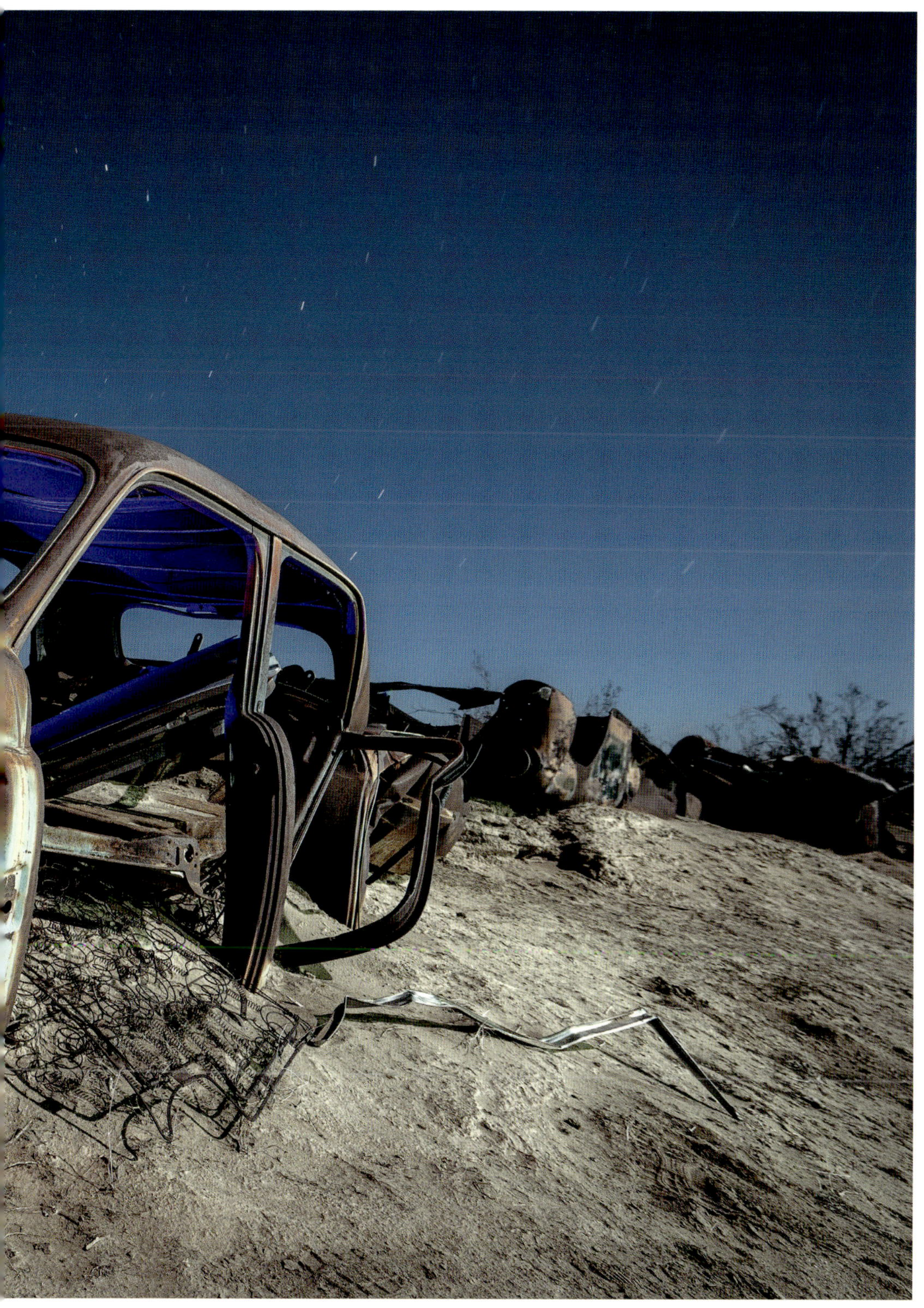

Nikon D610/14–24-mm f/2.8G lens. Three-minute forty-seven-second exposure f/8 ISO 200. March 2016. Full moon, warm white and blue light from ProtoMachines LED2.

Nike Missile Base

Growing up during the Cold War in Los Angeles with the threat of nuclear attack, residents knew that once a month on a Friday morning, they would hear the siren wail of the Civil Defense. Children practiced "duck and cover" drills or ran to fallout shelters.

Today, many Angelenos may not realize that from 1958 to 1974 there were army bases throughout the city armed with Nike Hercules missiles, ready to fire at enemy airplanes. In fact, there were actually sixteen missile bases around Los Angeles known as the "Ring of Steel," created during the Cold War to defend against attack. These were capable of launching missiles with an intercept range of 100,000 feet. However, none were ever launched against an enemy.

I am fascinated with this history, and I am wanting to photograph places near my house, trying not to travel far during the COVID-19 pandemic. I drive over to the abandoned missile base closest to my house. It is located near the Santa Susana Pass.

The first evening I visit is very cool. I am already thirsty from the steep walk up the hill, but I find the view exhilarating, at least until a coastal fog rolls in. I am immediately taken with how beautiful the mountainous area is.

During the second visit, the skies stay clear. It is near Independence Day. In the San Fernando Valley below, I hear the distant reverberation of fireworks crackling and booming, providing a soundtrack to my night of creative photography.

This particular location was the last of the sixteen Los Angeles Nike missile sites to be completed due to the rugged terrain and just one usable road. Construction crews needed to level a mountain peak and dig deep into the ground for the three underground missile launchers, which still can be seen today, along with a missile assembly building, dog sentry kennel, and other dilapidated structures.

Additionally, there are two heavily tagged city buses. They are also charred, a result of the Sesnon Fire in October of 2008. And if that is not enough, they are also riddled with bullet holes. The LAPD SWAT teams use the location for practice.

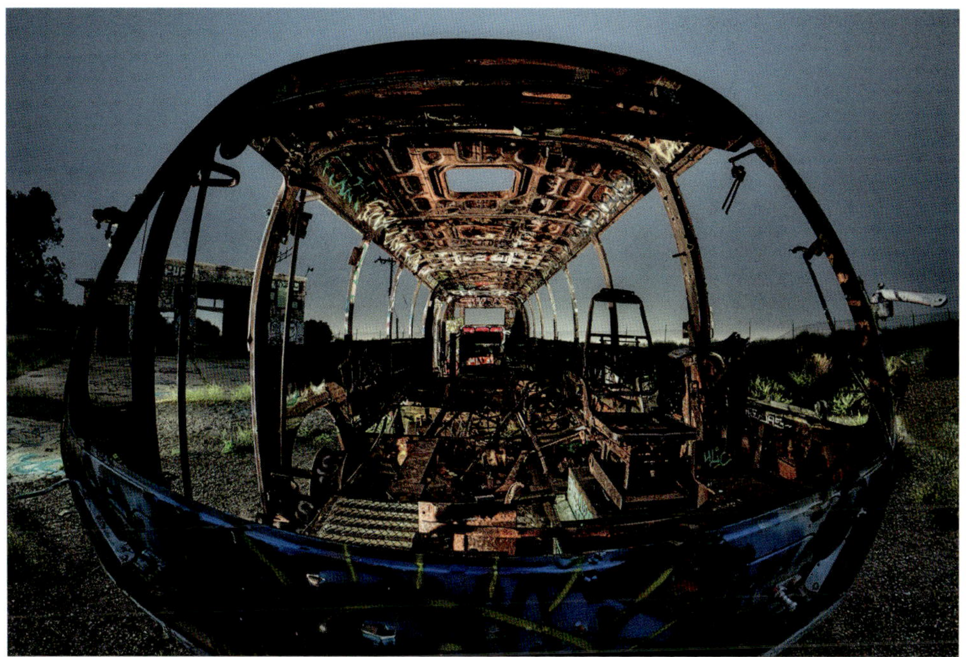

The Winter of our Deep Descent, the old missile assembly building in the back and the interior of one of two city buses. San Fernando Valley, Los Angeles.
Nikon D750/Rokinon 12-mm f/2.8 fisheye lens. Three-minute forty-eight-second exposure f/8 ISO 200. May 2020.
Full moon obscured by thick fog, warm white light from ProtoMachines LED2.

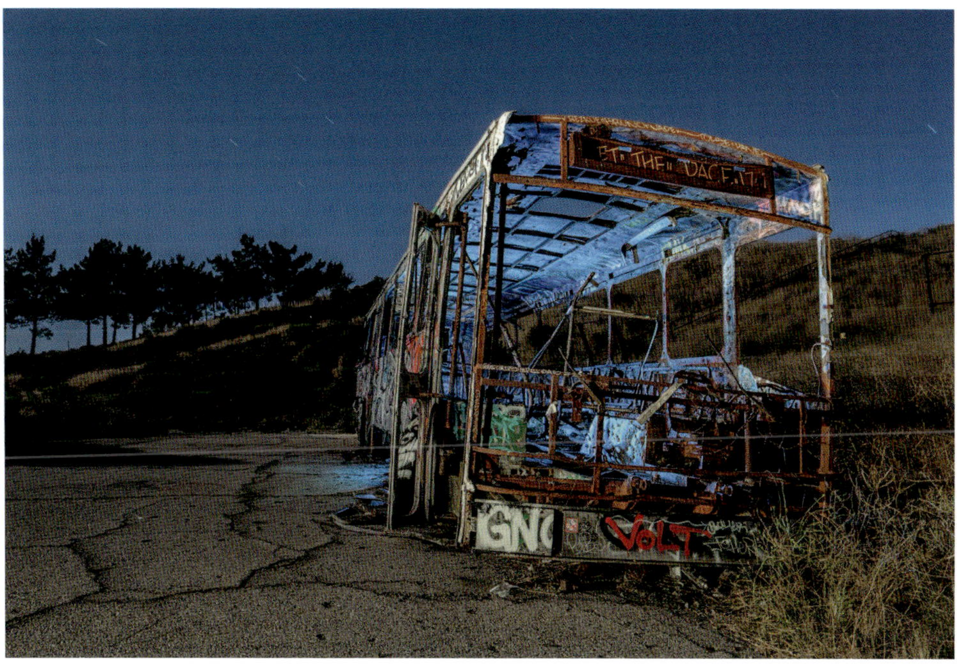

Get on the Bus, city bus near the launch area of the missiles. San Fernando Valley, Los Angeles.
Pentax K-1/15–30-mm f/2.8 lens. Three-minute exposure, f/8 ISO 200. July 2020.
Full moon, warm white and blue light from ProtoMachines LED2.

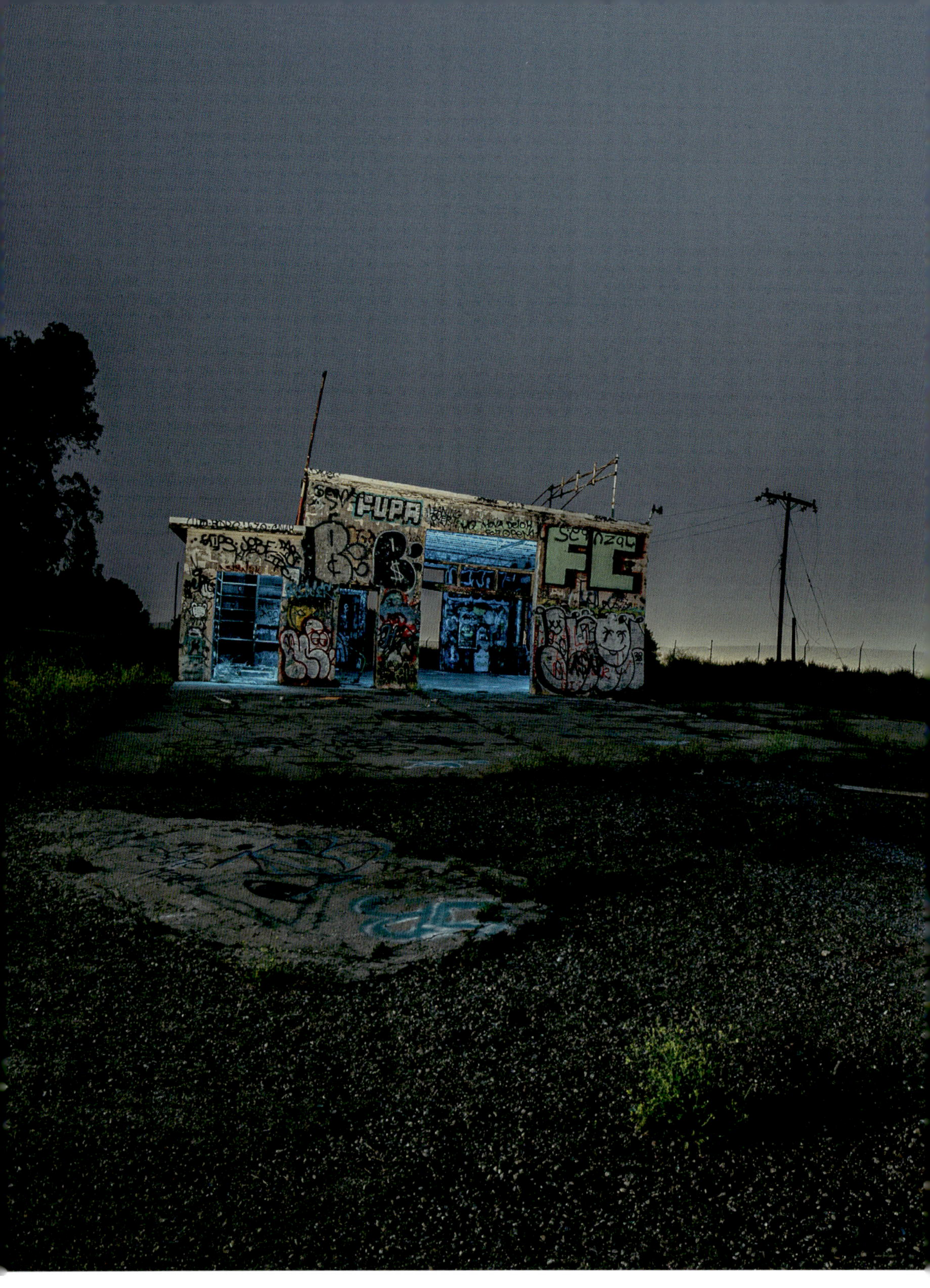

Nike Apocalypse, the old missile assembly building and one of two city buses. San Fernando Valley, Los Angeles.

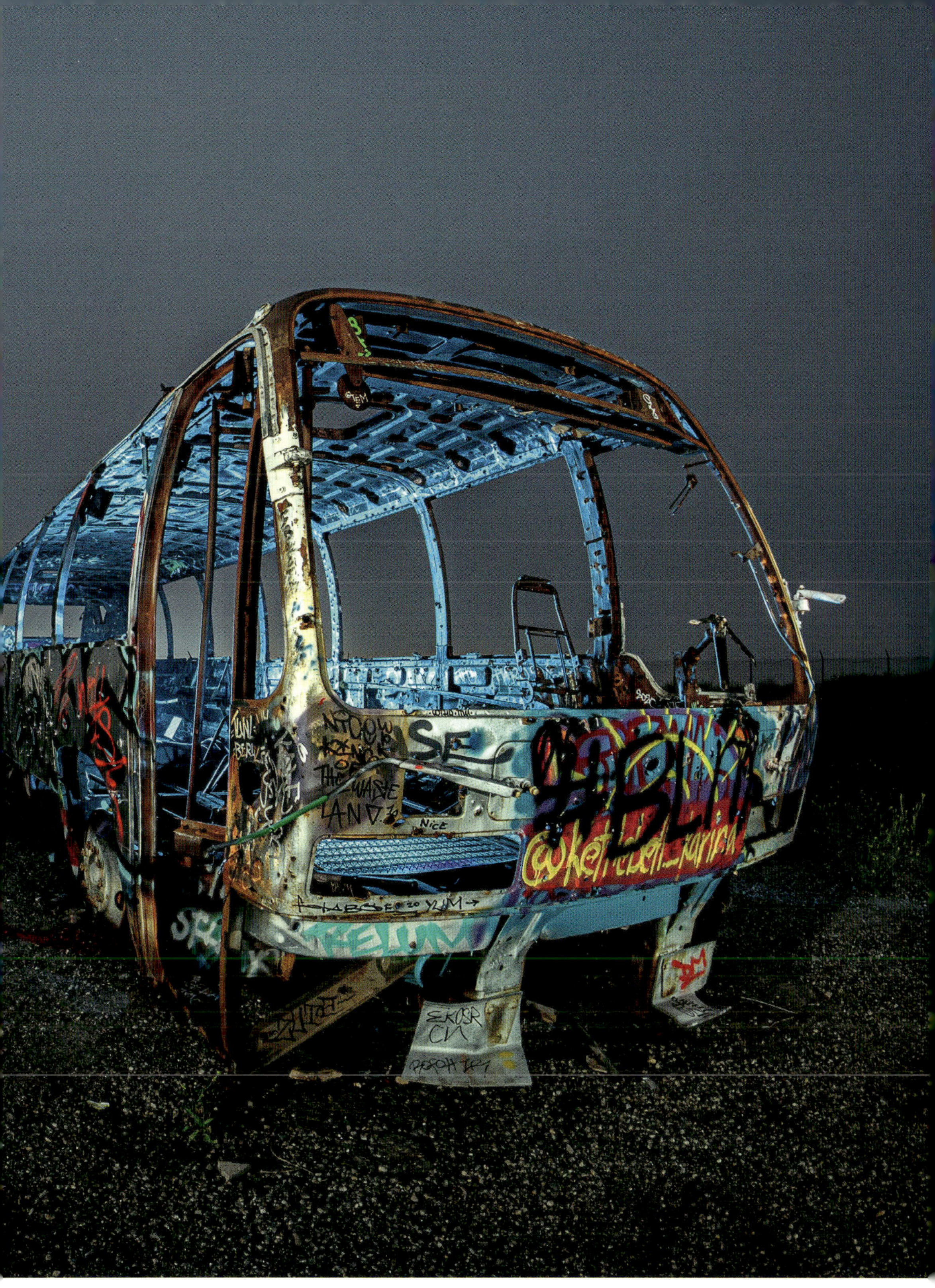

Nikon D750/Rokinon 12-mm f/2.8 fisheye lens. Fifty-seven-second exposure, f/8 ISO 200. May 2020. Full moon obscured by thick fog, warm white and teal light from ProtoMachines LED2.

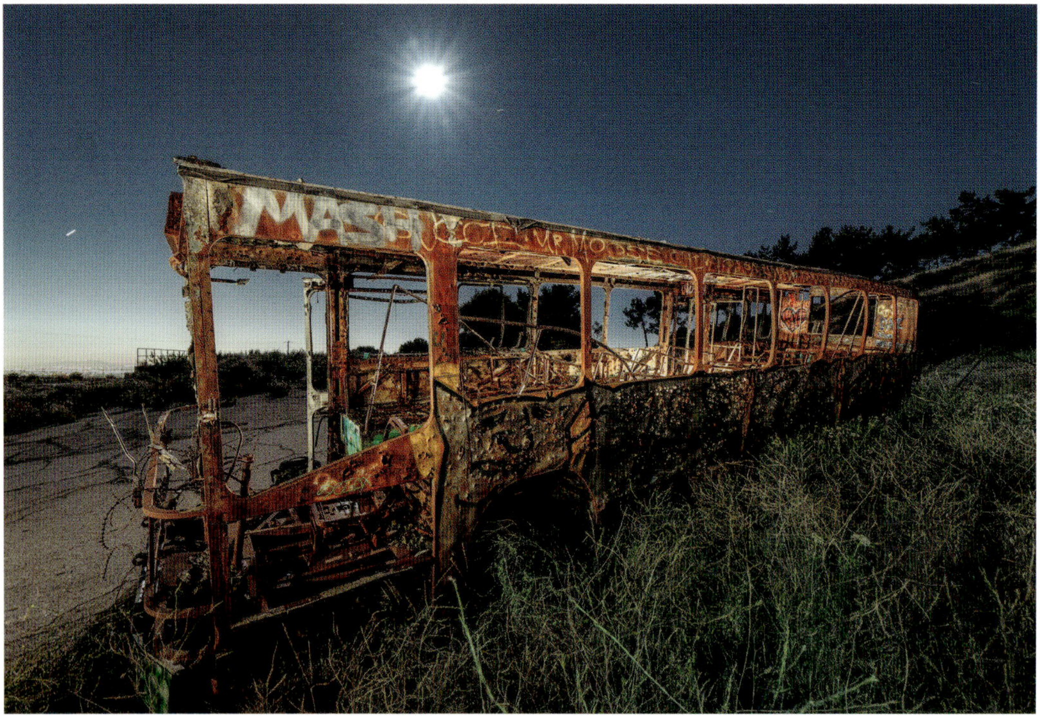

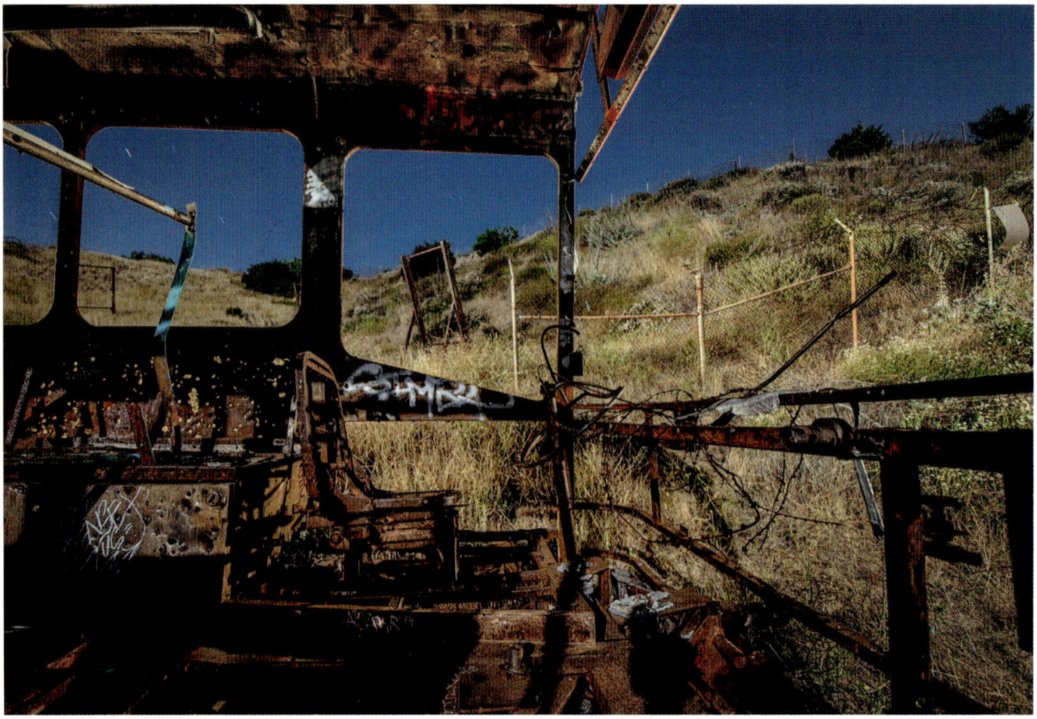

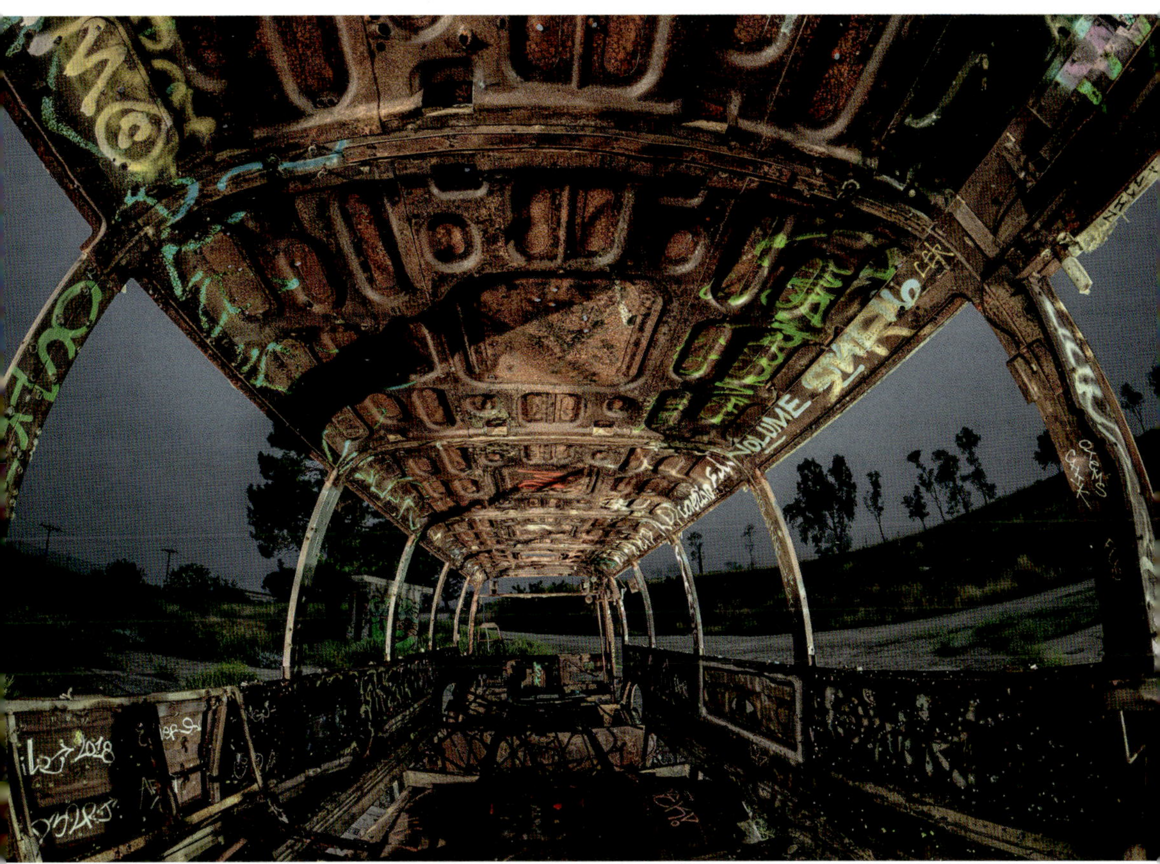

Riding on the Metro, the city bus near the former missile assembly building. San Fernando Valley, Los Angeles. Nikon D750/Rokinon 12-mm f/2.8 fisheye lens. Four-minute forty-four-second exposure f/8 ISO 200. May 2020. Full moon obscured by thick fog, warm white light from ProtoMachines LED2.

Opposite page

▲ **Glow Bus**, city bus near the launch area of the missiles. San Fernando Valley, Los Angeles. Pentax K-1/15–30-mm f/2.8 lens. Three-minute exposure, f/8 ISO 200. July 2020. Full moon, warm white light from ProtoMachines LED2.

▼ **Invisible Driver**, city bus near the launch area of the missiles. San Fernando Valley, Los Angeles. Pentax K-1/15–30-mm f/2.8 lens. Three-minute exposure, f/8 ISO 200. July 2020. Full moon, warm white light from ProtoMachines LED2.

Mojave Tropico

Mojave Tropico was an old desert movie set in the shadow of Soledad Mountain, which was being systematically torn apart for gold and silver, using a sodium cyanide solution to leach the precious metals from the rock.

Dave and I are photographing at night for only a few minutes when the inevitable security guard driving a white base-level pickup rolls up and tells us that we must leave. I am in the middle of a test exposure. I walk over to talk to them even though I know what they are saying. This is done to stall for time while my exposure finishes. The photo you will see is my only photo of Mojave Tropico. The place has since been torn down.

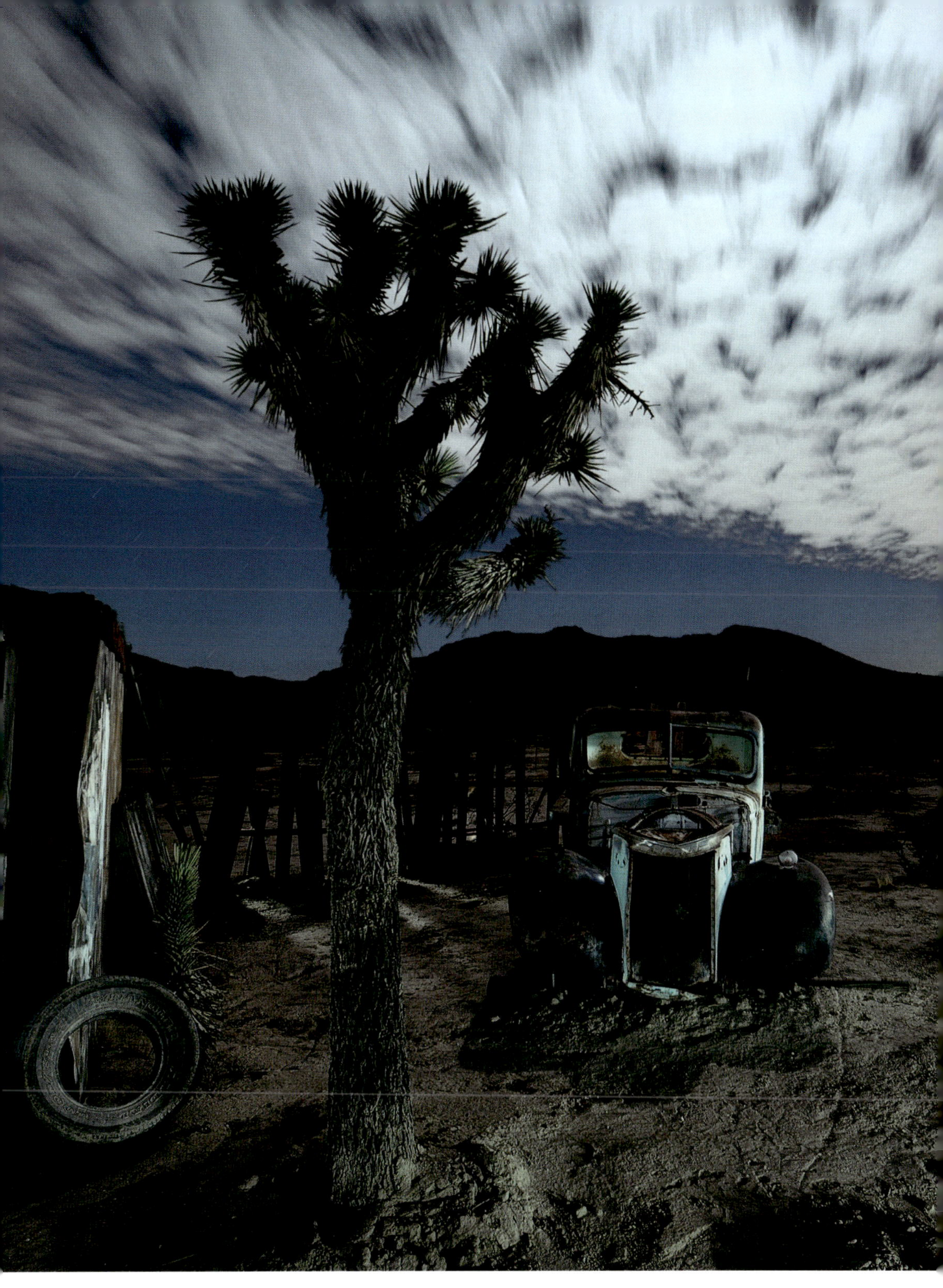

One Tree Flats, Mojave Tropico movie set near Soledad Mountain, Antelope Valley.
Nikon D610/14–24-mm f/2.8G lens. Three minutes one second f/8 ISO 200. November 2016.
Full moon on cloudy day, warm white and red light from ProtoMachines LED2.

SONOMA COUNTY

I am driving along a winding stretch of highway approaching Armstrong Redwoods State Natural Reserve. The second I lay eyes on this vintage Ford pickup truck along the side of the road, I know I will return. I just photographed the *M*A*S*H* ambulances a month before. Those had been the first vehicles I had photographed at night. I am excited to try this a second time.

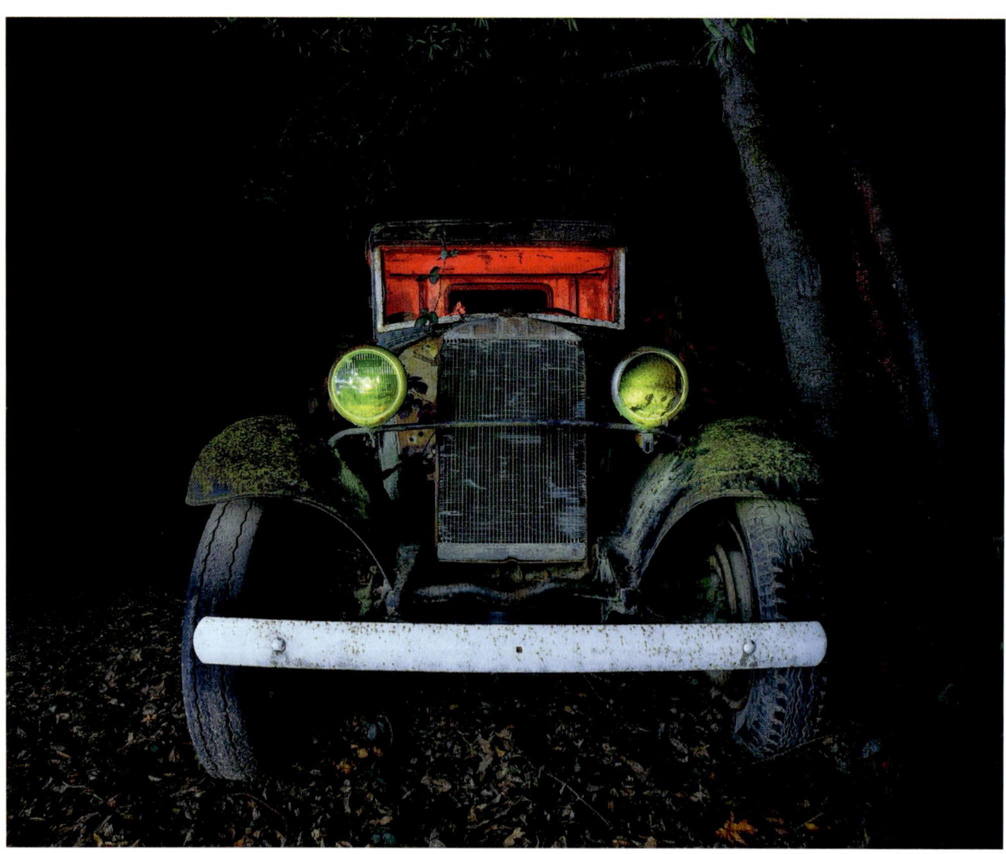

Sonoma Red, possibly a 1930 Ford Model AA pickup truck. Sonoma County.
Nikon D7000/Tokina 11–16-mm f/2.8 lens. Two minutes one second f/8 ISO 200. December 2013.
White and red light from Streamlight 88040 ProTac HL flashlight and Roscolux color gels.

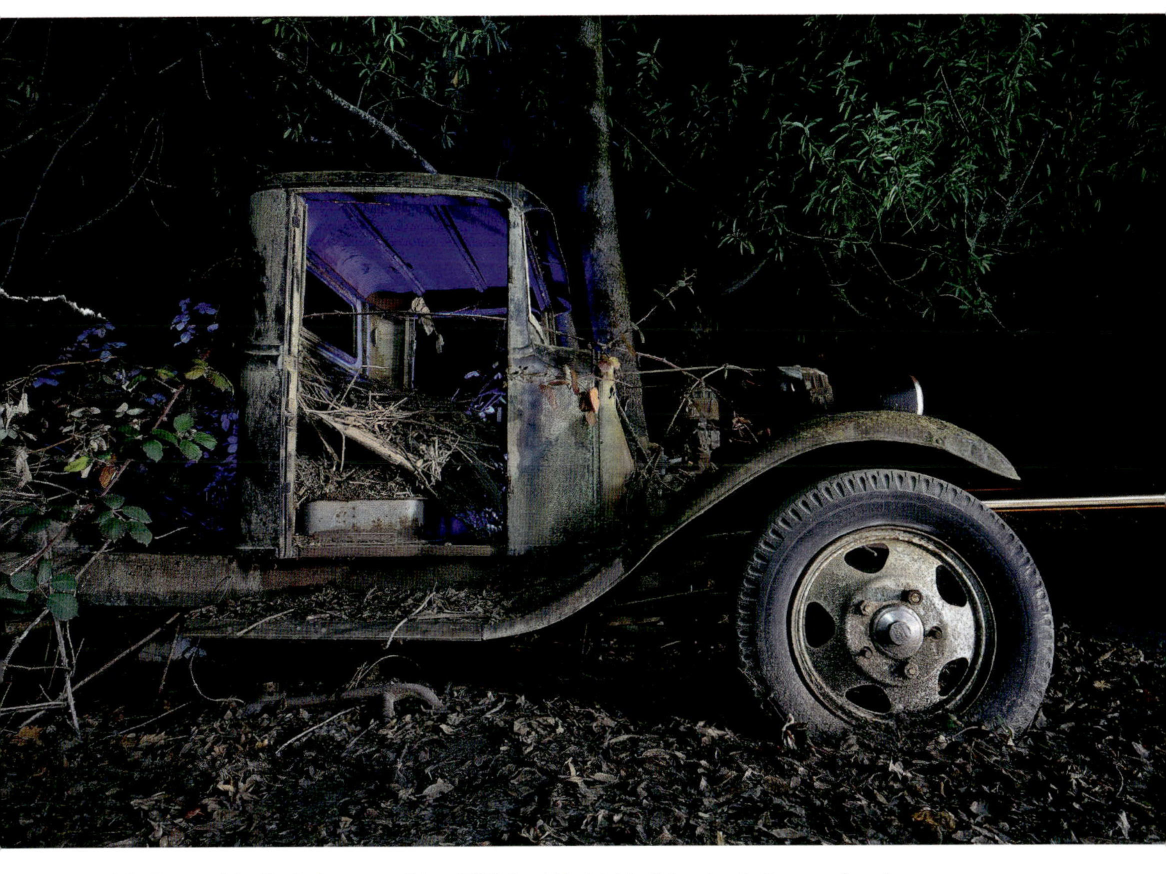

The Rust and the Mysterious, possibly a 1930 Ford Model AA pickup truck. Sonoma County.
Nikon D7000/Tokina 11–16-mm f/2.8 lens. Two minutes fifty-six seconds f/8 ISO 200. December 2013.
White and blue light from Streamlight 88040 ProTac HL flashlight and Roscolux color gels.

Laws Museum

This is a Model A alongside a vintage gravity pump at Laws Museum. I photographed this the same evening that I photographed the steam engine with Lance and friends.

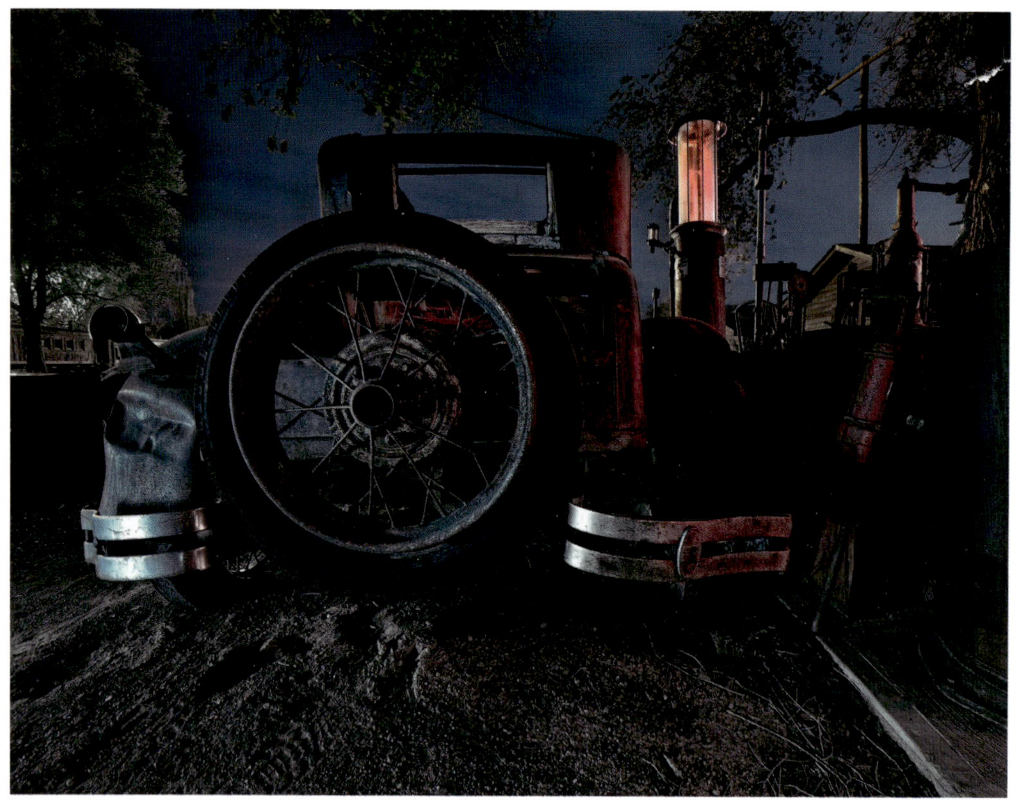

Midnight Gravity Pump, Model A and gravity gas pump. Laws Museum, Bishop. Nikon D610/Nikkor 14–24-mm f/2.8 lens. Two minutes f/8 ISO 200. November 2017. Full moon, warm white and red light from ProtoMachines LED2.

ZODIAC CAR

Charles Manson and the Manson Family lived at Spahn Ranch, an old Western town movie set, in the late 1960s. They left an indelible mark on Southern California, and movies such as *Once Upon a Time in Hollywood* show that they will not be forgotten.

When I first moved to the region, the neighborhood kids and I loved hiking in the hills south of Spahn Ranch, wondering if the Manson Family also wandered around in these parts. We would hike to a cave behind Castle Peak, which was then part of Ahmanson Ranch, then private property. All the kids called it "Bat's Cave," although now in literature, it is referred to as "The Cave of Munits." Regardless, local stories say that a Chumash shaman was slain here after murdering the son of a Chumash chief.

One of the times when returning from the cave, someone pulled up in a convertible Jeep, stood up, and began shooting at us. We took off running through sharp brush, scraping ourselves and ripping our clothing, finally ducking behind some large rocks. My friend, panting, arms bleeding, said maybe we should not run like this since he was only shooting salt pellets, which would hurt but not kill us. I asked, "Do salt pellets ricochet off rocks?"

The ranch was eventually acquired by the state and is now the Upper Las Virgenes Canyon Open Space Preserve, located less than eight miles from Spahn Ranch. I am happy to report that it is much safer to explore now.

As an adult, I heard rumors of a Corvair that was hidden up in the hills above Spahn Ranch. Manson had a right-hand man named Bruce Davis who drove a Corvair. Many believe that this rusty 1960s Corvair belonged to him. Some refer to this car as the Zodiac Car due to a popular myth that Bruce Davis was involved in the Zodiac killing, although this was never established. If this car could speak, would it tell tales of horror and violence?

My mind is awash in these thoughts as I hike through two miles of hillside on a warm breezy May evening, the rugged hills illuminated by the moon. I easily find the car. It is under a tree in a rocky canyon overlooking the lights of the San Fernando Valley. I examine the car for some sort of identification or VIN, but it has been stripped bare. I photograph the car from numerous angles for several hours. On the way back, I discover another car. Whether they are from the Manson family or stolen cars that were dumped there, I am not sure.

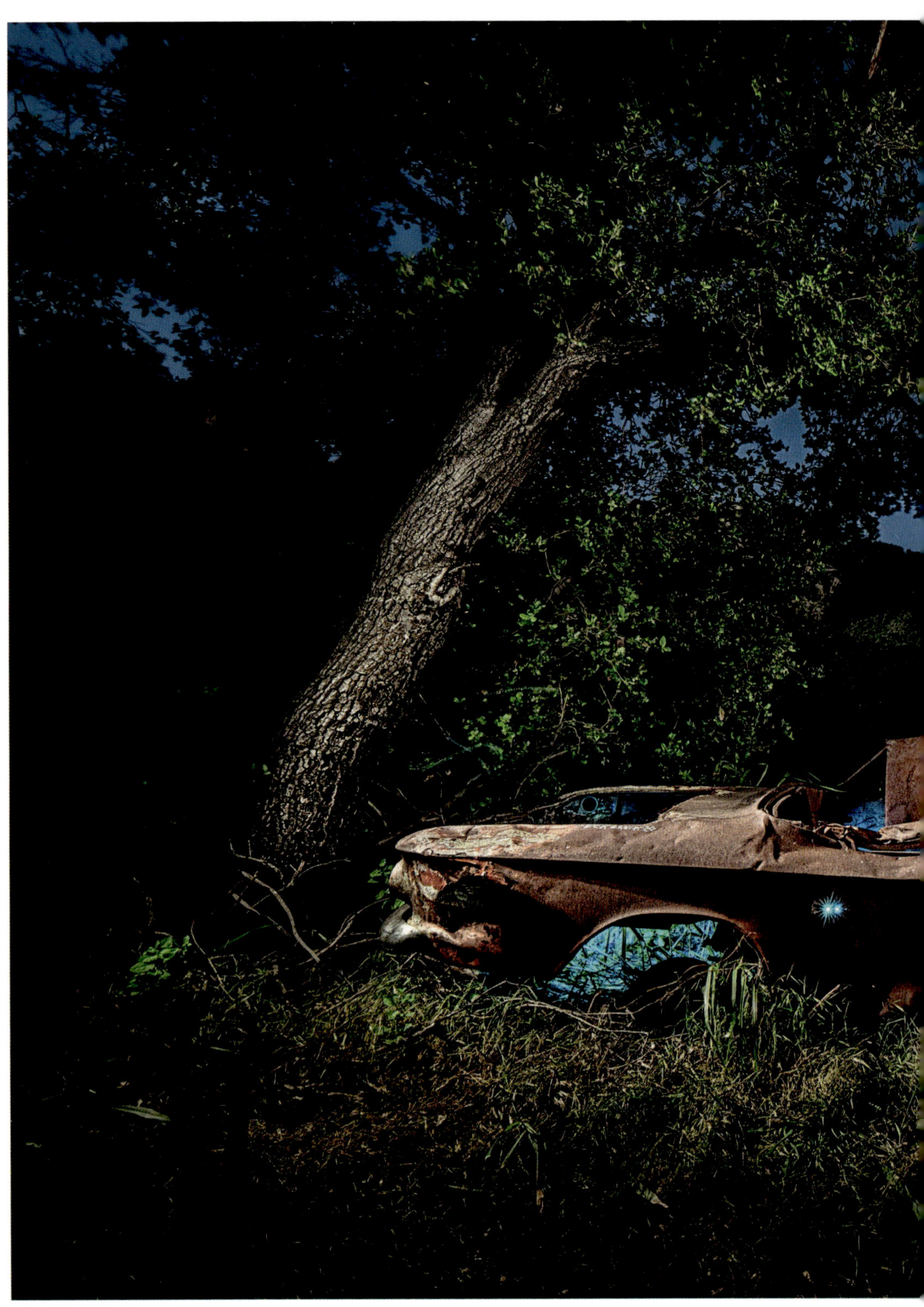

Never Say Never to Always, 1960s Corvair in the rocky hills above Spahn Ranch, San Fernando Valley, Los Angeles.

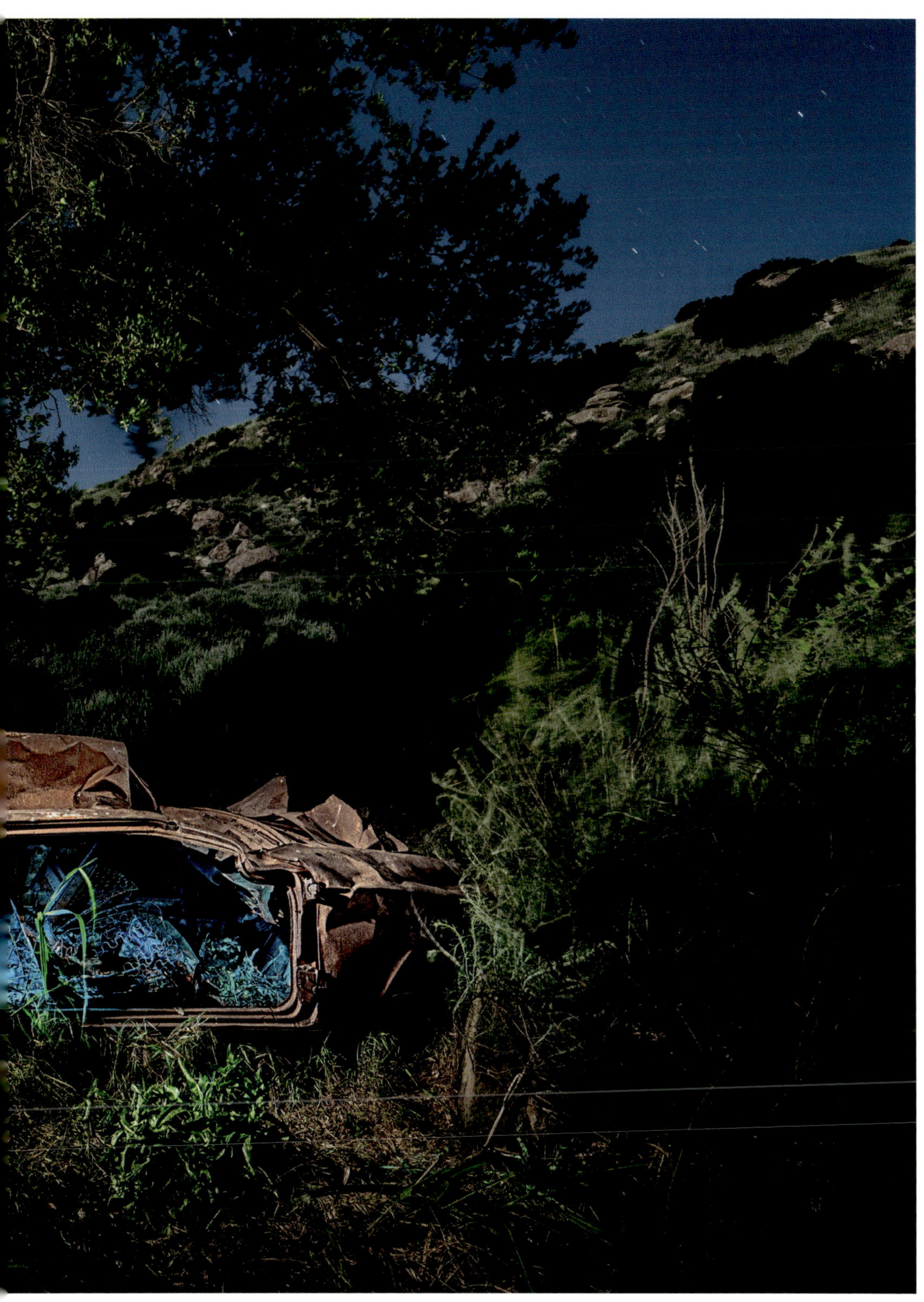

Pentax K-1/Pentax 15–30-mm f/2.8 lens. One minute thirty seconds f/8 ISO 200. May 2020.
Full moon obscured by shade, warm white and teal light from ProtoMachines LED2.

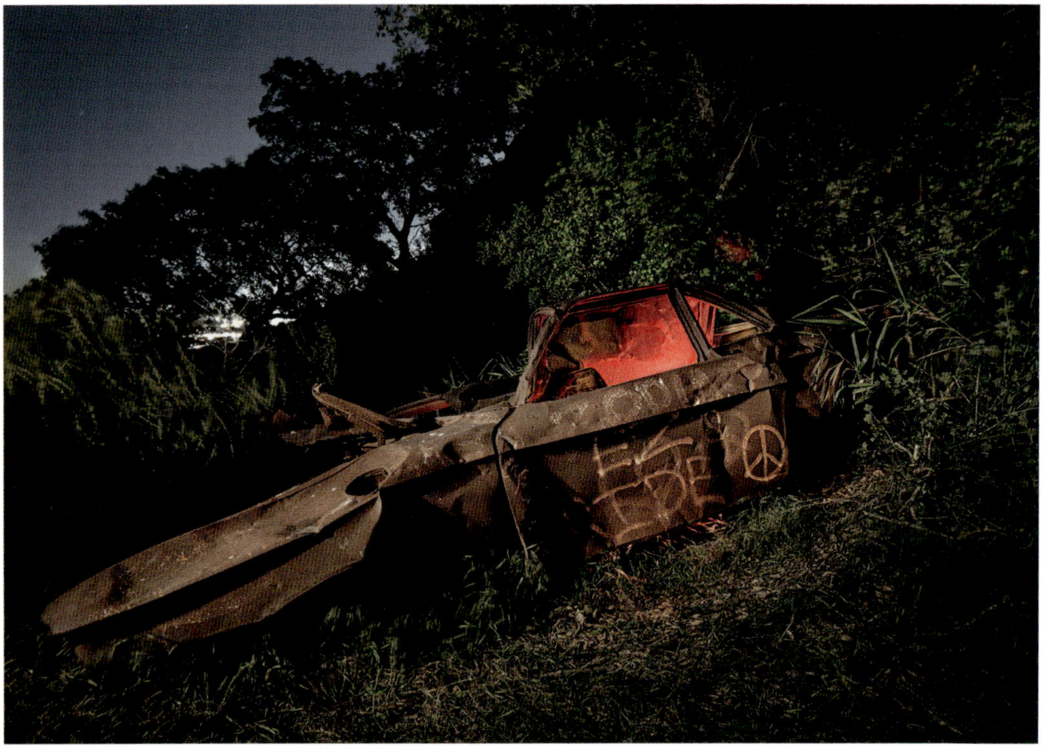

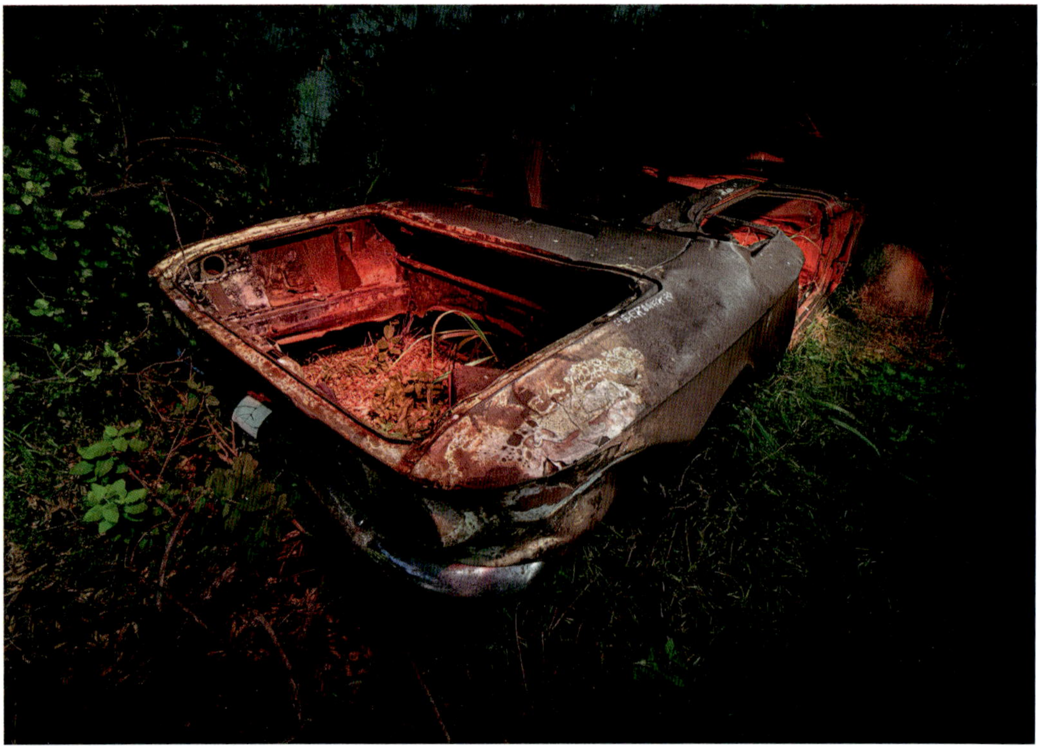

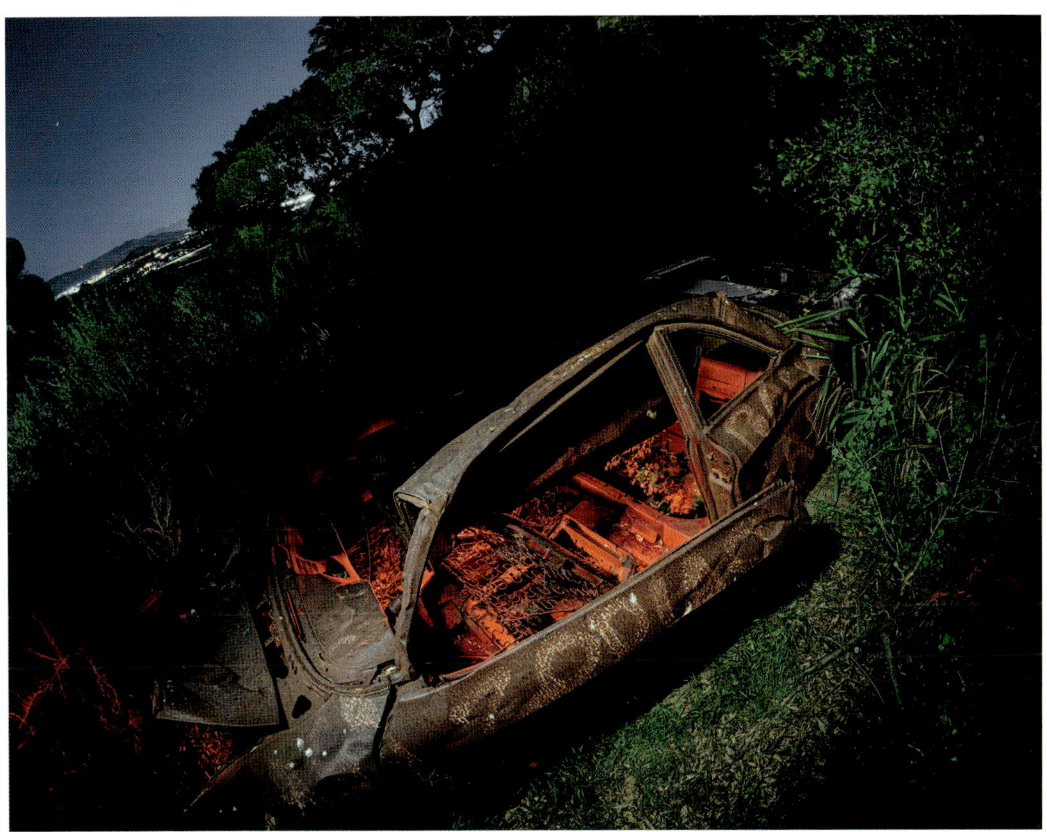

Zodiac City, a fisheye view of a 1960s Corvair and the valley lights in the rocky hills above Spahn Ranch, San Fernando Valley, Los Angeles.
Nikon D750/Rokinon 12-mm f/2.8 fisheye lens. One minute thirty seconds f/8 ISO 200. May 2020.
Full moon obscured by shade, warm white and red light from ProtoMachines LED2.

Opposite page

▲ **The Family Car**, 1960s Corvair in the rocky hills above Spahn Ranch, San Fernando Valley, Los Angeles.
Pentax K-1/Pentax 15–30-mm f/2.8 lens. One minute thirty seconds f/8 ISO 200. May 2020.
Full moon obscured by shade, warm white and red light from ProtoMachines LED2.

▼ **Mechanical Man**, the back of a 1960s Corvair in the rocky hills above Spahn Ranch, San Fernando Valley, Los Angeles.
Pentax K-1/Pentax 15–30-mm f/2.8 lens. One minute thirty seconds f/8 ISO 200. May 2020.
Full moon obscured by shade, warm white and red light from ProtoMachines LED2.

Eagle Field

The first thing you associate with Eagle Field are planes. It is, after all, a decommissioned World War II airfield, where a dedicated few stay busy restoring many magnificent planes to their former glory, and storing others. But they also have many military vehicles and automobiles from yesteryear in various states of disrepair.

Naturally, growing up on *Indiana Jones* movies, I am particularly enamored with the Aeropuerto de Nazca truck. I believe this is a 1937 Ford fuel truck. It was used when Indiana Jones visits Nazca in Peru in *Indiana Jones and the Kingdom of the Crystal Skull*. While this is arguably the worst of the franchise, well, it is still Indiana Jones. Every time I visit Eagle Field, I photograph this truck. Whether close, near, fisheye lens, wide angle lens, showing the stars streaking across the sky, it is all good. I keep the childlike sense of fun on the surface.

There is also a Chevrolet flatbed truck that I seem to love. It is the grill; they look like really large teeth.

► **Mater**, 1942 Chevrolet 1-ton truck. Eagle Field.
Nikon D610/Rokinon 12-mm f/2.8 fisheye lens. Seven minutes five seconds f/8 ISO 200. April 2019.
Full moon, warm white and blue light from ProtoMachines LED2.

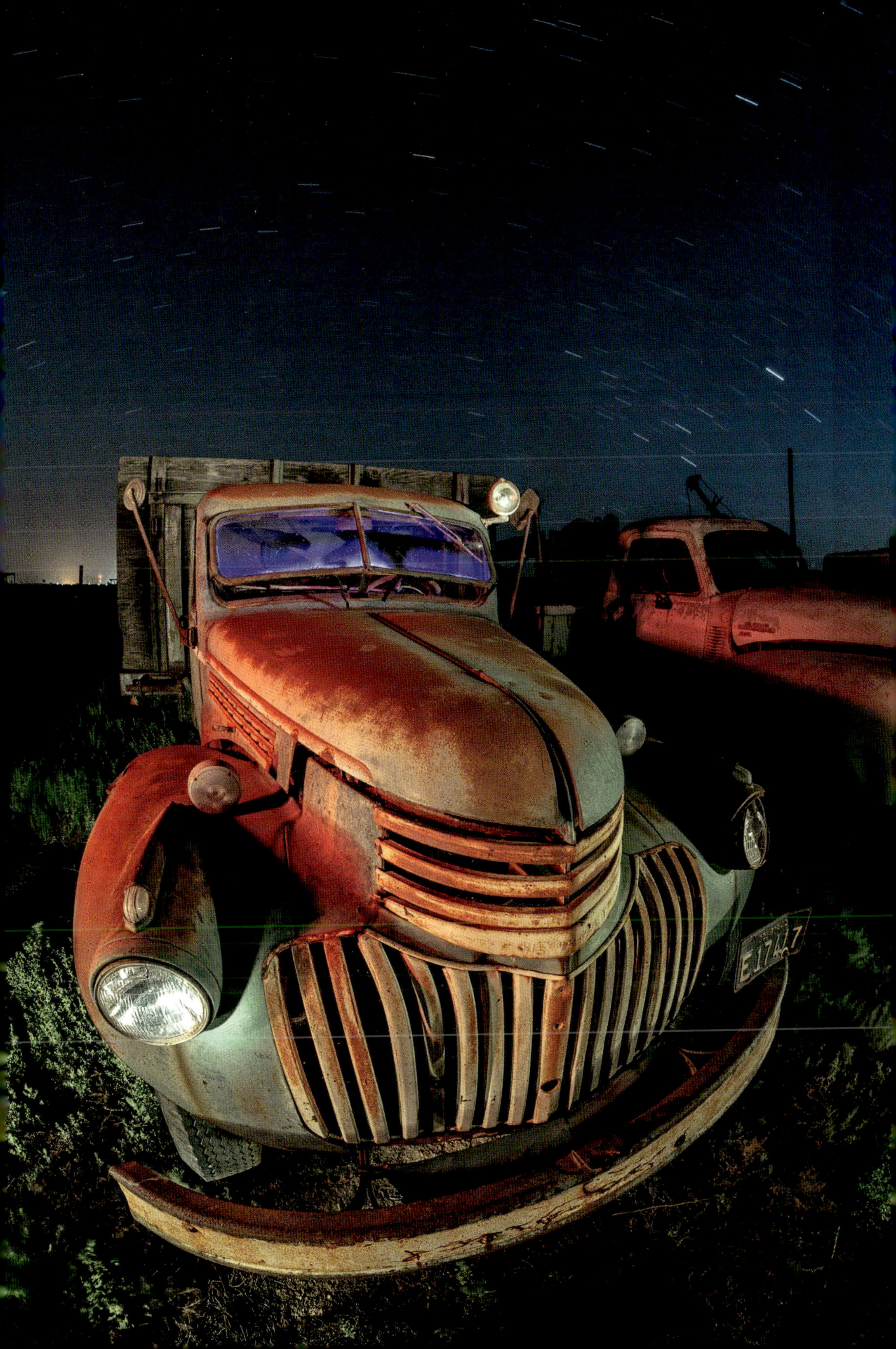

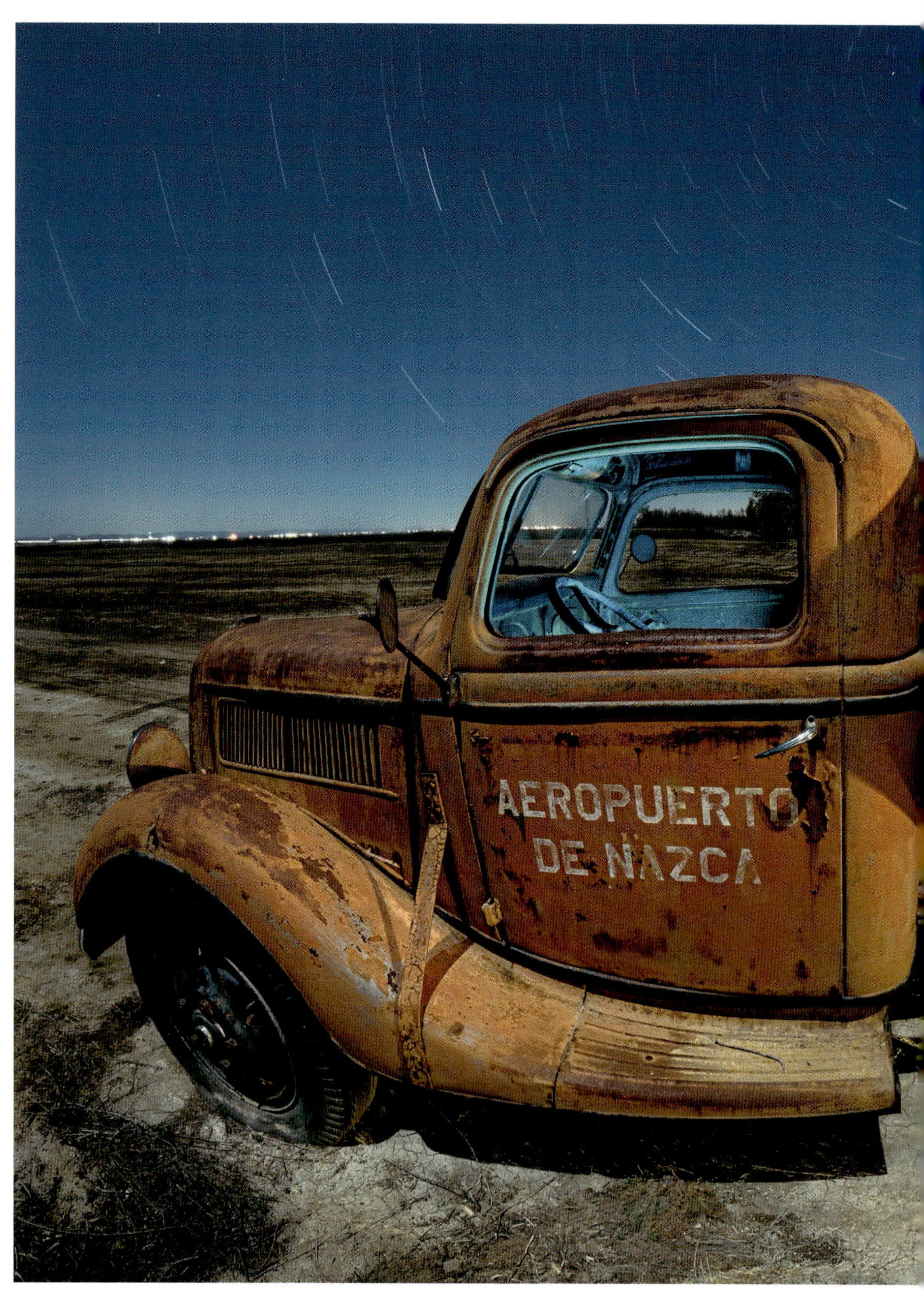

Calavera de Cristal, most likely a 1937 Ford fuel truck used in an *Indiana Jones* movie. Eagle Field.
Nikon D750/Rokinon 12-mm f/2.8 fisheye lens.

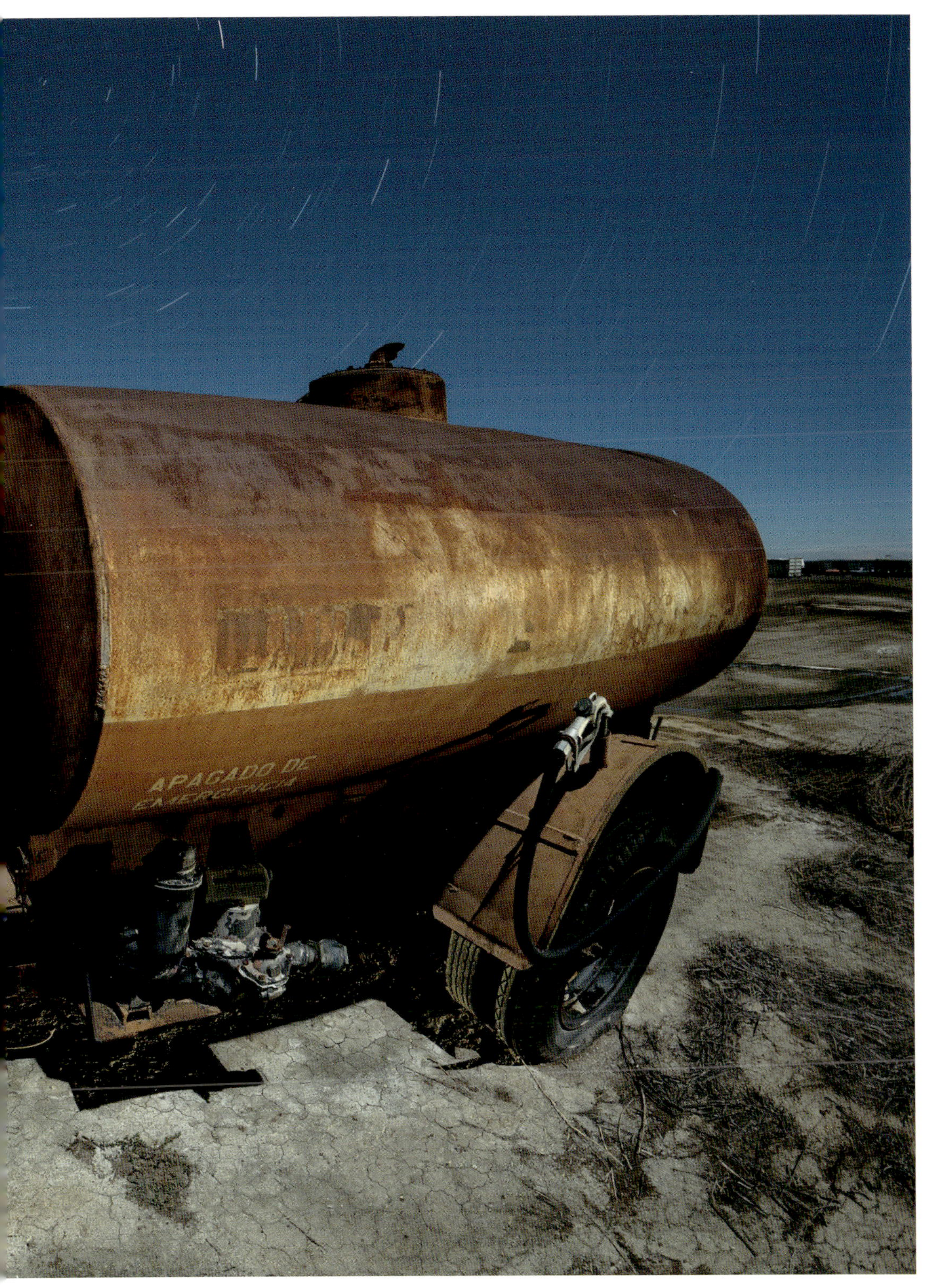

Thirty minutes total “stacked”; each image two minutes f/8 ISO 200. February 2020. Full moon, warm white and teal light from ProtoMachines LED2.

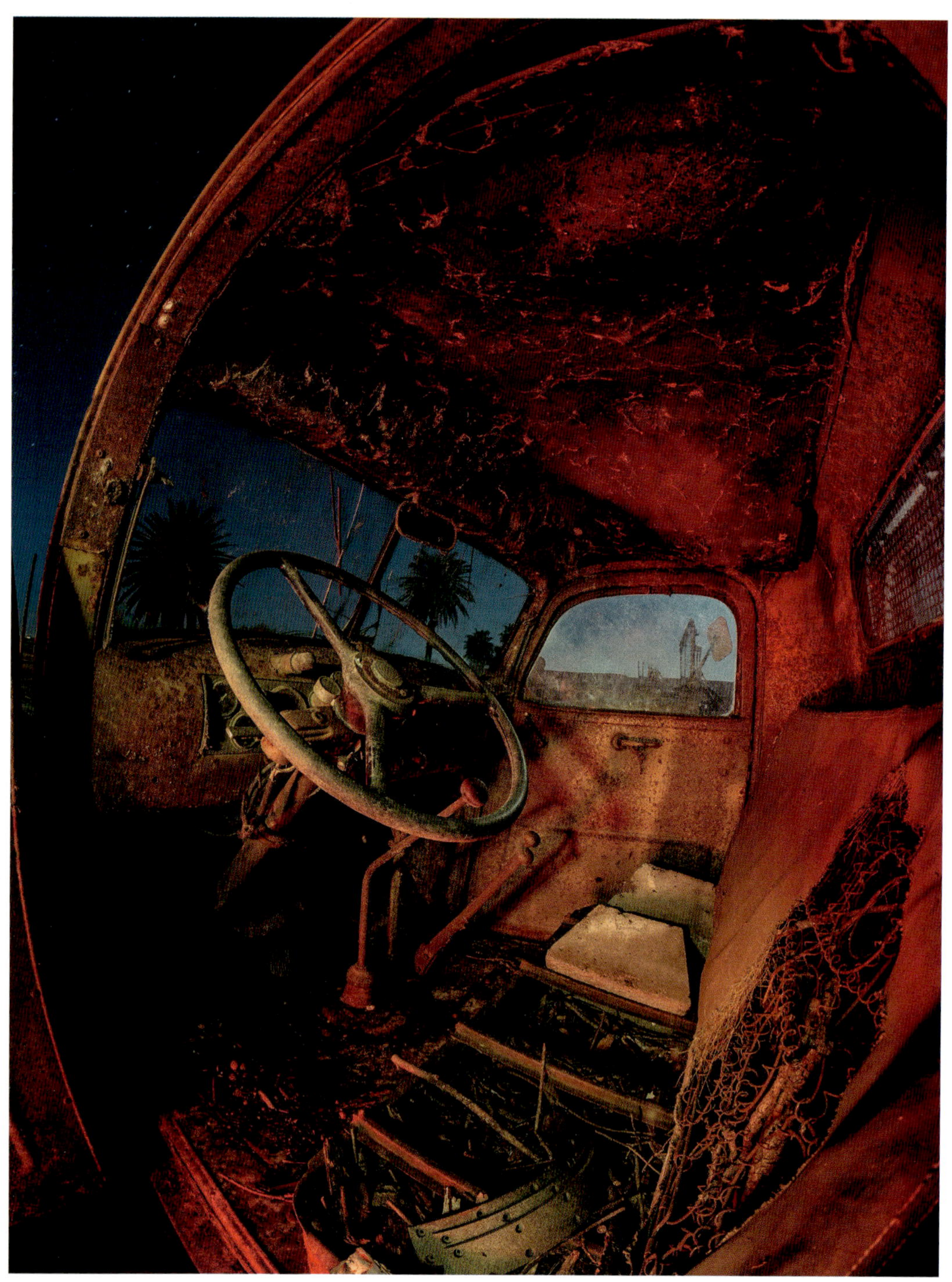

Red Lorry Red Lorry, the uncomfortable-looking interior of a 1938 Ford fuel tanker truck. Eagle Field. Nikon D610/Rokinon 12-mm f/2.8 fisheye lens. One minute thirty seconds f/8 ISO 320. April 2019. Full moon, red light from ProtoMachines LED2.

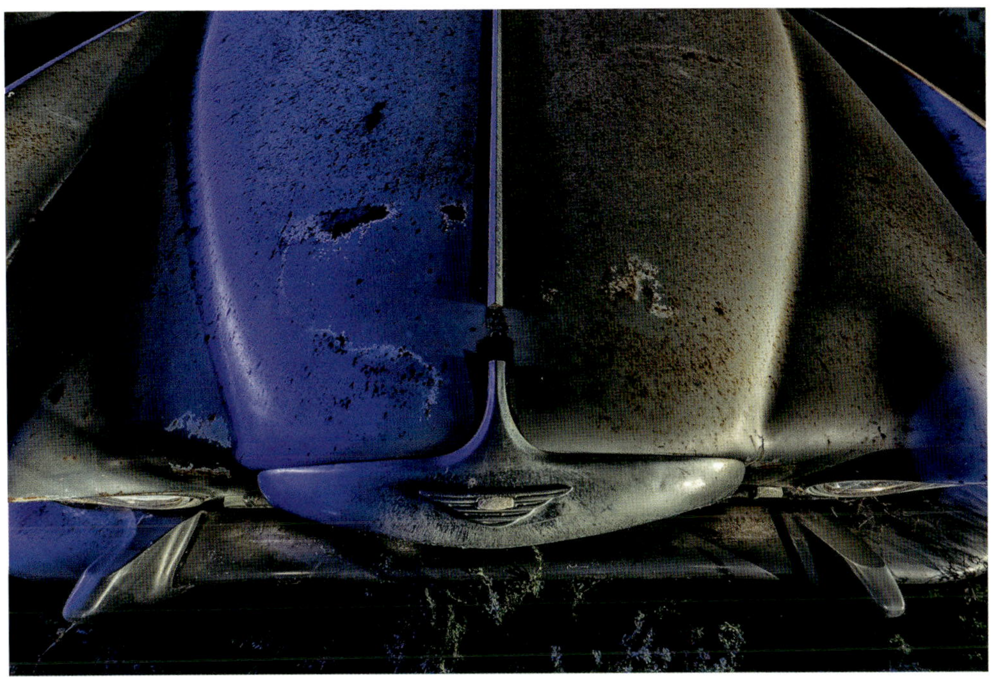

Bumper Bloom, night wildflowers hugging the bumper of a 1960s Jaguar Mark X 420G. Eagle Field. Nikon D750/Nikkor 14–24-mm f/2.8 lens. One minutes thirty-eight seconds f/8 ISO 400. April 2019. Full moon, warm white and blue light from ProtoMachines LED2.

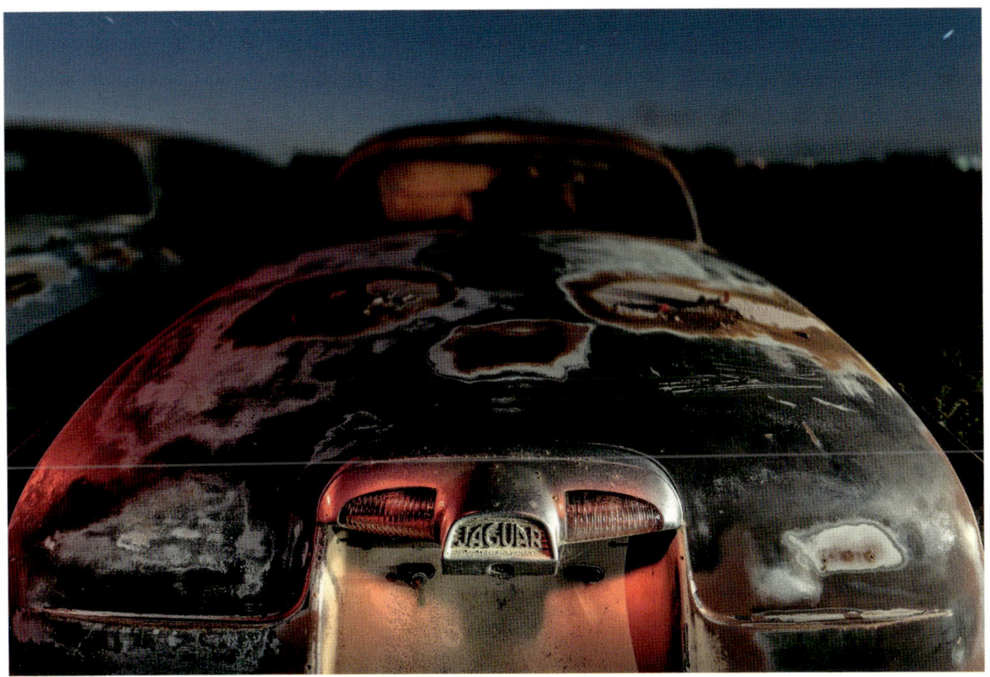

Under the Jaguar Moon, vintage Jaguar missing a couple of coats of paint. Eagle Field. Nikon D750/Nikkor 14–24-mm f/2.8 lens. Two minutes fifty-three seconds f/8 ISO 200. April 2019. Full moon, red light from ProtoMachines LED2.

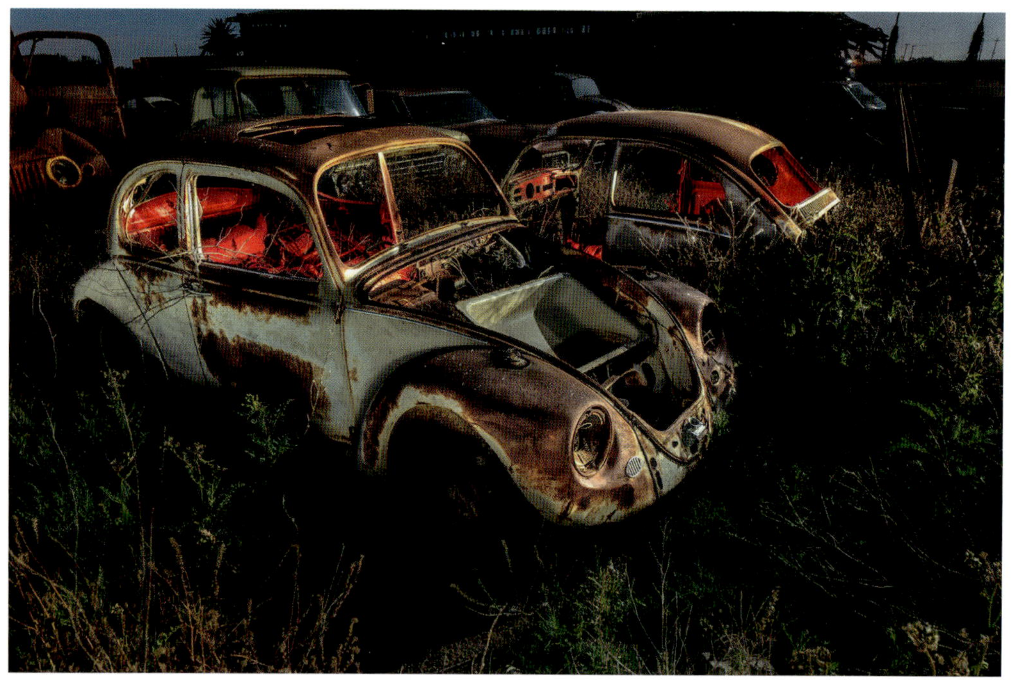

Bug Club, nature reclaiming a couple of VWs. Eagle Field.
Nikon D750/Nikkor 14–24-mm f/2.8 lens. Three minutes f/8 ISO 200. April 2019.
Full moon, warm white and red light from ProtoMachines LED2.

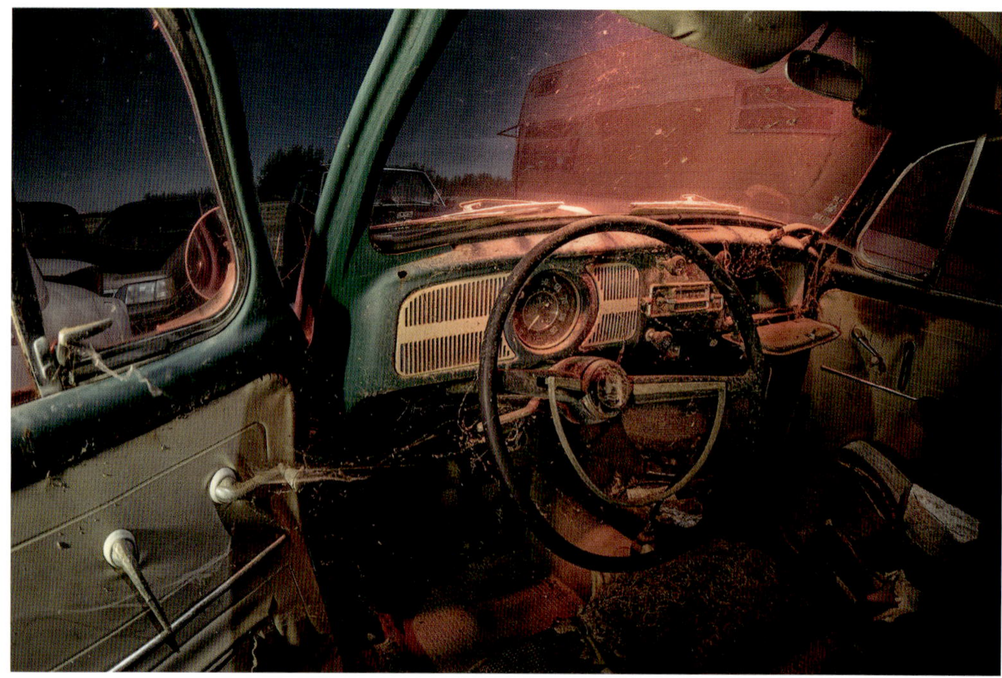

Bugs in a Bug, an old VW. Eagle Field.
Nikon D750/Rokinon 12-mm f/2.8 fisheye lens. Two minutes f/8 ISO 200. February 2020.
Full moon, warm white and red light from ProtoMachines LED2.

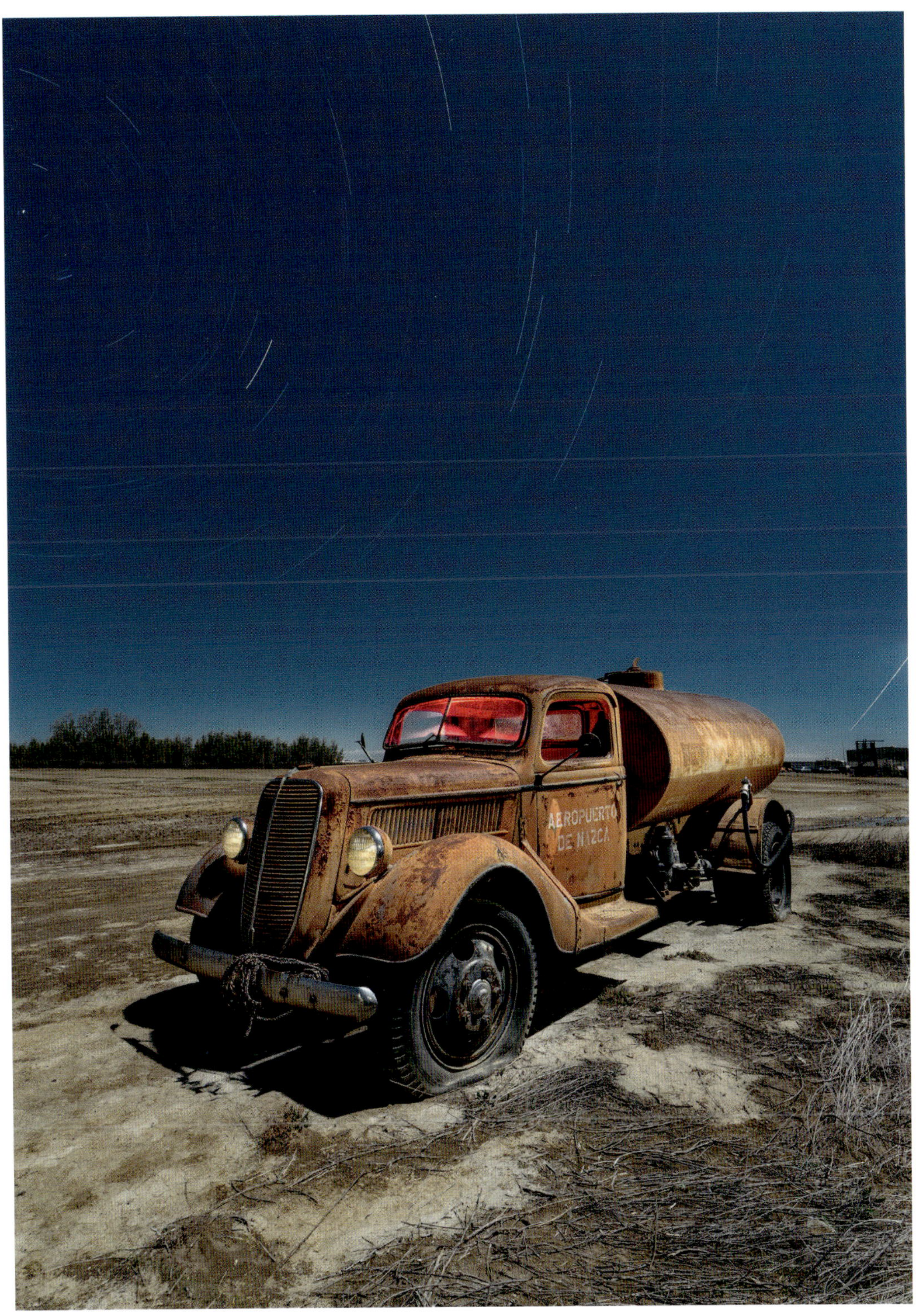

Moon Over Nazca, most likely a 1937 Ford fuel truck used in an *Indiana Jones* movie. Eagle Field.
Pentax K-1 and 15–30-mm f/2.8 lens. One hour total "stacked." Each photo five minutes f/8 ISO 200. February 2020.
Full moon, warm white and red light from ProtoMachines LED2.

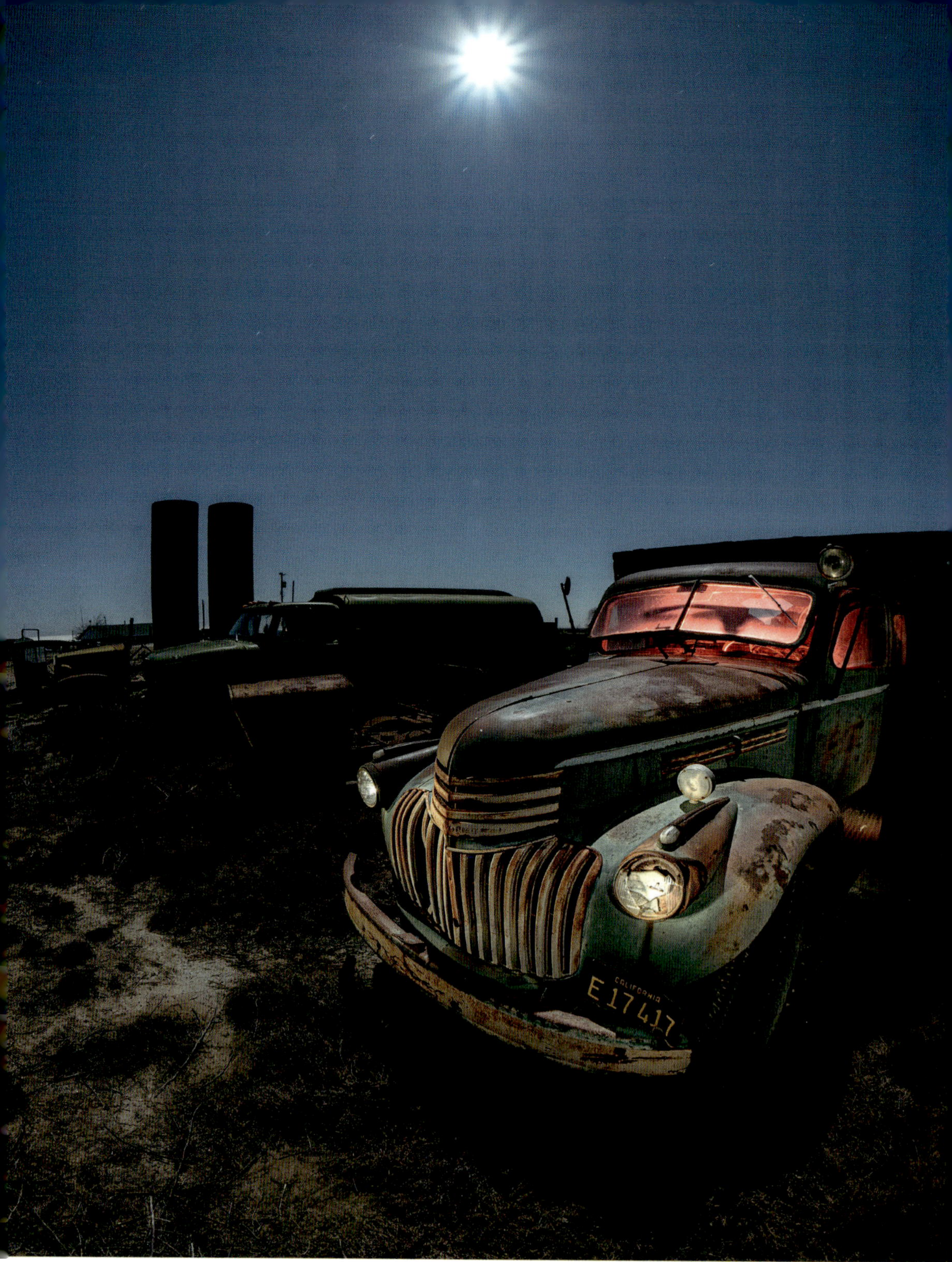

Under the Snow Moon Sky, an old Chevrolet flatbed.
Nikon D750/Rokinon 12-mm f/2.8 fisheye lens. Each image two minutes f/8 ISO 200. February 2020.
Full moon, warm white and red light from ProtoMachines LED2.

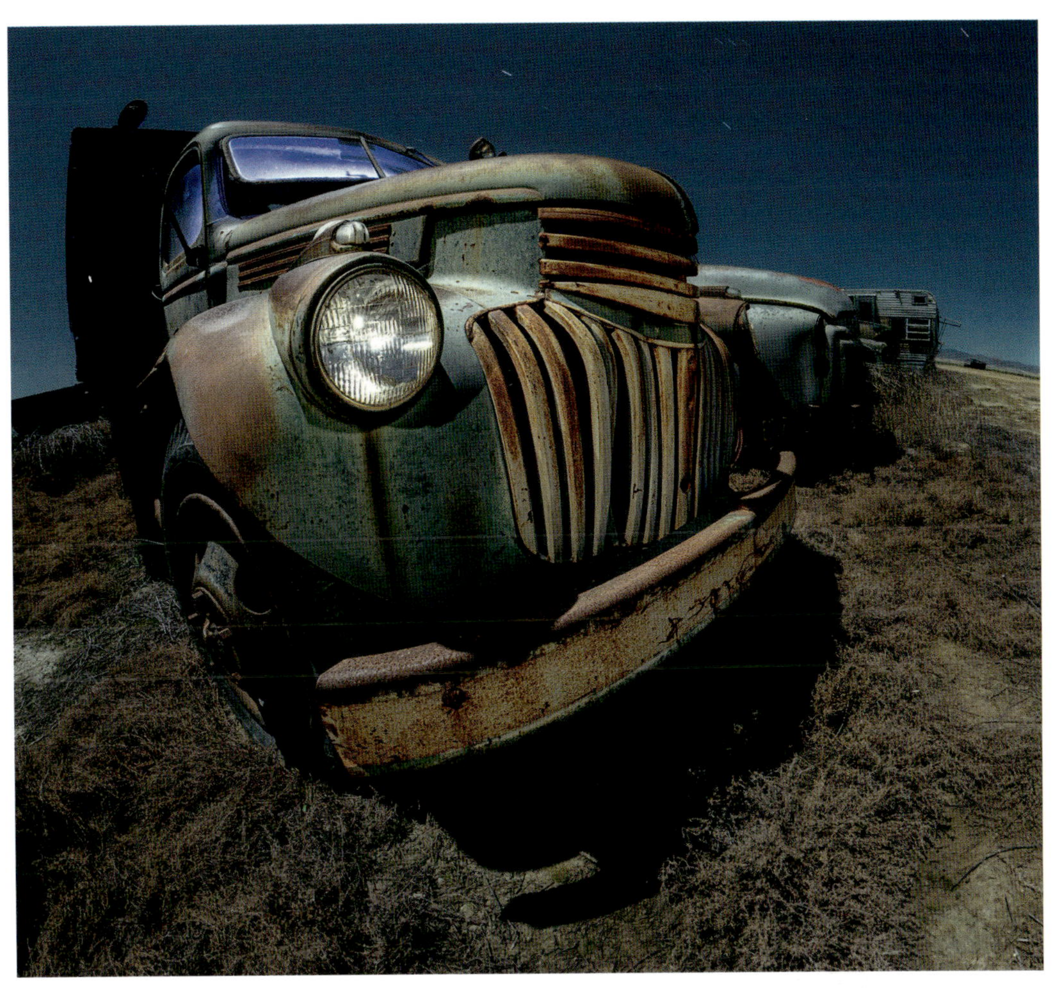

Drove my Chevy to the Levee, an old Chevrolet flatbed. Eagle Field.
Nikon D750/Rokinon 12-mm f/2.8 fisheye lens. Four minutes fifteen seconds f/8 ISO 200. February 2020.
Full moon, warm white and blue light from ProtoMachines LED2.

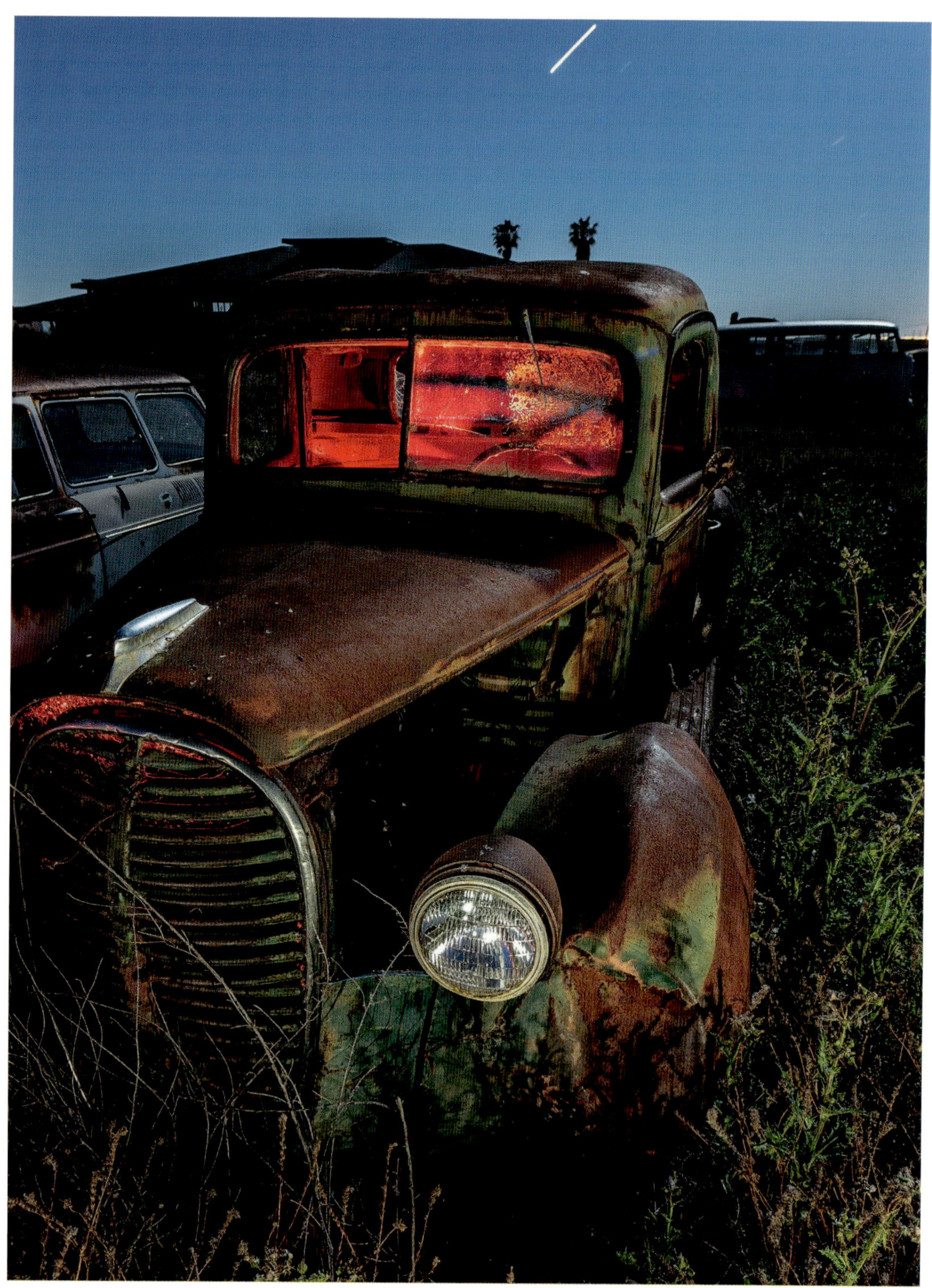

Clark, beautiful texture on the windshield of this 1938 Ford fuel tanker truck.
Nikon D750/Nikkor 14–24-mm f/2.8 lens. Three minutes f/8 ISO 200. April 2019.
Full moon, warm white and red light from ProtoMachines LED2.

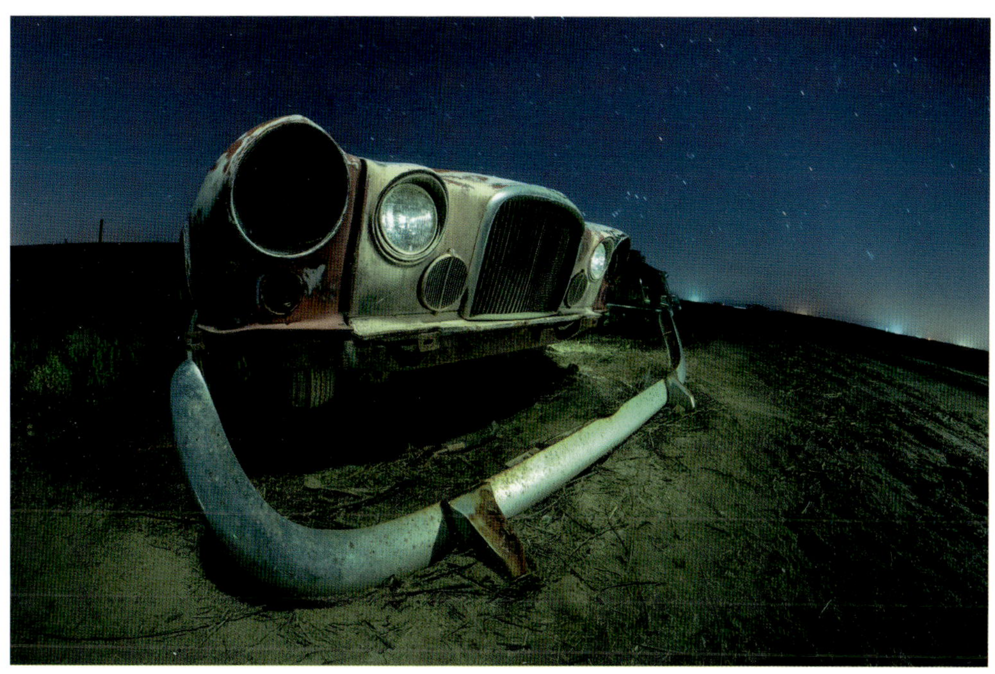

Parallel, a vintage 1963 Mark 10 Jaguar. Eagle Field.
Nikon D610/Rokinon 12-mm f/2.8 fisheye lens. Two minutes fifteen seconds f/8 ISO 1000. April 2019.
Full moon, warm white light from ProtoMachines LED2.

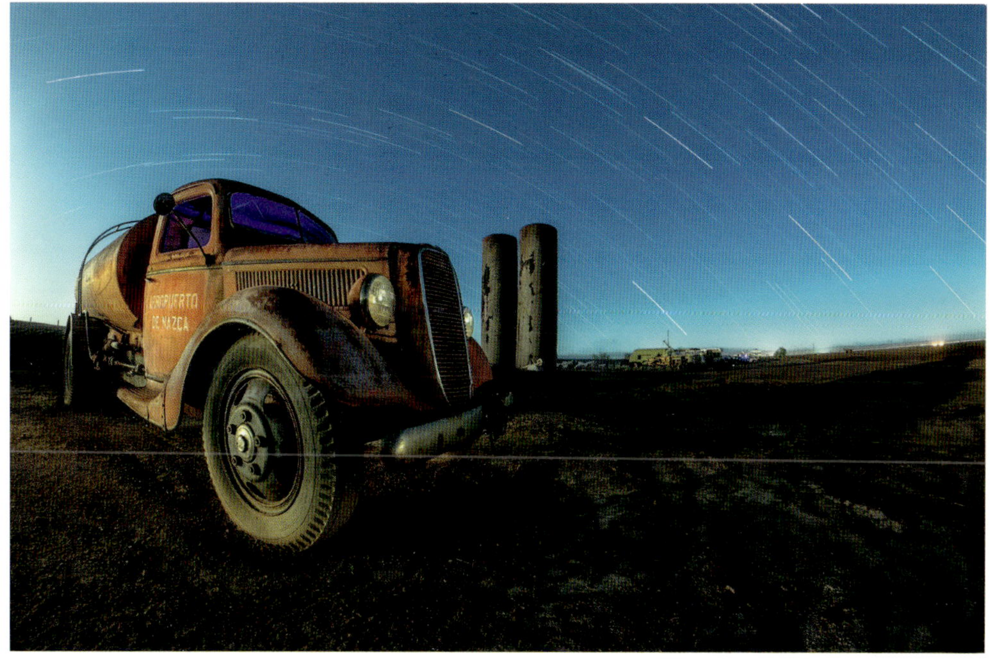

Luna Amarilla Sobre Nazca, most likely a 1937 Ford fuel truck used in an *Indiana Jones* movie. Eagle Field.
Nikon D610/Rokinon 12-mm f/2.8 fisheye lens. Fifty-one minutes total “stacked”; each photo three minutes f/8 ISO 640. April 2019.
Full moon, warm white and blue light from ProtoMachines LED2.

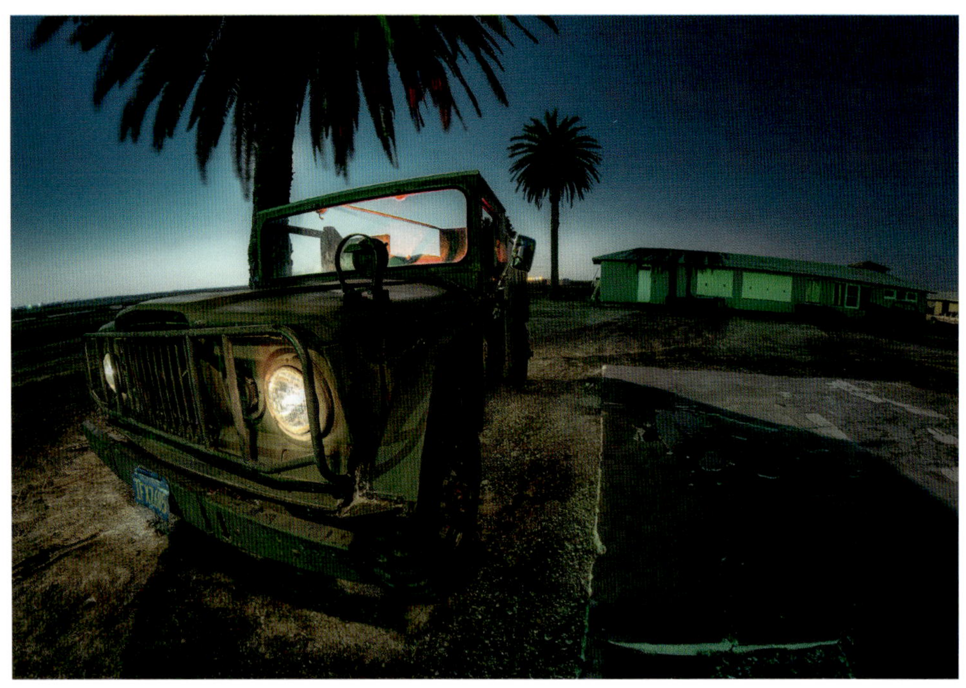

Under the Palms, vintage Army jeep. Eagle Field.
Nikon D750/Rokinon 12-mm f/2.8 fisheye lens. Three minutes f/8 ISO 200. February 2020.
Full moon, warm white and yellow light from ProtoMachines LED2.

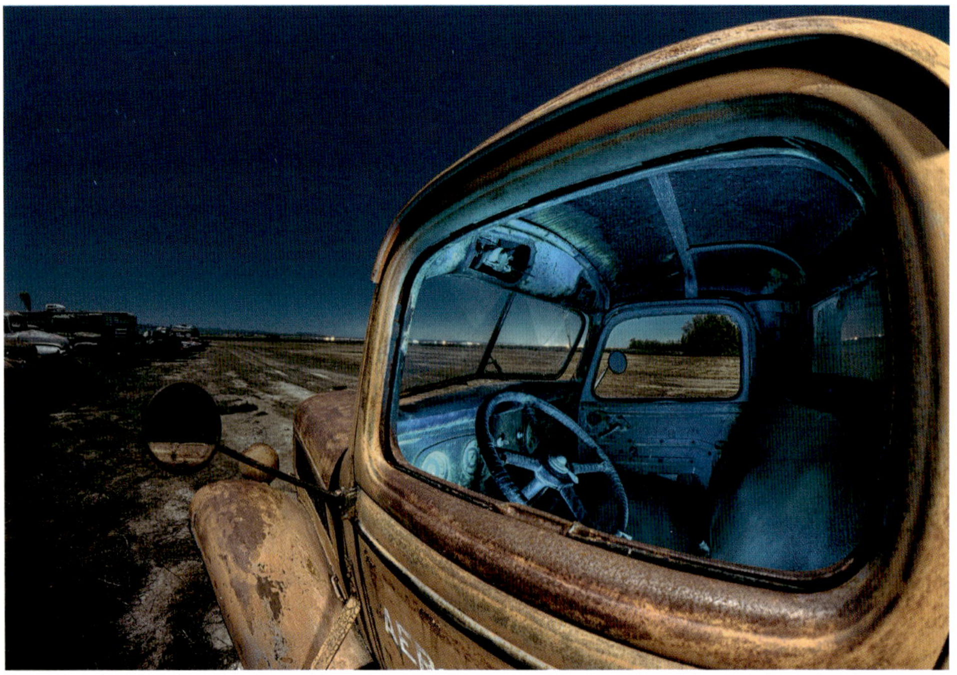

Waiting for Nazca, most likely a 1937 Ford fuel truck used in an *Indiana Jones* movie. Eagle Field.
Nikon D750/Rokinon 12-mm f/2.8 fisheye lens. Two minutes f/8 ISO 200. February 2020.
Full moon, warm white and teal light from ProtoMachines LED2.

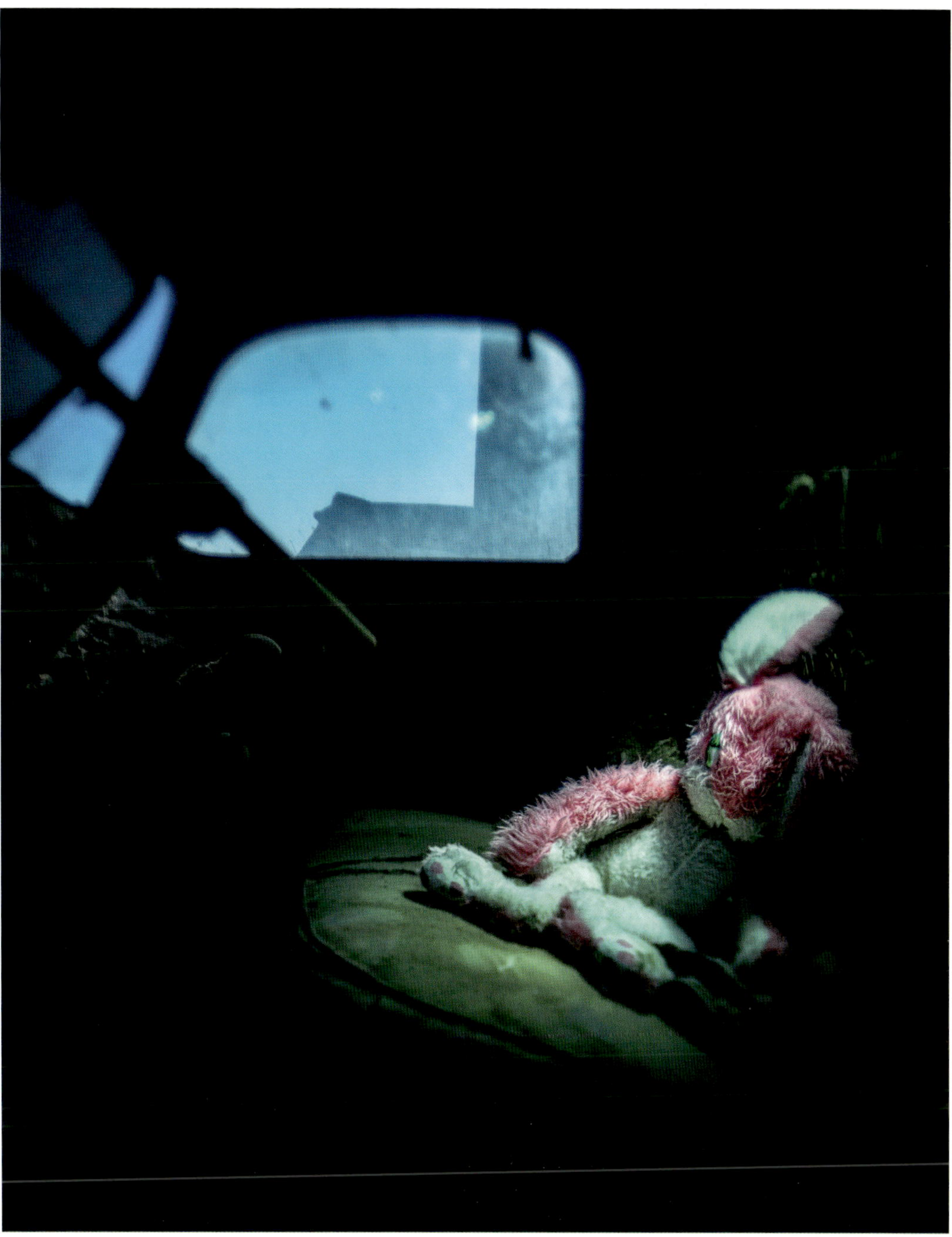

Tale of the Abandoned, interior of a Chevy flatbed during a spontaneous trip to a decommissioned WWII airfield on Halloween night. Eagle Field.
Pentax K-1/Lensbaby Edge 35 Optic lens. One minute fifteen seconds f/4 ISO 200. October 2020.
Full moon, warm white light from ProtoMachines LED2.

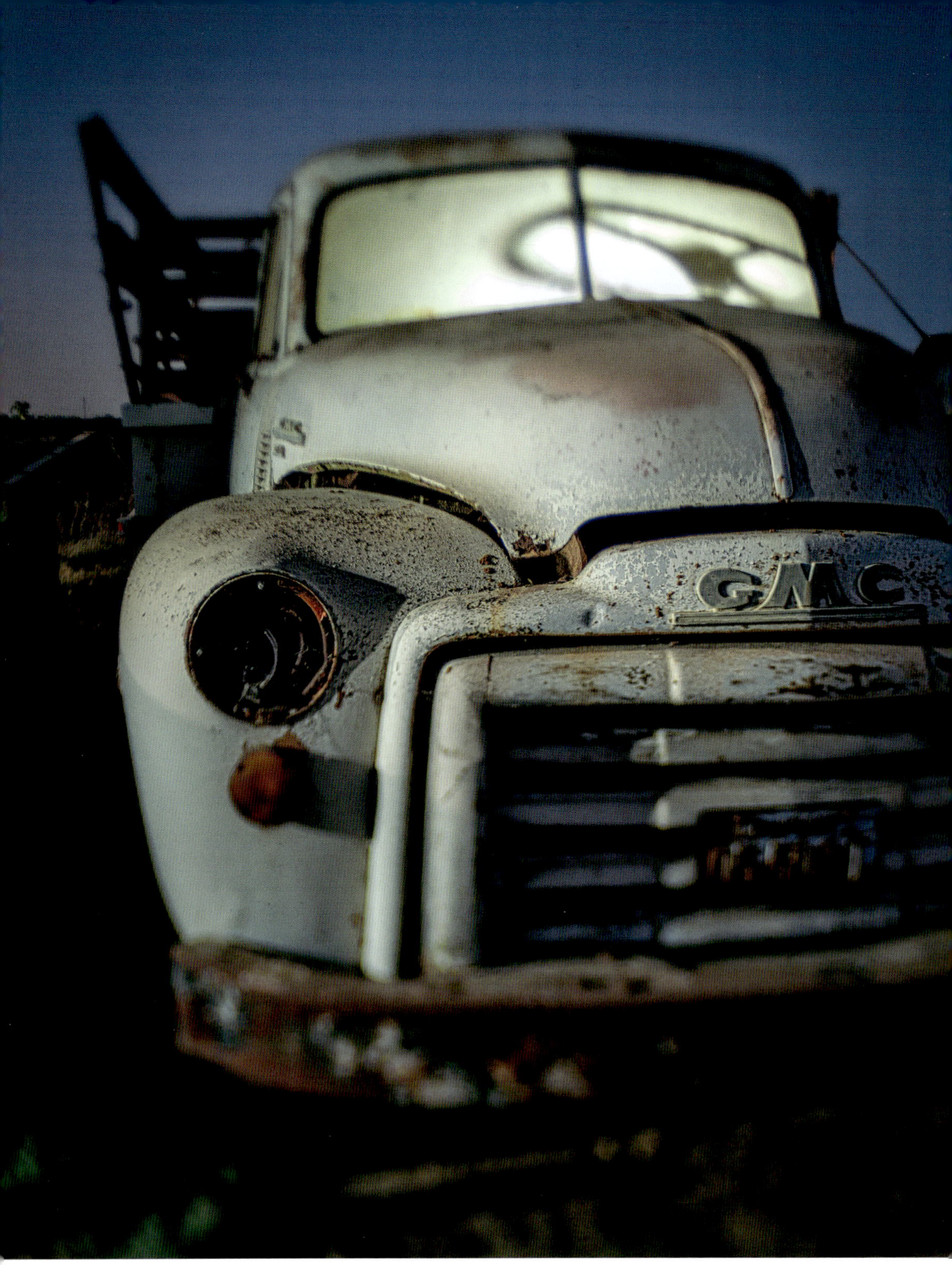

Ghostly Motor Company, old white GMC flatbed, Eagle Field. I wanted to create a haunting effect through a combination of lighting and selective focusing, particularly since it was Halloween night.
Pentax K-1/Lensbaby Edge 35 Optic lens. Seventy-one seconds f/4 ISO 200. Halloween 2020.
Full moon, warm white light from ProtoMachines LED2.

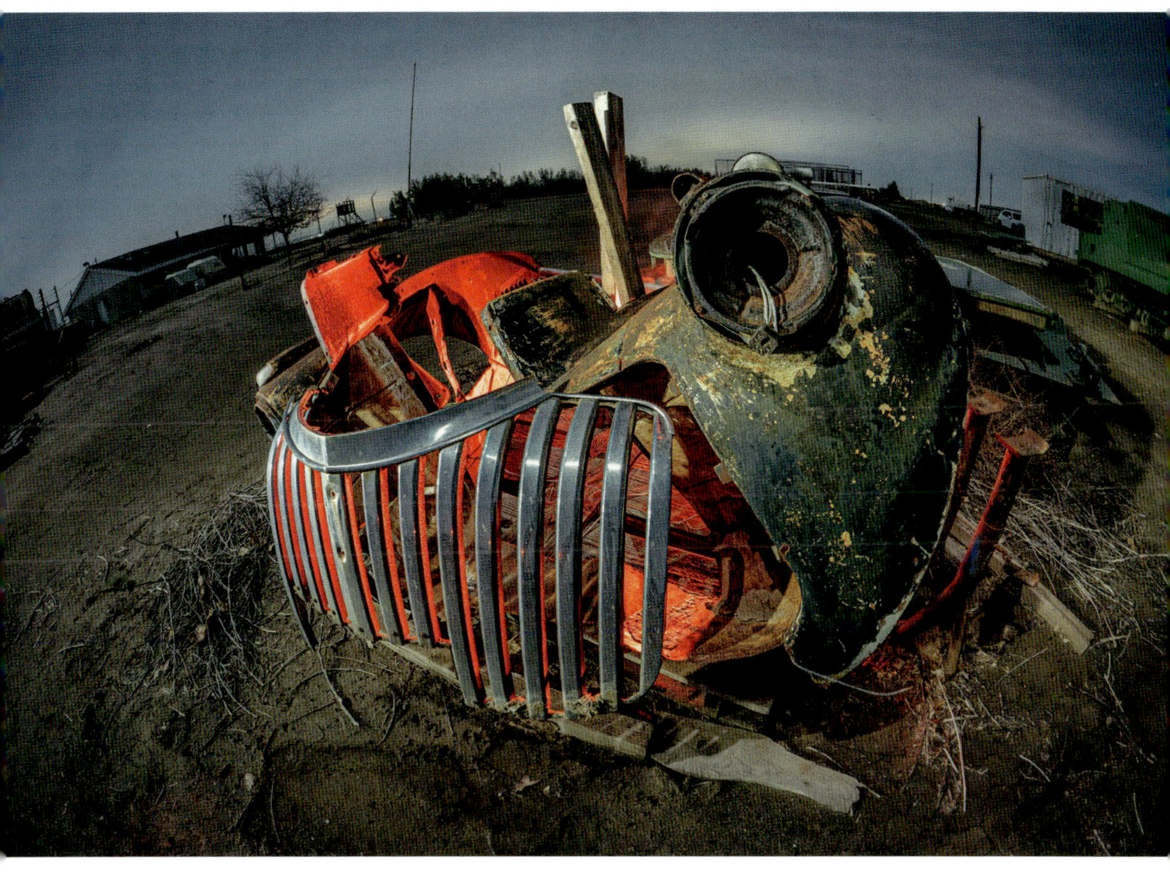

Not Quite Dead Yet, most likely a 1945 or 1946 Chevy truck, or possibly a grass-eating monster, Eagle Field. Either way, it looks like it's seen better days.
Nikon D750/Rokinon 12mm f/2.8 fisheye lens. 107 seconds f/8 ISO 320. December 2020.
Full moon on a hazy evening, warm white and red light from ProtoMachines LED2.

Motor Transport Museum

I meet Bryan at the Motor Transport Museum. For him, collecting and restoring vehicles is a way of life, and his knowledge is encyclopedic. We connect through our love of electronic and outsider music over pizza and gyro sandwiches. The site is nestled in a beautiful, rugged, rocky region of the Sonoran Desert several miles from the border of Mexico, quite close to the South Terminus of the Pacific Crest Trail.

I wander the lot. It is crammed full of vintage trucks, buses and other vehicles such as Pickwick, Mack, International, Federal, Nash, Commerce, and Austin. The owners have been accumulating discarded vehicles, motors and even olive presses for scrap metal, restoration, history, or perhaps for reasons that will reveal themselves later. I am just happy they are here. I relish the beautiful evening and set about experimenting with a Lensbaby tilt-shift lens that I have just purchased. I stay until almost three in the morning. It is a good evening.

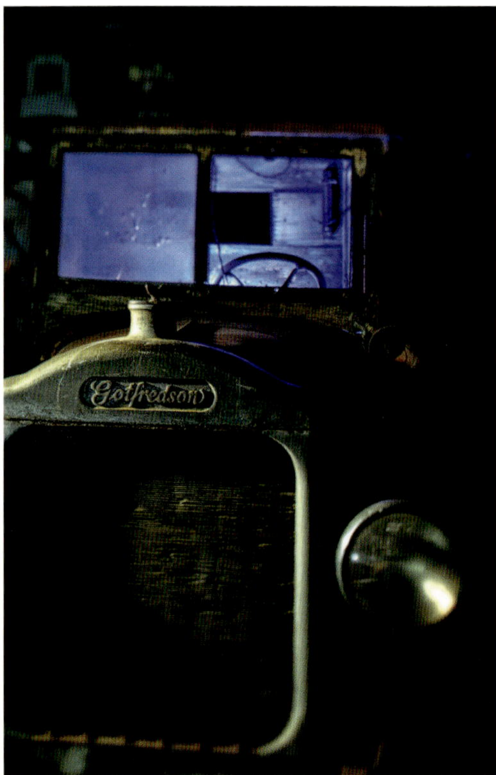

Blue Gotfredson, odd tilt-shift-style night photo of a rare 1927 Gotfredson Model 20B stake bed truck. Motor Transport Museum, Campo.
Pentax K-1/Lensbaby Edge 35 Optic lens. One minute eighteen seconds f/3.5 to f/5.6 (not sure, the lens is manual) ISO 200. October 2020.
Warm white and blue light from ProtoMachines LED2, lit in almost total darkness.

▶
Rust Never Sleeps, night photo of the interior of what is most likely a 1928 Moreland truck. Motor Transport Museum, Campo.
Nikon D750/Rokinon 12-mm f/2.8 fisheye lens. Eighteen minutes total "stacked"; each photo three minutes f/8 ISO 200. October 2020.
Full moon, warm white light from ProtoMachines LED2.

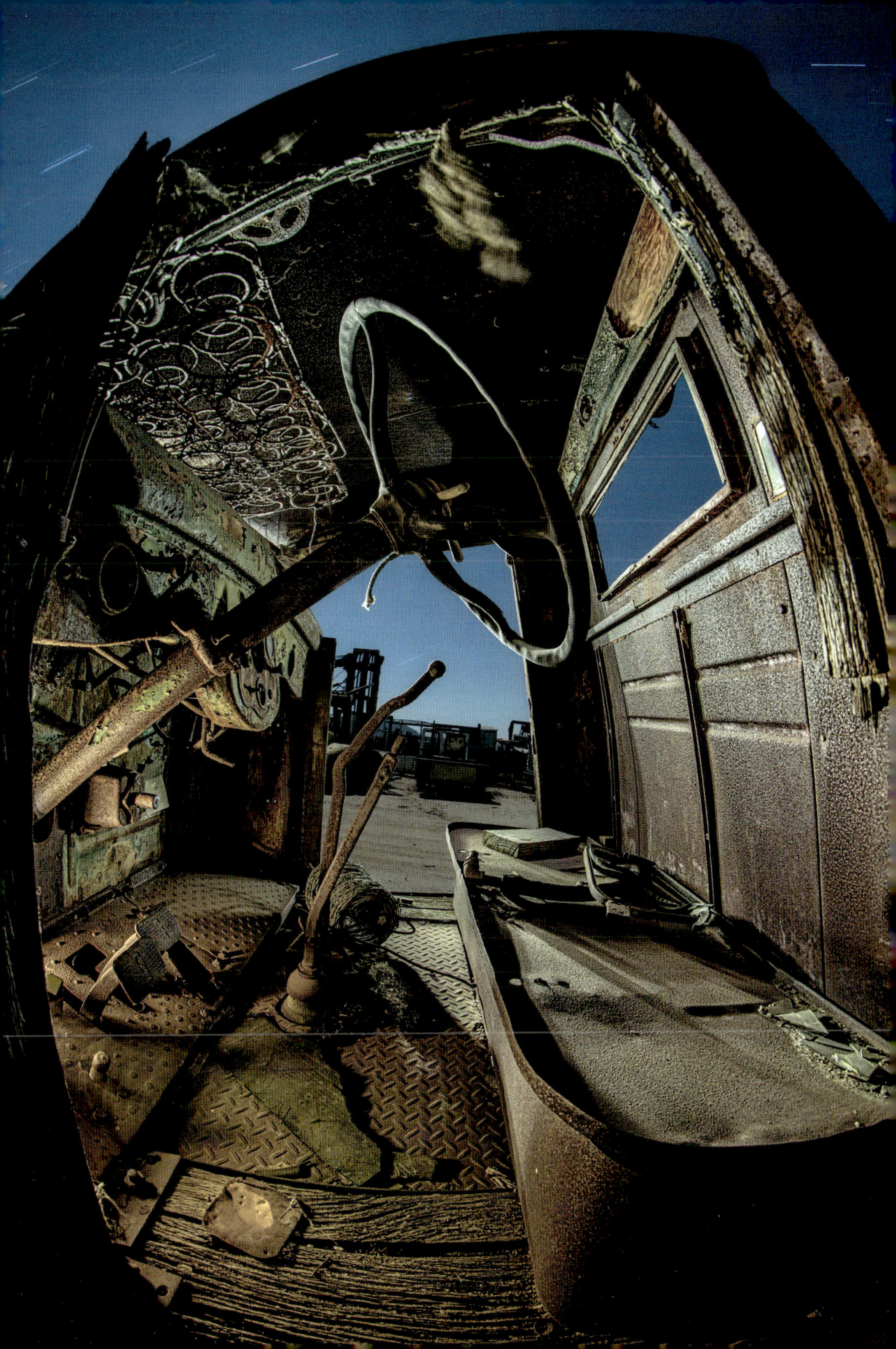

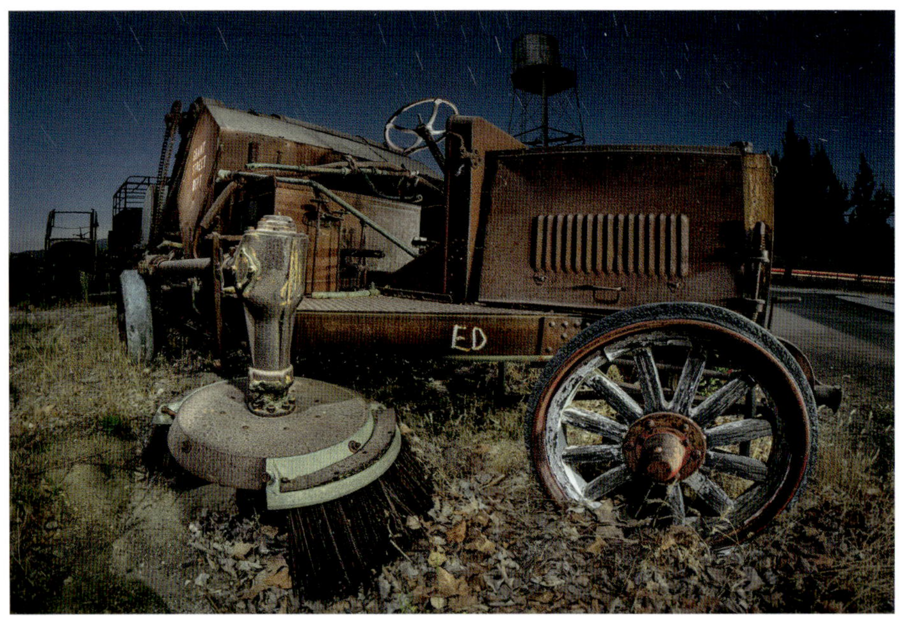

Sweep by Sweepwest, 1926 Austin Street Sweeper. Almost 100 years old, the tech is not terribly different from modern street sweepers. Motor Transport Museum, Campo.
Nikon D750/Rokinon 12-mm f/2.8 fisheye lens. Fifteen minutes total "stacked"; each photo three minutes f/8 ISO 200. October 2020.
Full moon, warm white light from ProtoMachines LED2.

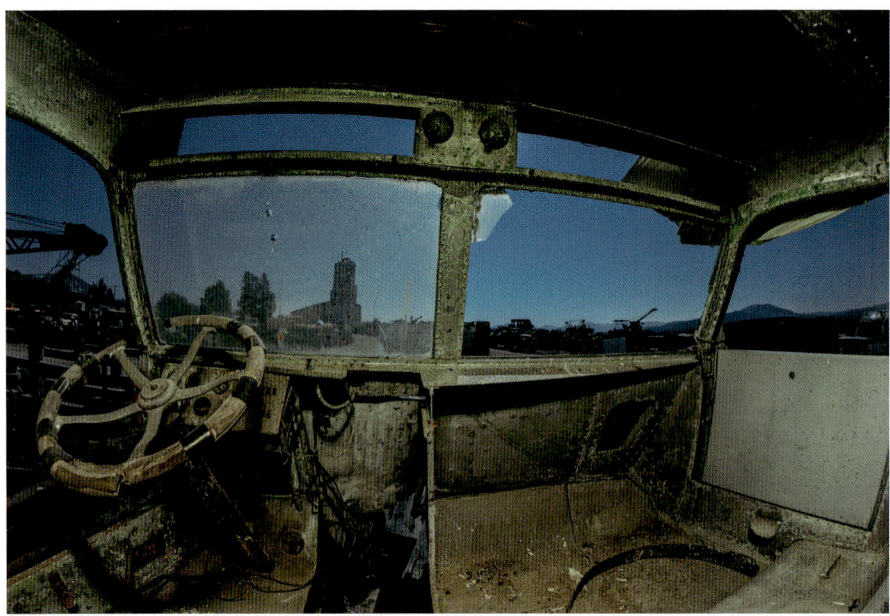

Tatooine Express, this is an extremely rare double-decker breadbox-style 1930 Nite Coach made by Pickwick from aircraft aluminum. In the upper deck, people would sit and eat. The bottom level had beds, bathrooms, and showers. Motor Transport Museum, Campo.
Nikon D750/Rokinon 12-mm f/2.8 fisheye lens. Three minutes f/8 ISO 200. October 2020.
Full moon, warm white light from ProtoMachines LED2.

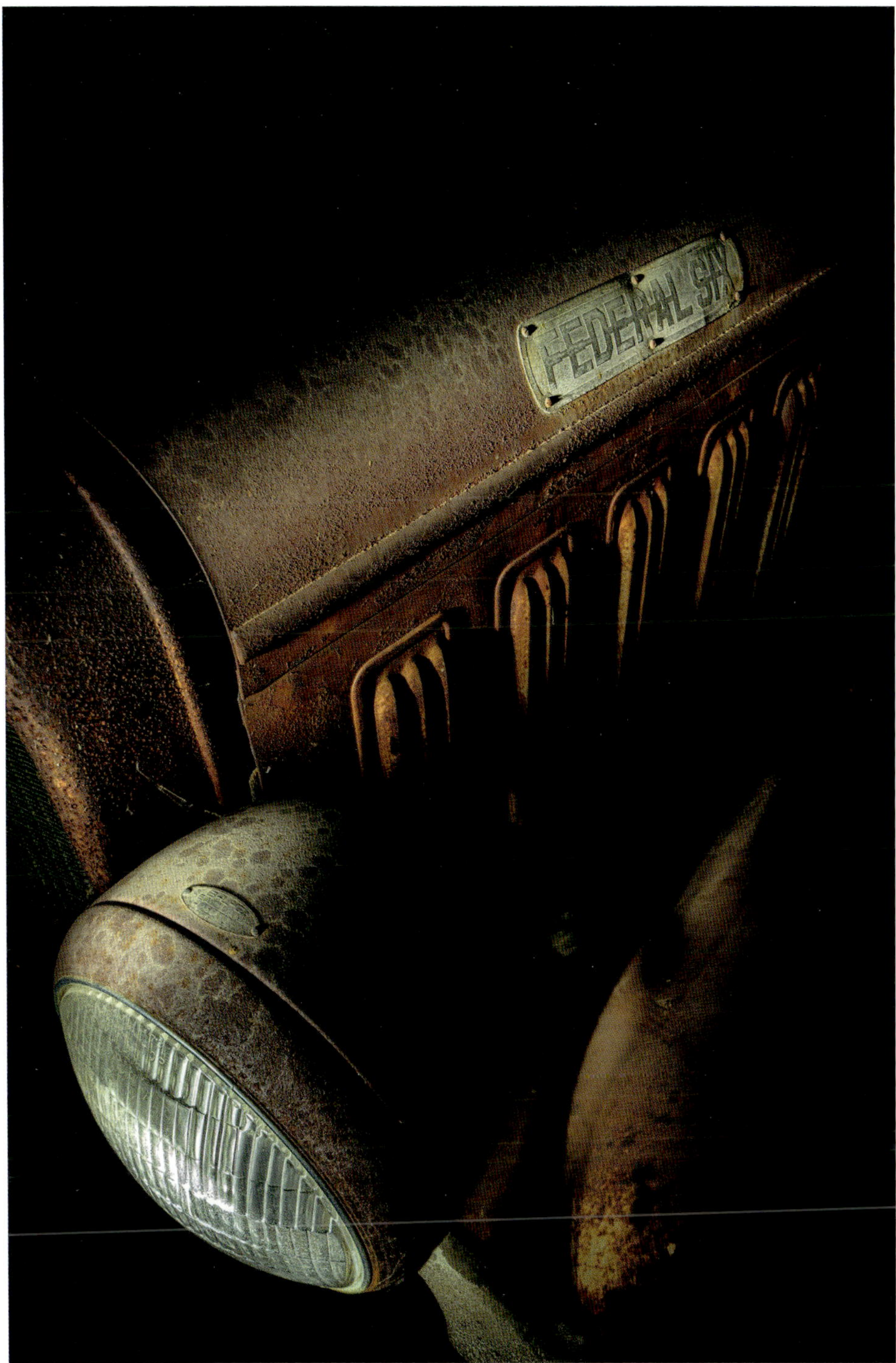

The Federal Six, 1929 Federal school bus, possibly the first motorized school bus in Campo. Motor Transport Museum.
Pentax K-1/15–30-mm f/2.8 lens. Forty-two seconds f/8 ISO 200. October 2020.
Warm white light from ProtoMachines LED2. Full moon was present but not used to create starker lighting with a shorter exposure.

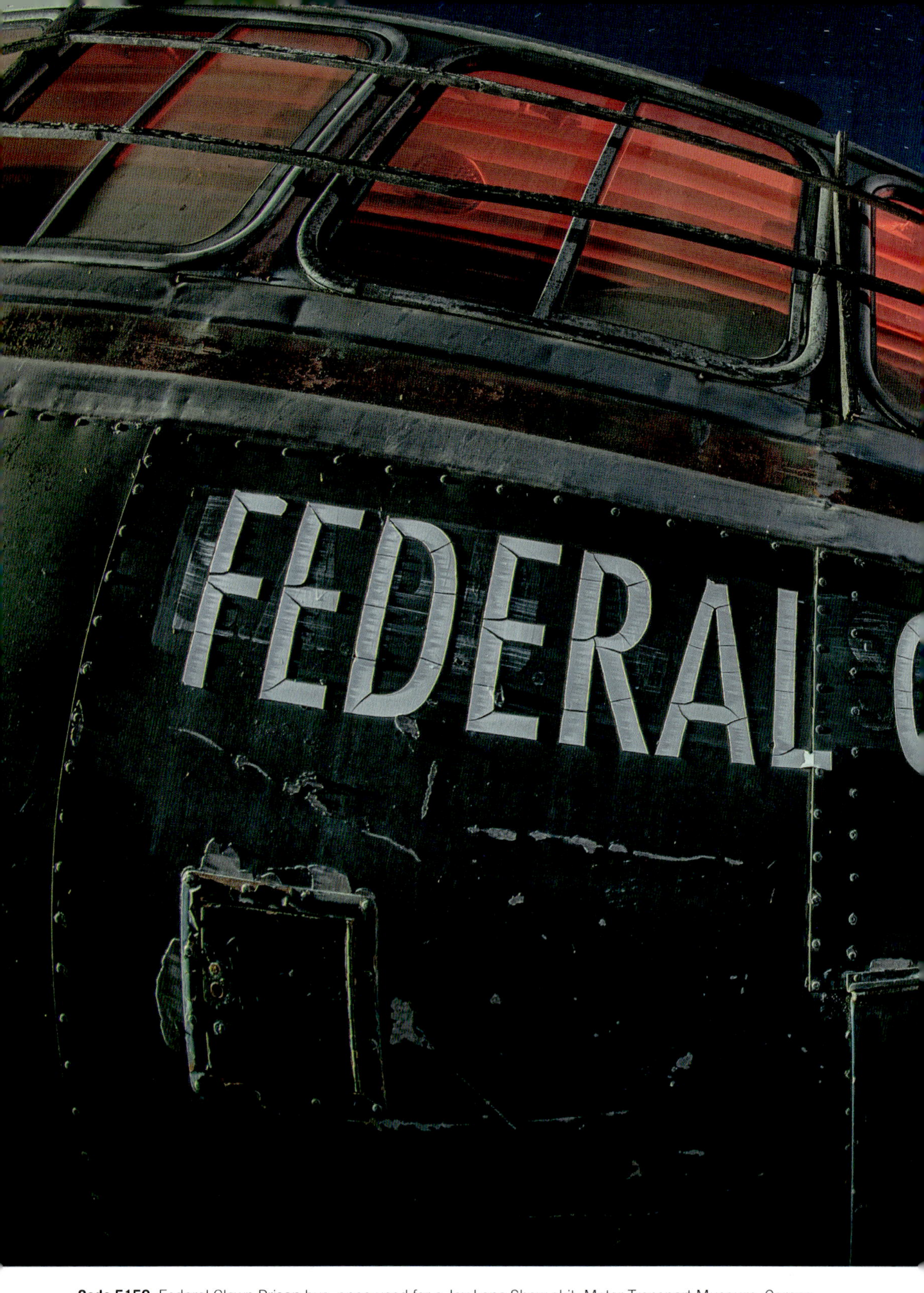

Code 5150, Federal Clown Prison bus, once used for a Jay Leno Show skit. Motor Transport Museum, Campo.

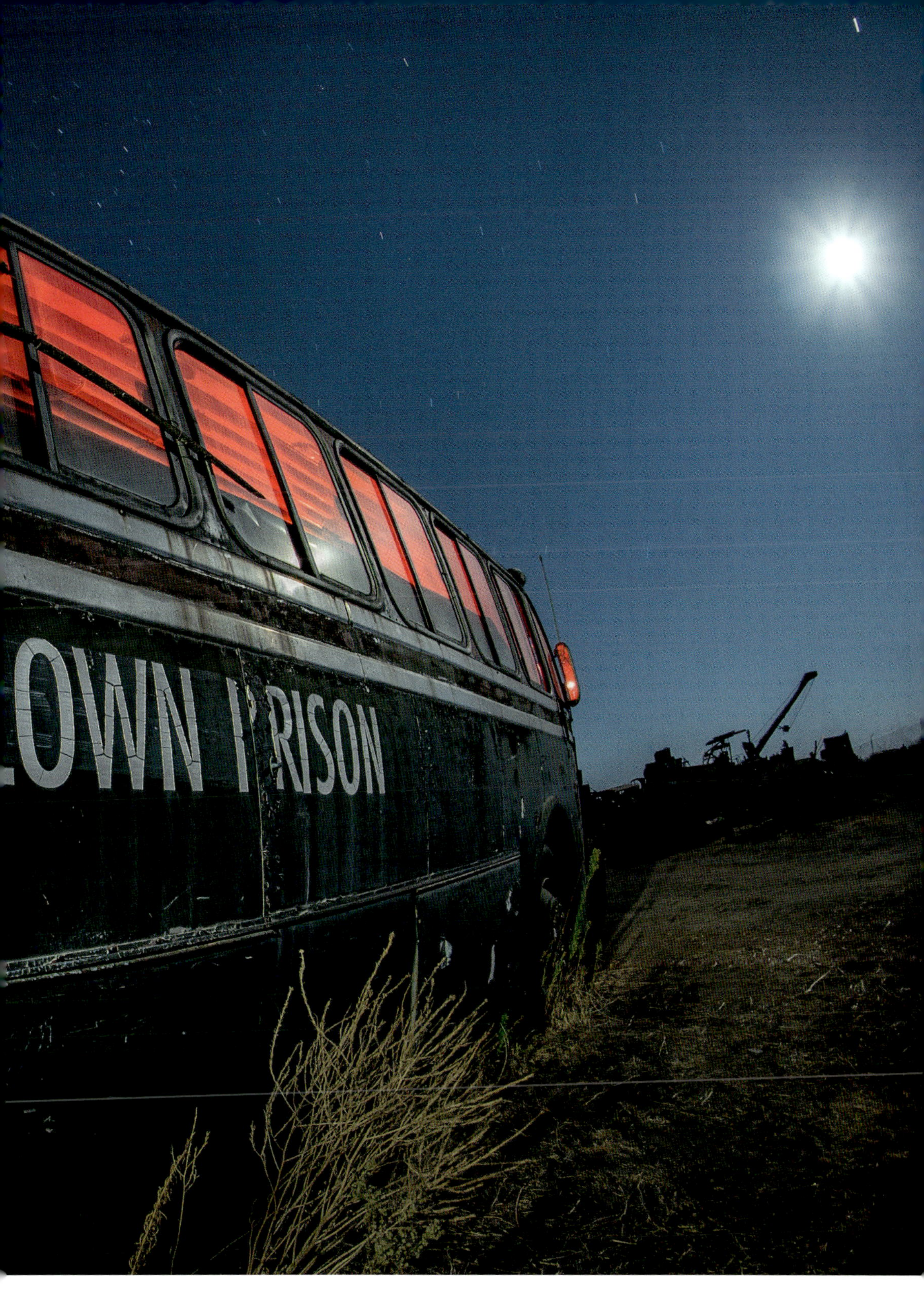

Nikon D750/Rokinon 12-mm f/2.8 fisheye lens. Three minutes f/8 ISO 200. October 2020. Full moon, warm white and red light from ProtoMachines LED2.

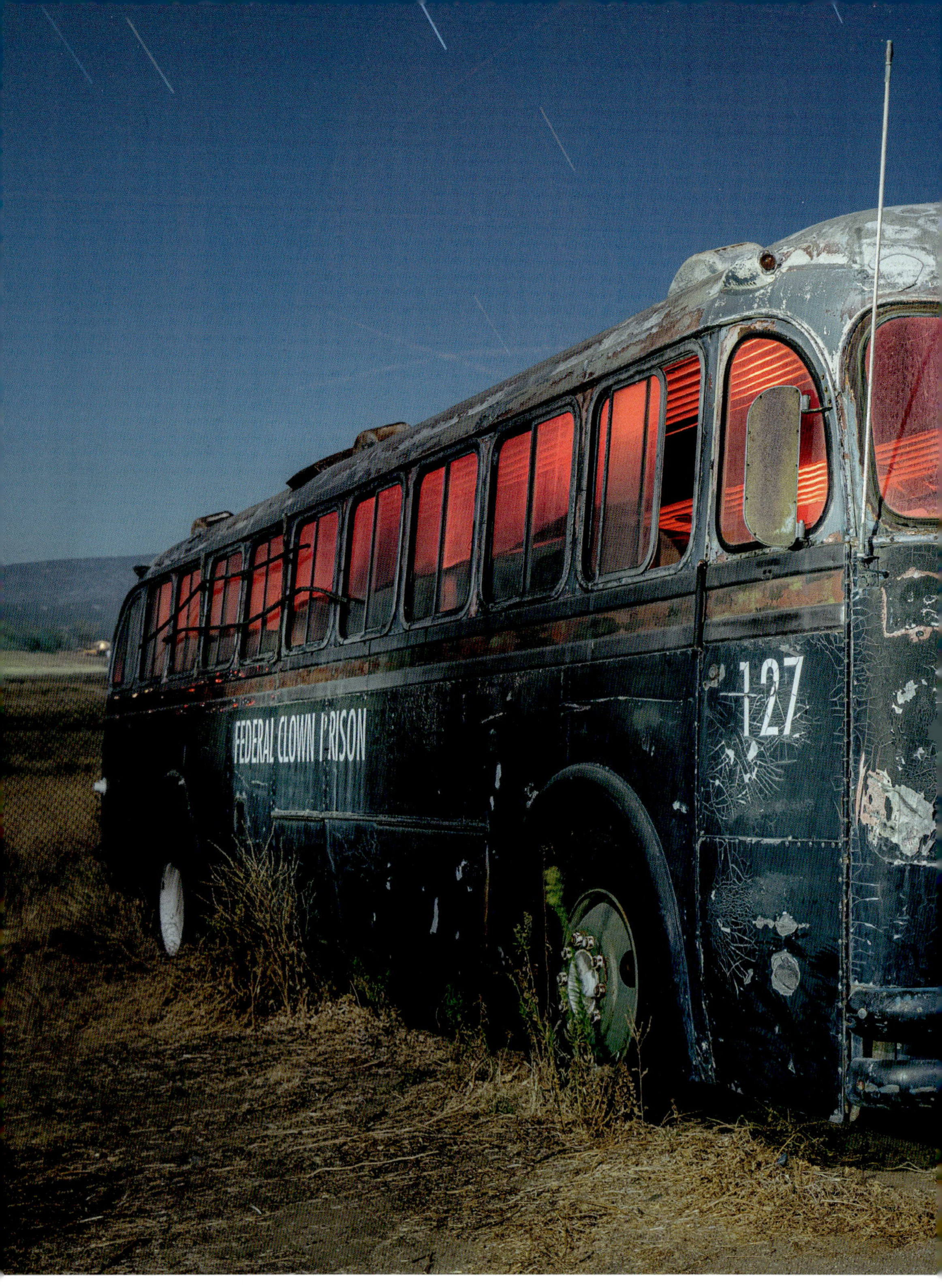

Better than a Clown Car, Federal Clown Prison bus, once used for a Jay Leno Show skit. Motor Transport Museum, Campo.

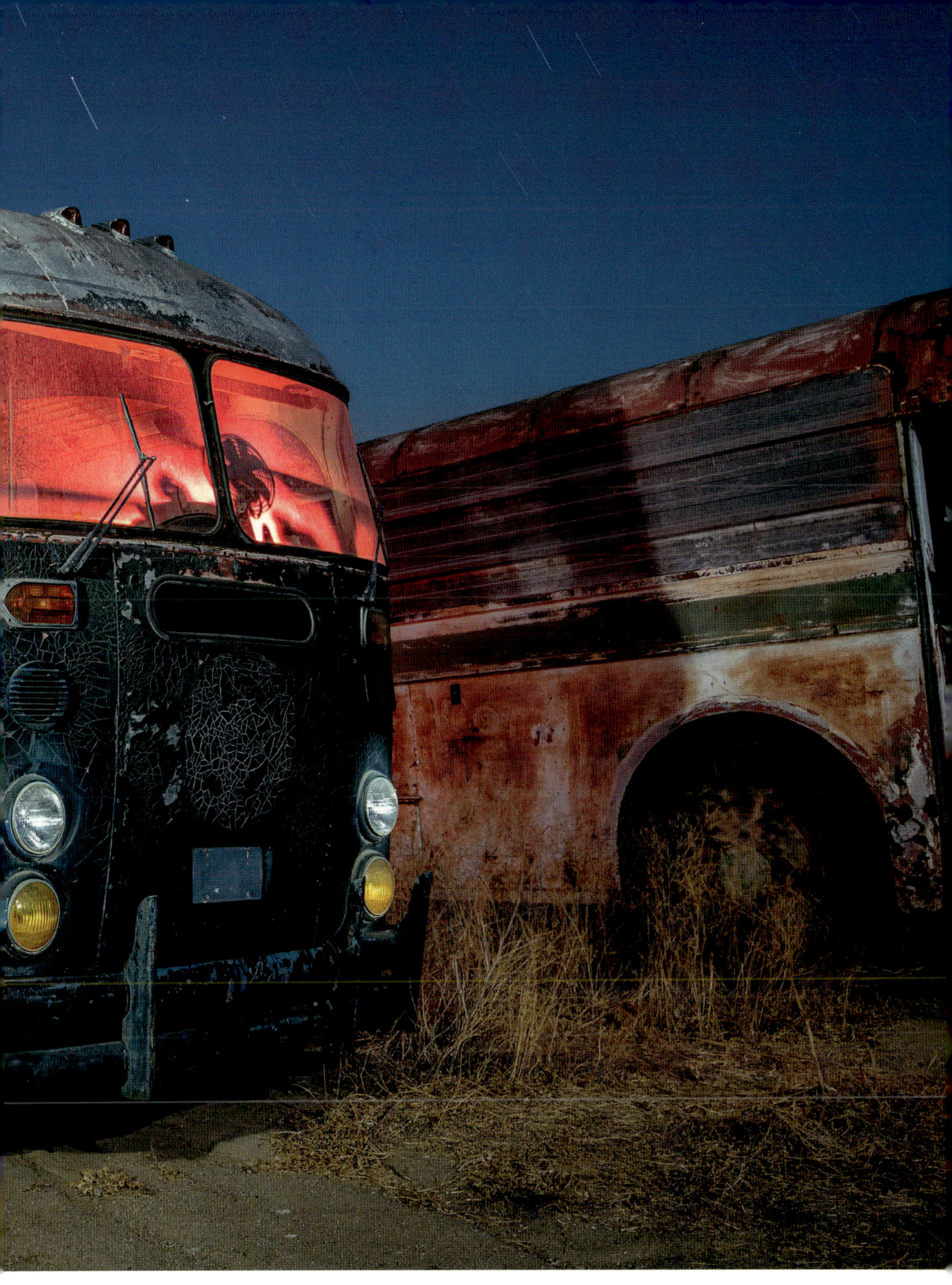

Pentax K-1/Tamron 15–30-mm f/2.8 lens. Nine minutes total "stacked"; each photo three minutes f/8 ISO 200. October 2020.
Full moon, warm white and red light from ProtoMachines LED2.

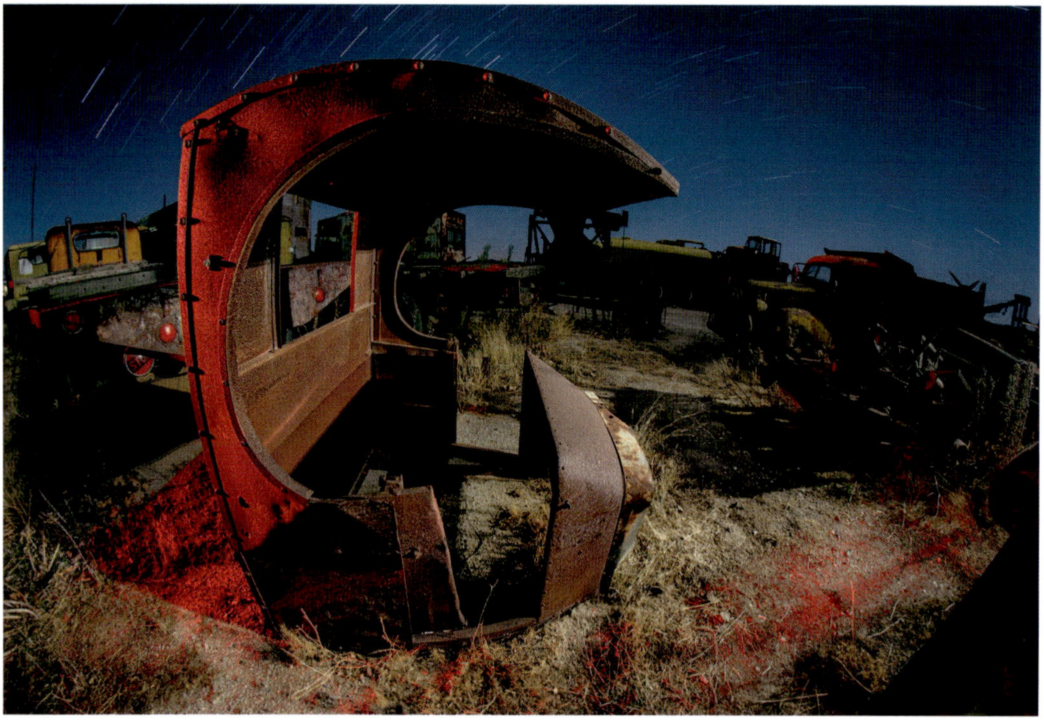

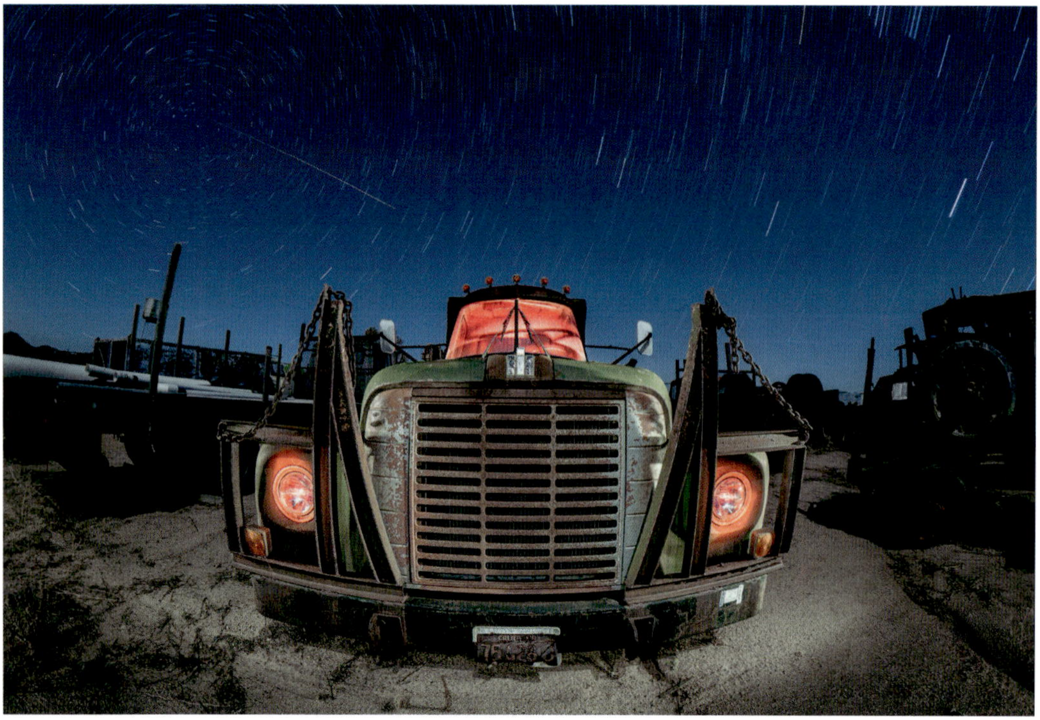

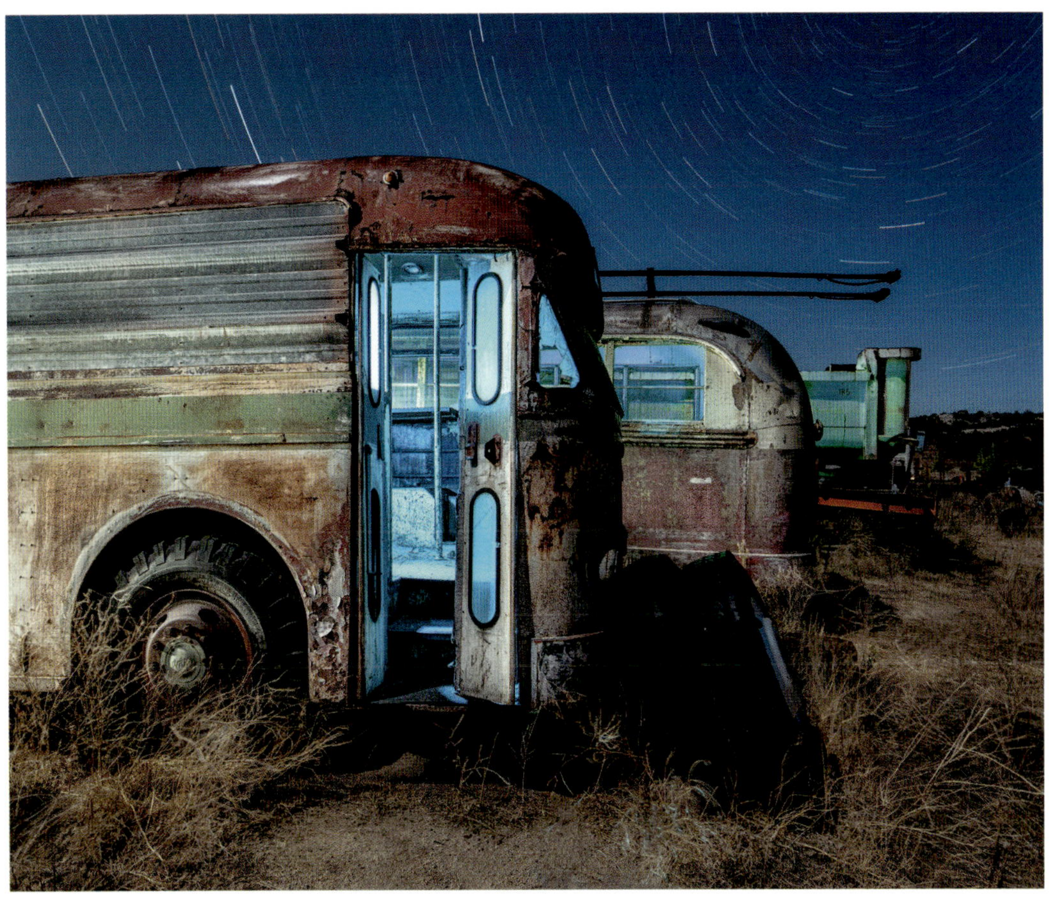

Ready to Retire, night photo of a couple of old abandoned city buses underneath the heavenly bodies perpetually in motion during my second trip here on Thanksgiving Eve. I drove back home just in time for our holiday celebration. Motor Transport Museum.
Pentax K-1/15-30mm f/2.8 lens. Forty minutes total "stacked"; each photo 160 seconds f/8 ISO 200. November 2020.
Full moon, warm white and Gas Station Teal (Trademark, Tim Little) from ProtoMachines LED2.

Opposite page

▲ **Dangerous Curves**, the grounded remains of what I believe is a rare and rusty 1920s Fageol truck cab, Motor Transport Museum. Although warm and sunny during the day, by the time I packed up, it was below freezing and I had ice on my windshield. This was during my second trip here.
Nikon D750/Rokinon f/2.8 fisheye lens. Twenty-one minutes total "stacked"; each photo 3 minutes f/8 ISO 250. November 2020.
Full moon, warm white and red light from ProtoMachines LED2.

▼ **The Red Crown**, seeming like a rather menacing night encounter between my fisheye lens and the massive International Loadstar 1600 truck, wearing a five-point crown of red...with a shooting star for good measure. Motor Transport Museum.
Nikon D750/Rokinon f/2.8 fisheye lens. Eight minutes total "stacked". 19.8 minutes total "stacked"; each photo 149 seconds f/8 ISO 250. November 2020.
Full moon, warm white and red light from ProtoMachines LED2.

Golden Cactus

The EAT sign greets you as you enter the magnificent Owens Valley, formed by the Sierras to the west and the Inyo Mountains and White Mountains to the east. Most people from Los Angeles do not know about the Owens Valley, despite siphoning off its water for decades, unless they are outdoor enthusiasts or like to ski in Mammoth.

Golden Cactus in Pearsonville is a roadside attraction of sorts, part refurbished miners' cabins, part museum crammed full of amazing vintage cameras, typewriters, and artifacts from yesteryear. Included in that is a collection of fascinating vehicles, including a Model T, a rare Tucker with three headlights, a large-finned Cadillac, and a Plymouth DeSoto.

The attraction is run by Ricardo and his brother, who are happy to show you around and tell stories. His brother, James, is a rather philosophical sort. Ricardo and James hang out with me, showing active interest in the process of night photography. Our conversation swings from questions about the cosmos to philosophy to restoring vintage automobiles, all under a cold February night sky.

I take a liking to the 1948 Tucker immediately. How could I not? I have never seen one before. And little wonder since only fifty-one, including the prototype, were ever made, according to *Road & Track Magazine*. And it is unusual. The third "Cyclops" headlight in the middle really makes it for me. This was designed by Preston Tucker to swivel, lighting the way around corners. The car had other innovations, such as a padded dashboard for safety, a rear engine, a pop-out windshield designed to eject during a crash to protect passengers, a steering wheel box located behind the front axle to protect the driver from head-on collisions, and a parking brake with its own key to provide additional theft protection.

Golden Cactus has since gone through numerous misfortunes, including the devastating Ridgecrest earthquakes. Ricardo sent me photos of the destruction of the museum, and it was heartbreaking. The coronavirus pandemic has not done them any favors either.

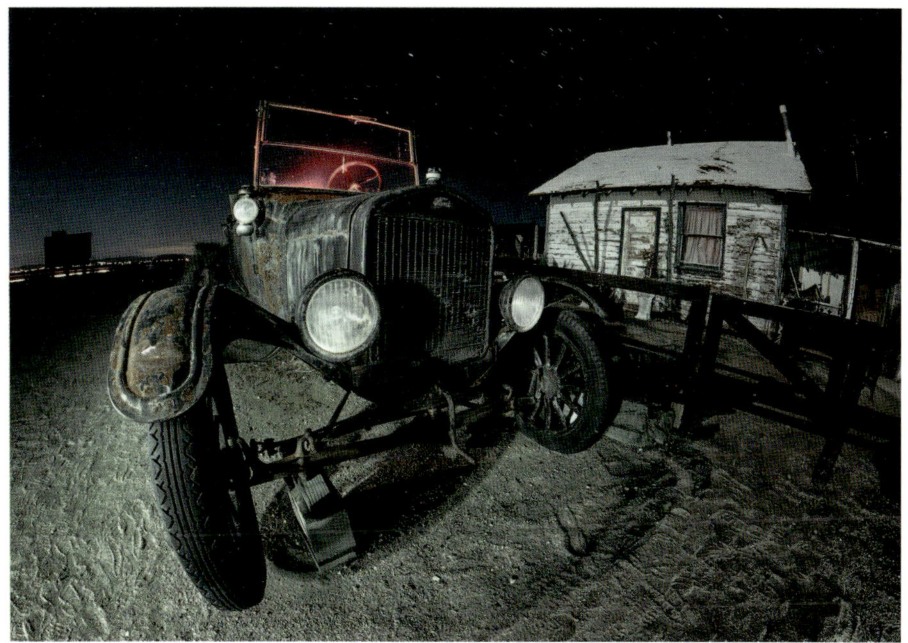

Kukla and Ollie, Ford Model T and an 1800s miner's cabin, Golden Cactus, Pearsonville.
Nikon D610/Rokinon 12-mm f/2.8 fisheye lens. Two minutes thirty seconds f/8 ISO 200. February 2018.
Full moon, warm white and red light from ProtoMachines LED2.

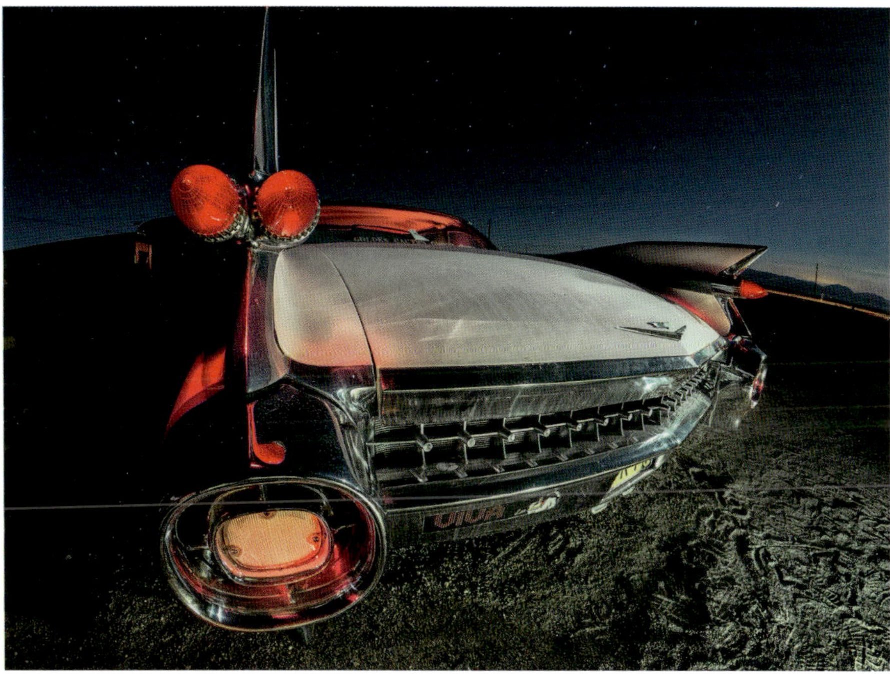

Fins and Lights and Stuff, a vintage Cadillac, made back when people let the tail lights and the fins fly.
Golden Cactus, Pearsonville.
Nikon D610/Rokinon 12-mm f/2.8 fisheye lens. Two minutes thirty seconds f/8 ISO 200. February 2018.
Full moon, warm white and red light from ProtoMachines LED2.

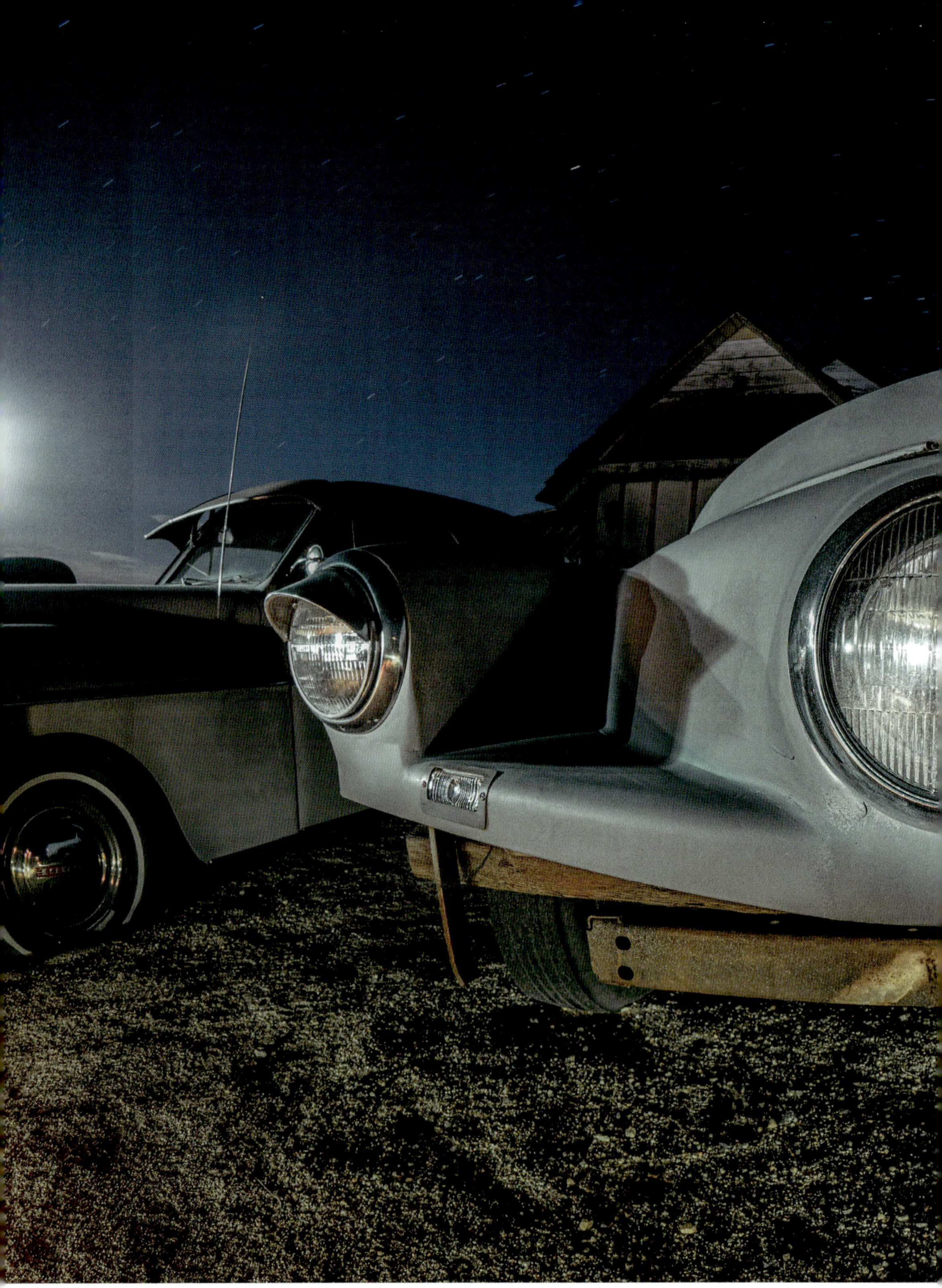

Eye See You, a rare 1948 Tucker with three headlights and other innovative features. Golden Cactus, Pearsonville.

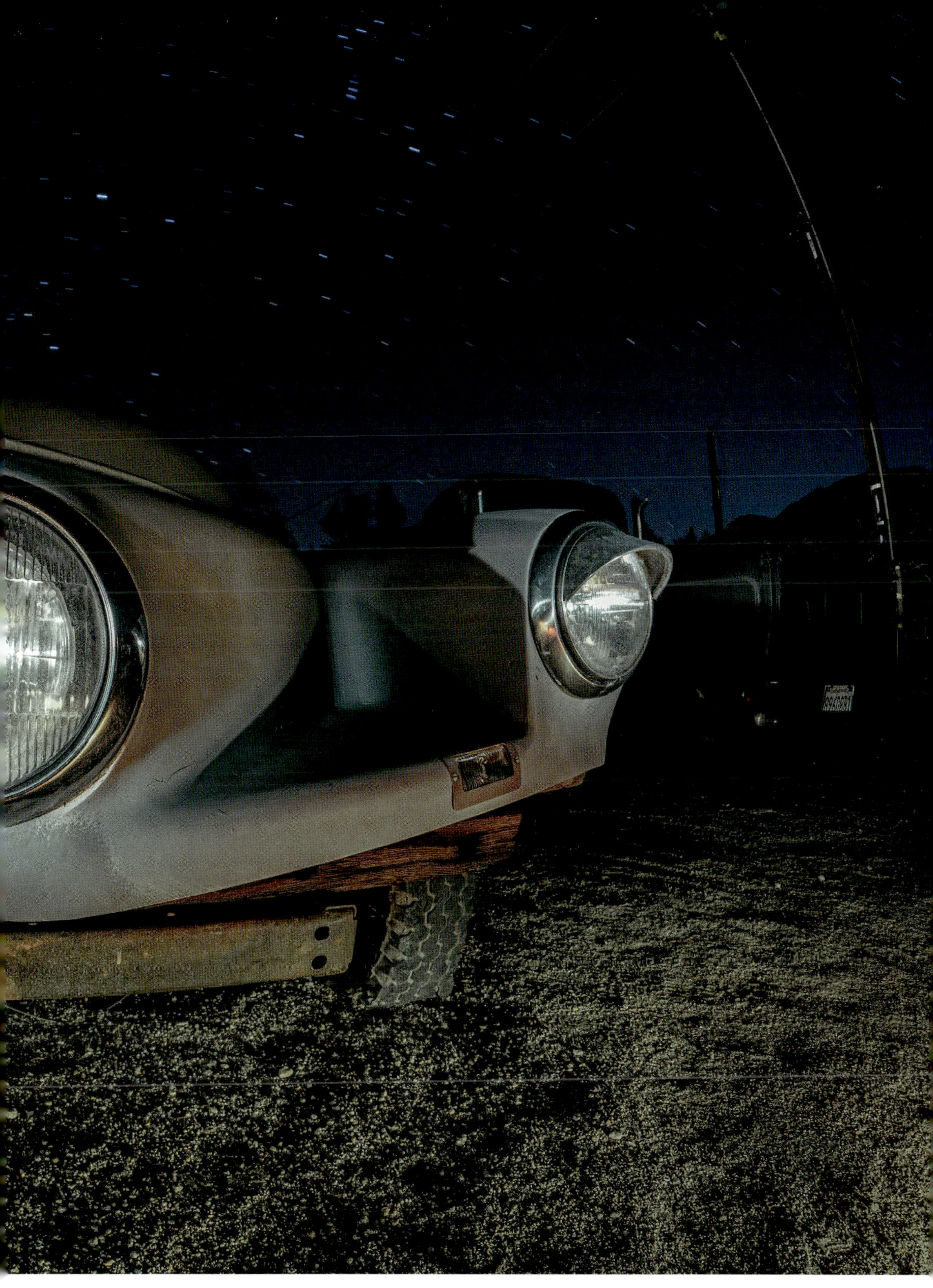

Nikon D610/Rokinon 12-mm f/2.8 fisheye lens. Two minutes thirty seconds f/8 ISO 200. February 2018. Full moon, warm white and red light from ProtoMachines LED2.

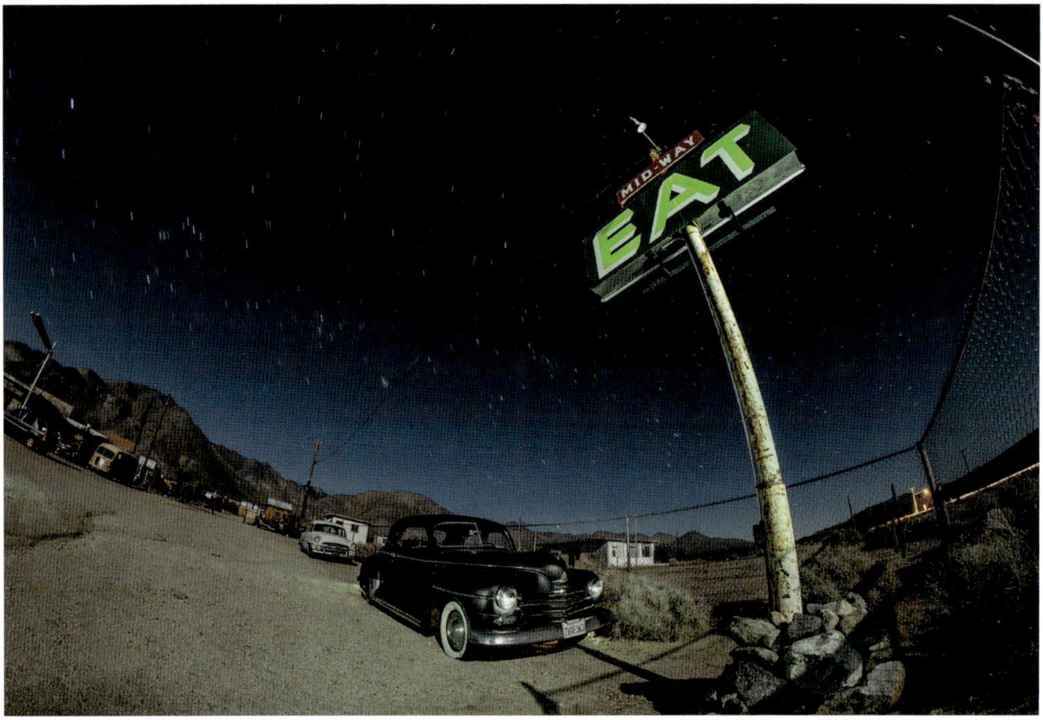

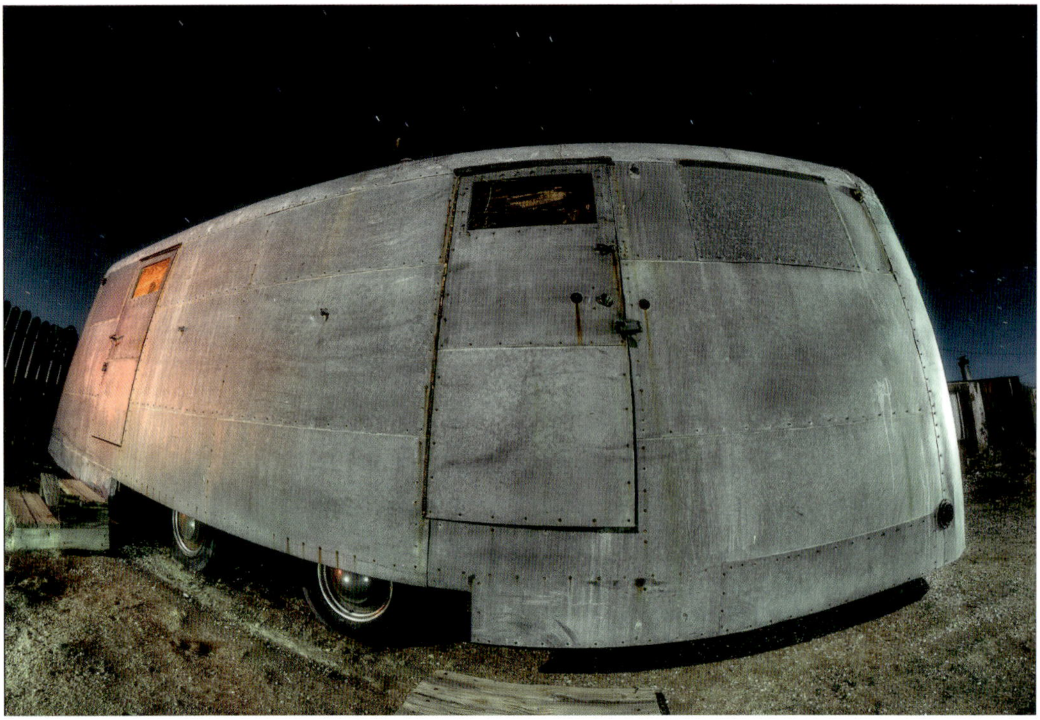

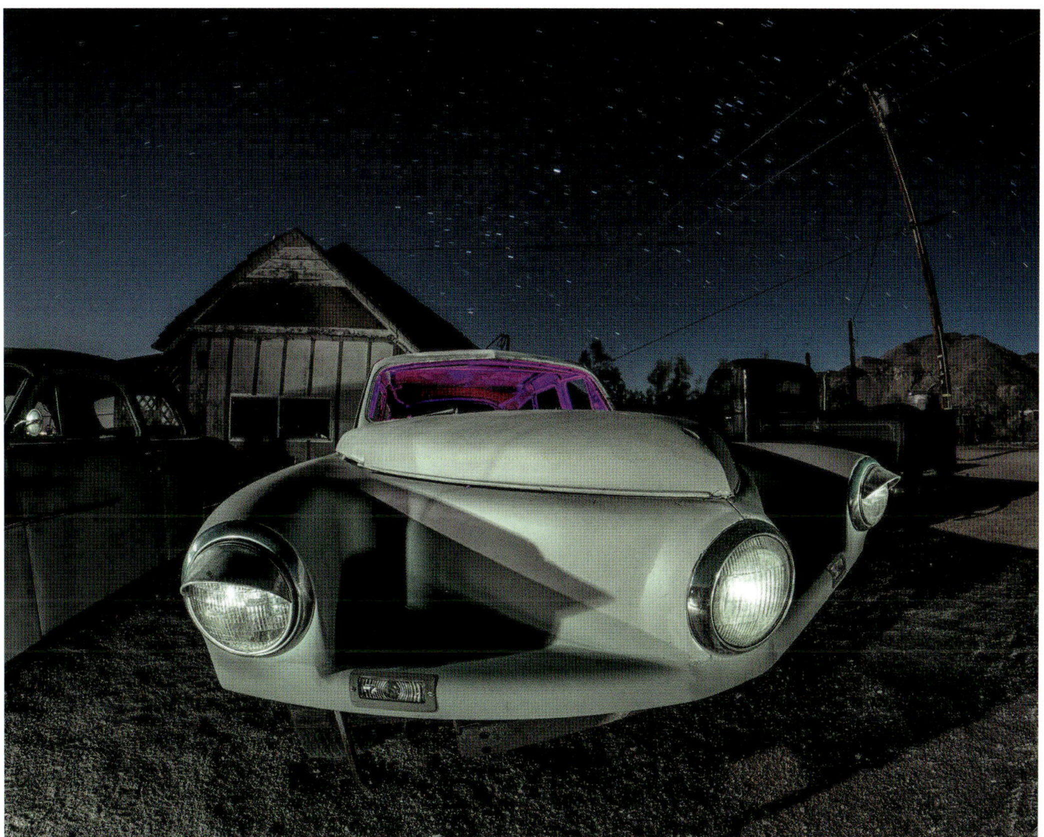

The Cyclops Three, a rare 1948 Tucker with three headlights and other innovative features. Golden Cactus, Pearsonville.
Nikon D610/Rokinon 12-mm f/2.8 fisheye lens. Two minutes thirty seconds f/8 ISO 200. February 2018.
Full moon, warm white and blue light from ProtoMachines LED2.

Opposite page

▲ **Mid-Way EAT**, 1950s Plymouth Special Deluxe and the Mid-Way Eat sign from a defunct 1970s restaurant. Golden Cactus, Pearsonville.
Nikon D610/Rokinon 12-mm f/2.8 fisheye lens. Two minutes thirty seconds f/8 ISO 200. February 2018.
Full moon, warm white light from ProtoMachines LED2.

▼ **Single Wide Paradise**, this is a homemade trailer from the 1930s. Golden Cactus, Pearsonville.
Nikon D610/Rokinon 12-mm f/2.8 fisheye lens. Three minutes f/8 ISO 200. February 2018.
Full moon, warm white and red light from ProtoMachines LED2.

Pearsonville

The 18-foot Uniroyal Girl with faded blond hair wearing a fiberglass skirt greets me with a wave of her hand. I have seen her for years, since we used to drive up to Lone Pine to paint my father's rental house. International Fiberglass made these giant statues for the Uniroyal Tire Company. The sculptor modeled his creation after Jackie Kennedy. And why not? Each statue was bikini-clad, but snap-on clothes were available for a more modest appearance.

My lady friend stands tall in Pearsonville, the Hubcap Capital of the World—gateway to Owens Valley. Every time I pass this way, I pull off the highway to take a photo of her, knowing that great times are just ahead. I might explore the Alabama Hills, Ancient Bristlecone Pine Forest, Mammoth, the Eastern Sierra, or, yes, Pearsonville itself.

In 2016, I am still just beginning my experiments in light painting vehicles. I have not had much opportunity to photograph abandoned cars. I have just done it twice, and more than two years ago. I meet Tim and Steve, fellow night photographers who speak about the auto salvage yard in Pearsonville in warm, reverential terms. They speak of Lucy Pearson, one of the founders of the town, and her collection of 80,000 used hubcaps, buying, selling, and trading them. They speak of how there were 4,000 cars and a raceway. They speak of epic workshops with pioneering night photographers Troy Paiva and Joe Reifer. They speak of beautiful vintage cars, rusting in the open.

I have seen photos of this place before. But nothing prepares me for the sheer diversity, even with less than 1,000 cars remaining: old Edsels, Corsairs, Cosmopolitans, bread trucks, GM buses, long Checker Aerobuses, Cadillac campers, and more. Pearsonville is still a gold mine for night photography. My friends greet this place with great affection, intimately familiar with many of the vehicles and their locations. And quickly, the place casts its spell on me. I am in awe of the amazing clouds swooping over the jagged South Sierra. I hand-light these rusty treasures while my camera soaks in the images. The hours evaporate quickly. We just began photographing, did we not? I return numerous times. This place is special.

But now in my most recent visit, I feel a twinge of sadness. The lots are eerily empty. However, the few cars that remain often have more space around them, allowing me to pull back or get angles not possible before. But I know that these will also not be long for this world. I hope my 18-foot lady friend will continue to wave hello for longer.

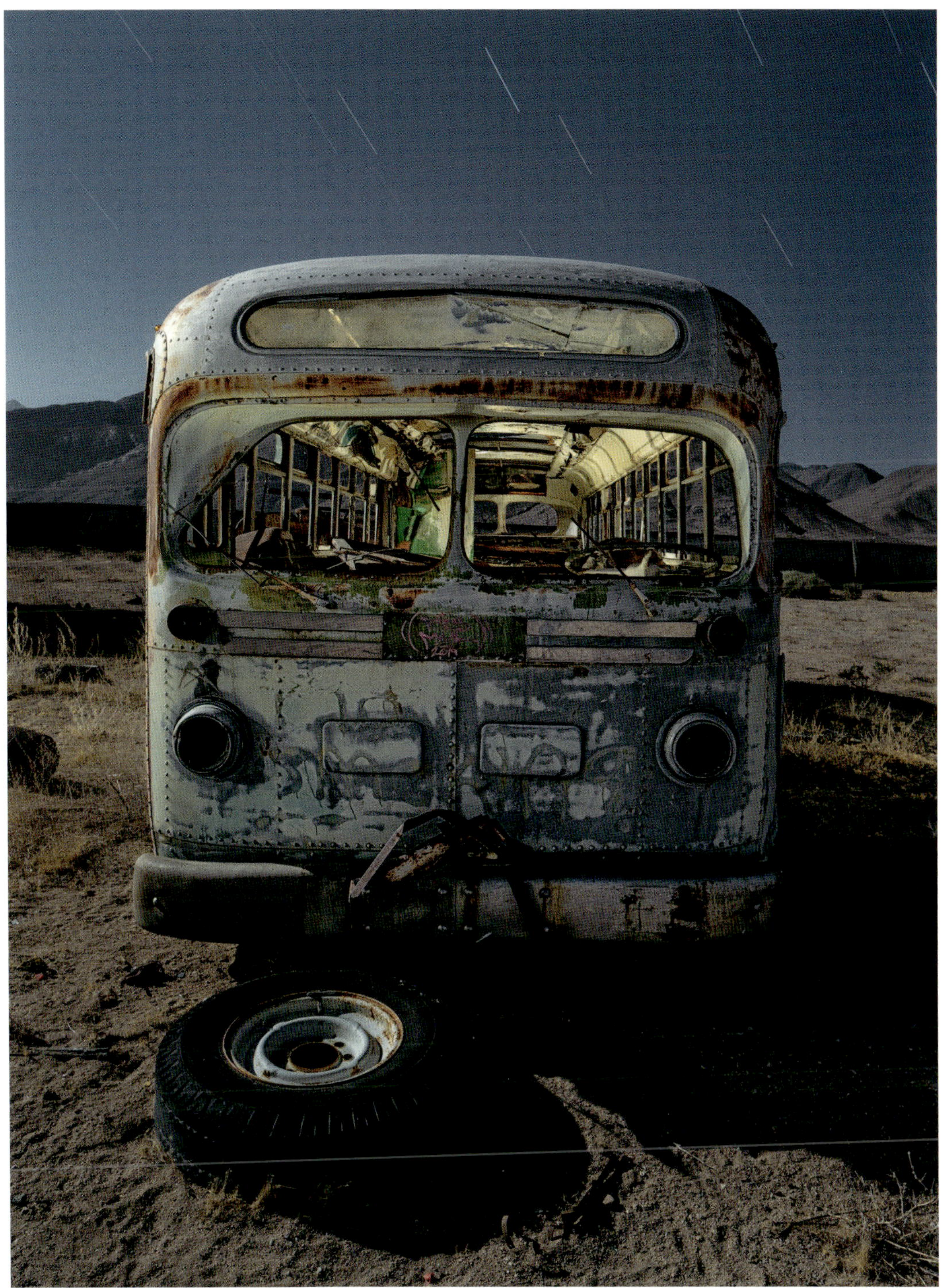

The Mojave Express Rides Again, "The Bus," as we sometimes call it, welcoming night photographers to Pearsonville for years.
Pentax K-1/15–30-mm f/2.8 lens. Fifteen minutes total "stacked." Each photo three minutes f/8 ISO 200. Early August 2020
Full moon, warm white light from ProtoMachines LED2.

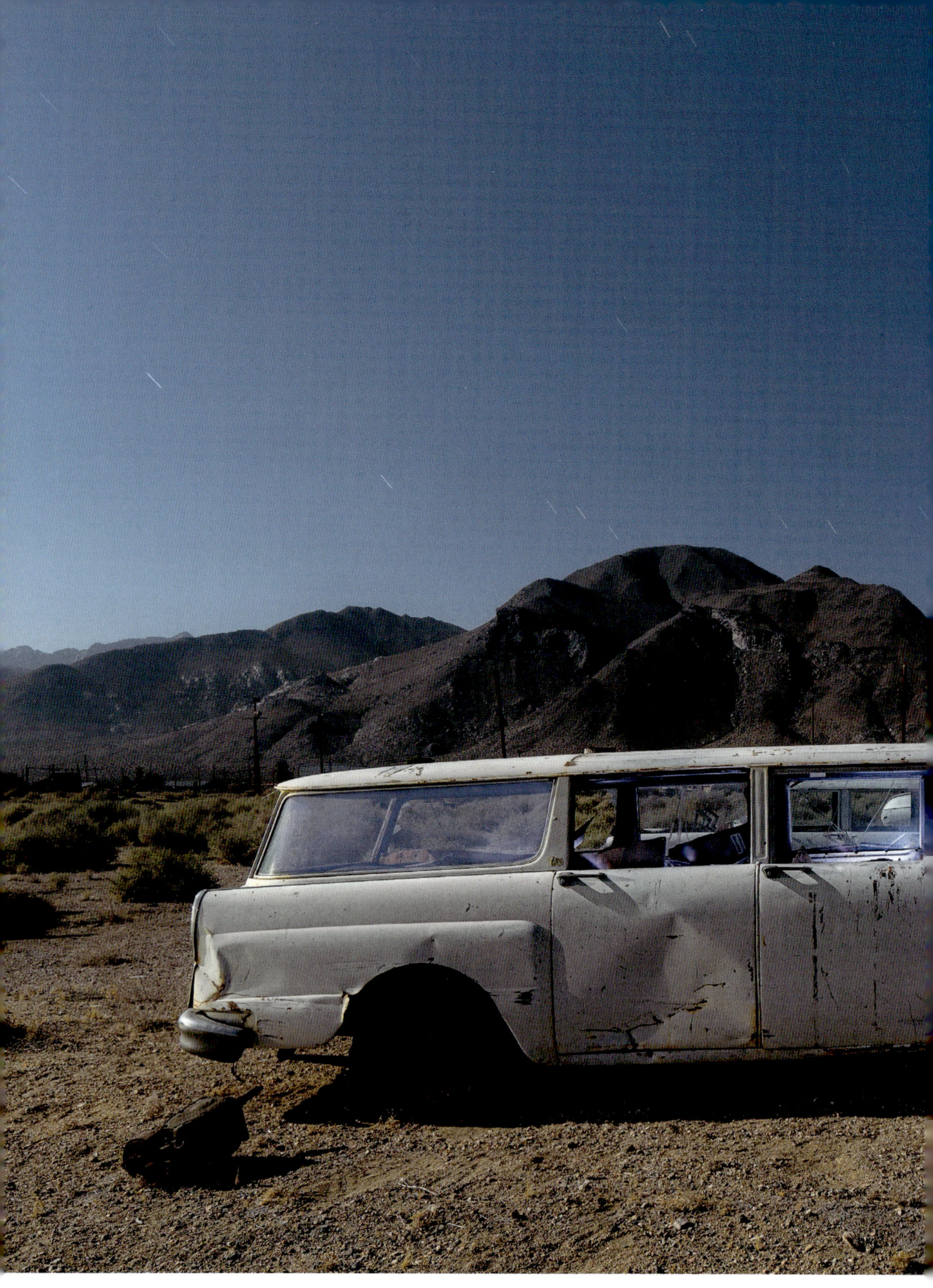

Stretch, Checker Aerobus, likely serving as an airport shuttle; was an extended version of the Checker Marathon. Pearsonville during a brutally hot and gusty night.

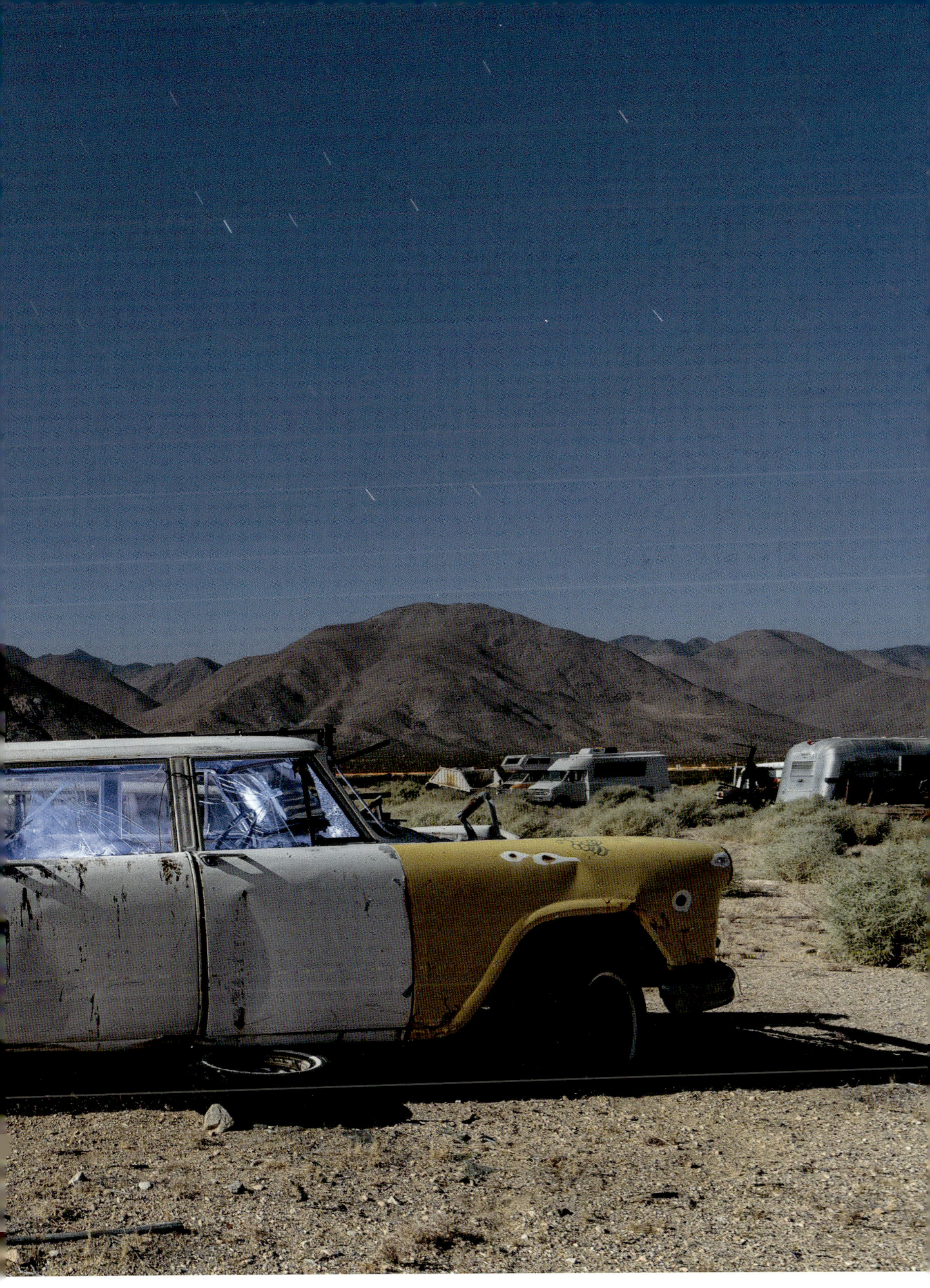

Pentax K-1/15–30-mm f/2.8 lens. Nine minutes total "stacked"; each photo three minutes f/8 ISO 200. August 2020. Full moon, warm white and blue light from ProtoMachines LED2.

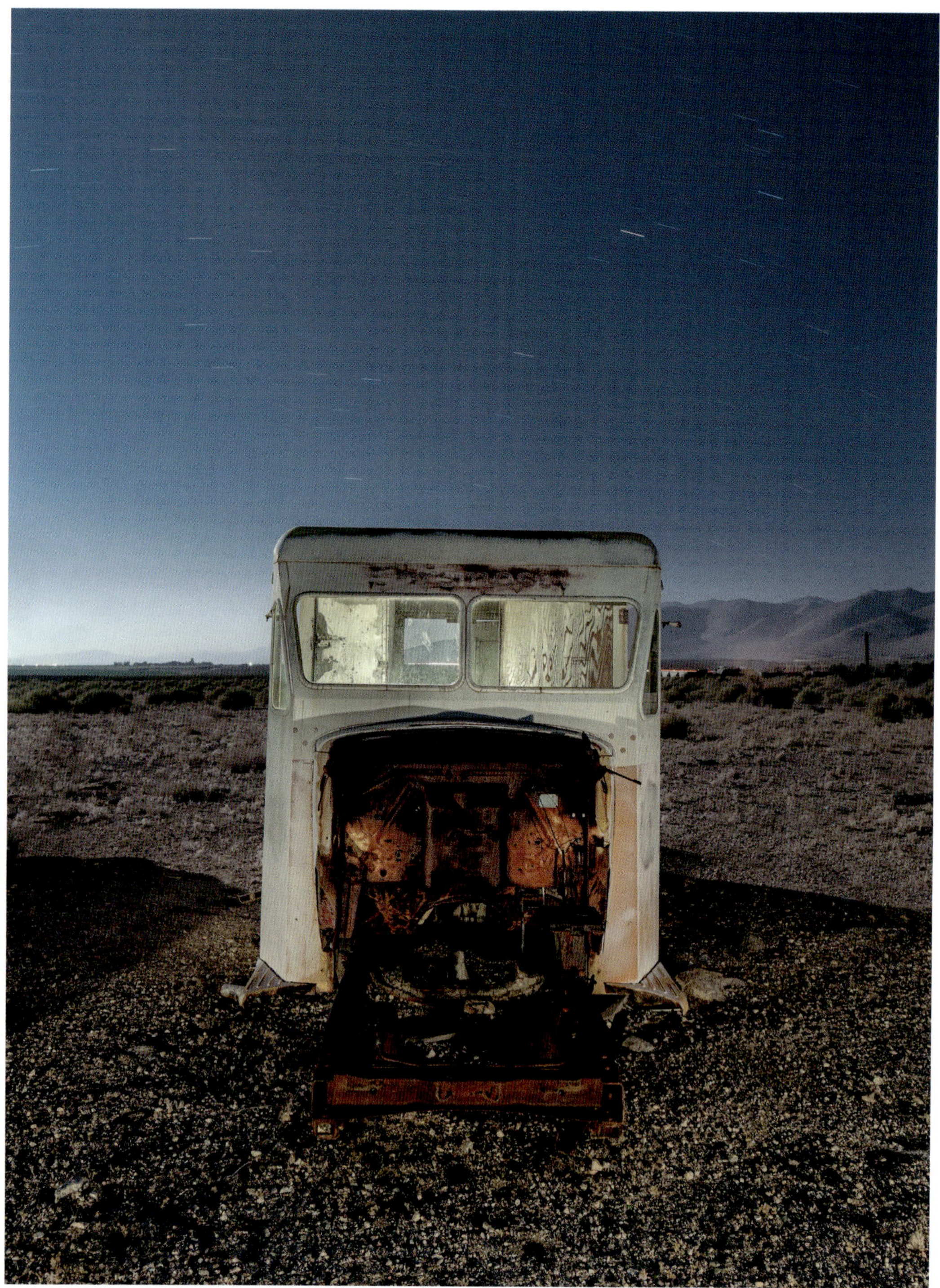

No Ice Cream Today, a wickedly hot and brutally gusty summer night—perfect for ice cream. But none here. This is the remains of a Foremost dairy truck. Pearsonville.
Pentax K-1/15–30-mm f/2.8 lens. Nine minutes total "stacked." Each photo three minutes f/8 ISO 200. Early August 2020.
Full moon, warm white light from ProtoMachines LED2.

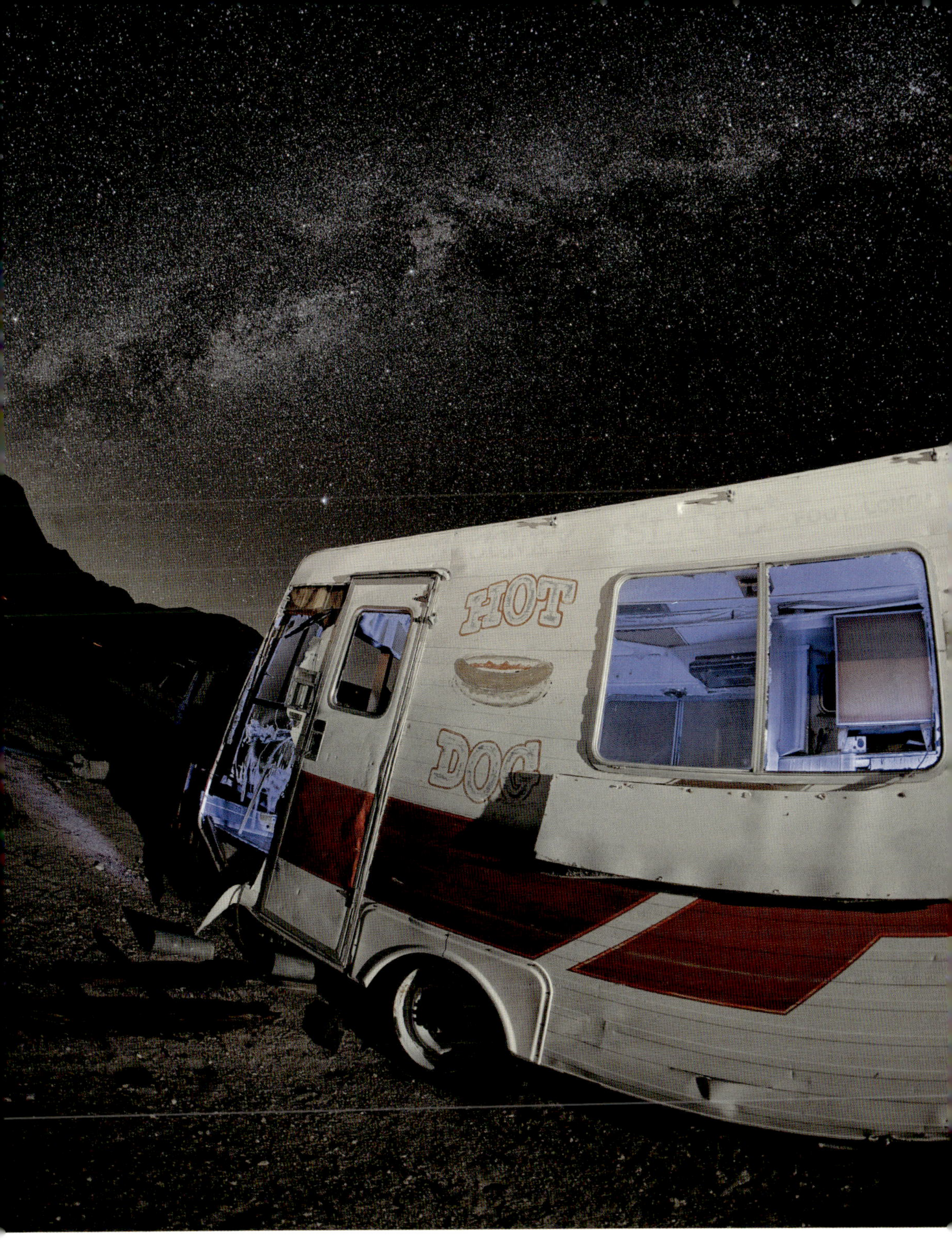

Hot Dog Heaven, RV underneath the northern part of the winter Milky Way. Pearsonville.
Nikon D750/Rokinon 12-mm f/2.8 fisheye lens. Ground: three minutes f/2.8 ISO 400. Sky: "stack" of thirty, each twenty seconds f/2.8 ISO 4000. December 2019.
Warm white and blue light from ProtoMachines LED2.

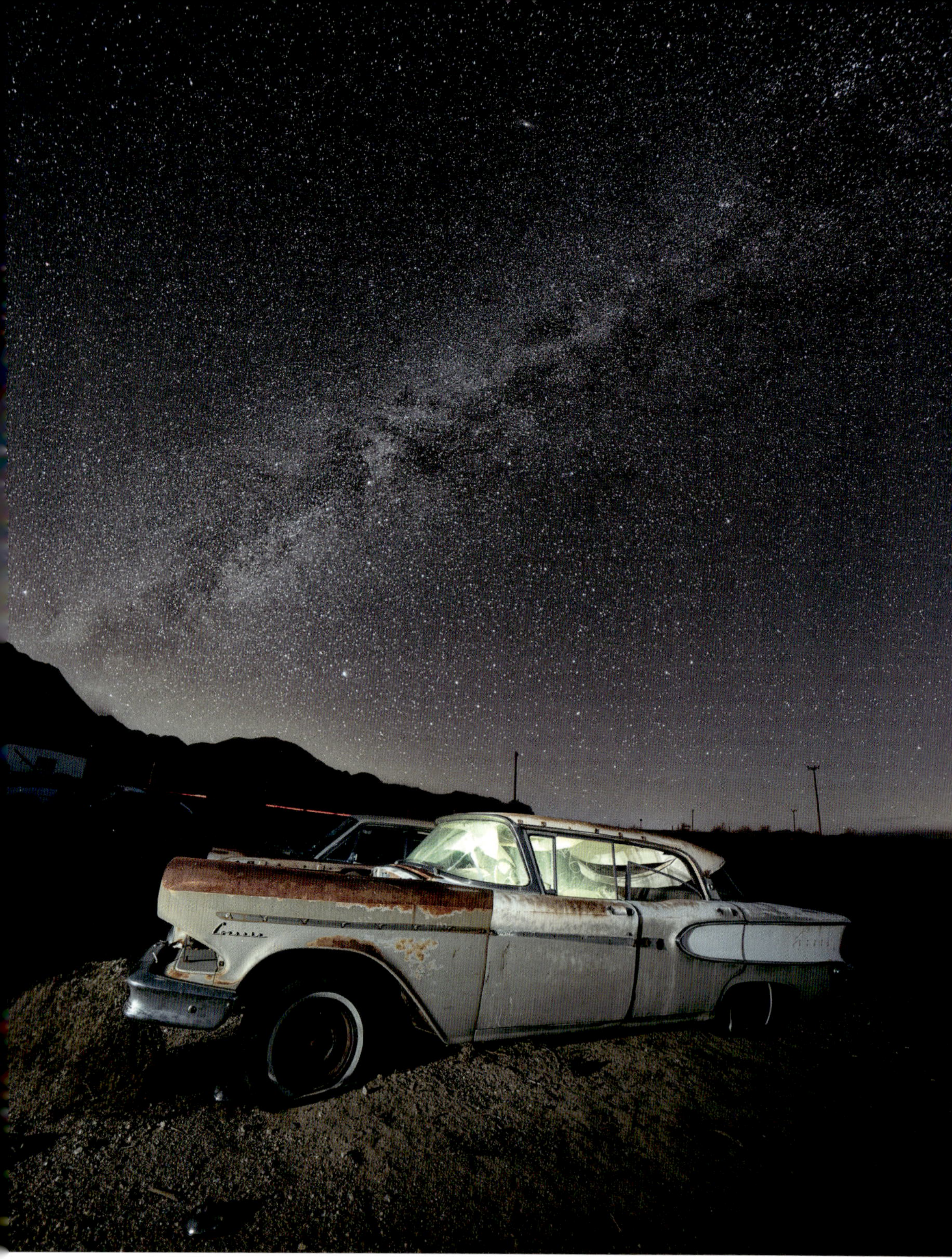

The Car's the Star, a late 1950s Edsel Corvair underneath the northern part of the winter Milky Way. Pearsonville. Nikon D750/Rokinon 12-mm f/2.8 fisheye lens. Ground: three minutes f/2.8 ISO 400. Sky: "stack" of thirty photos, each twenty seconds f/2.8 ISO 4000. December 2019.
Warm white light from ProtoMachines LED2.

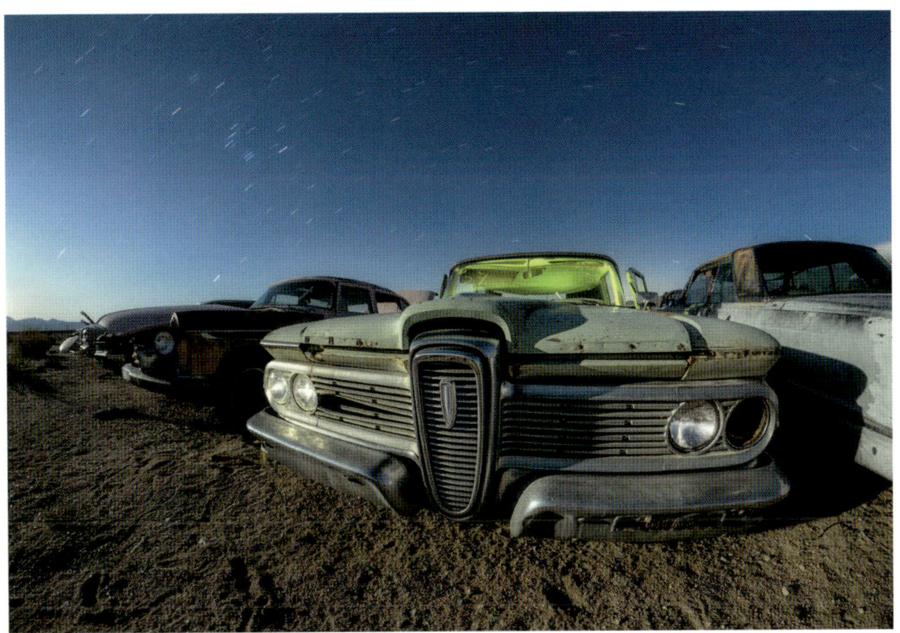

A Taste of Lemon, 1950s Edsel. Less than 10,000 Edsels were manufactured, and now, one in good shape is considered a valuable collector's item. Pearsonville.
Nikon D750/Rokinon 12-mm f/2.8 fisheye lens. Six minutes total "stacked"; each photo three minutes f/2.8 ISO 500. December 2019.
Full moon, warm white light from ProtoMachines LED2.

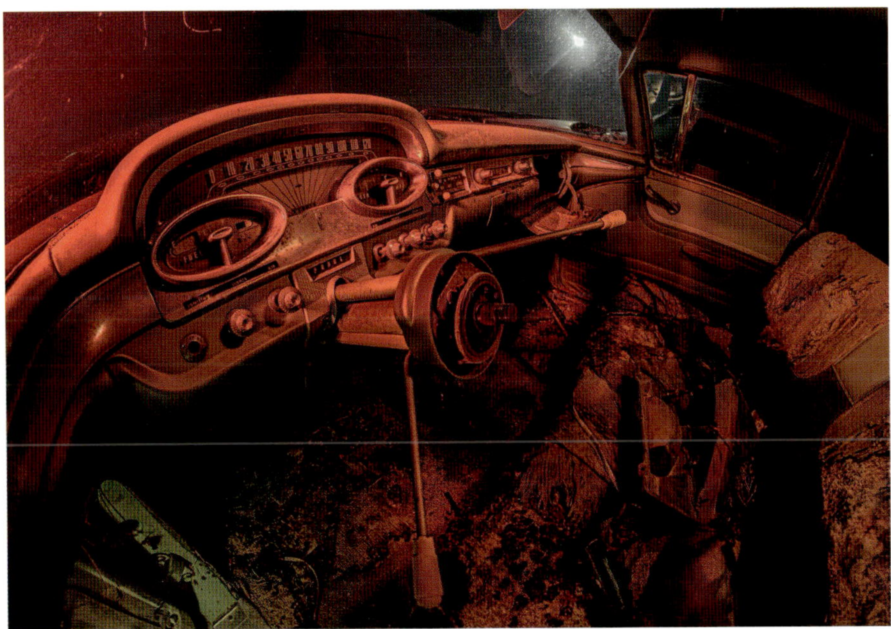

Rama Lama Ding Dong, 1950s Edsel interior. Pearsonville.
Nikon D750/Rokinon 12-mm f/2.8 fisheye lens. Thirty-seven seconds f/8 ISO 200. December 2019.
Full moon, red light from ProtoMachines LED2.

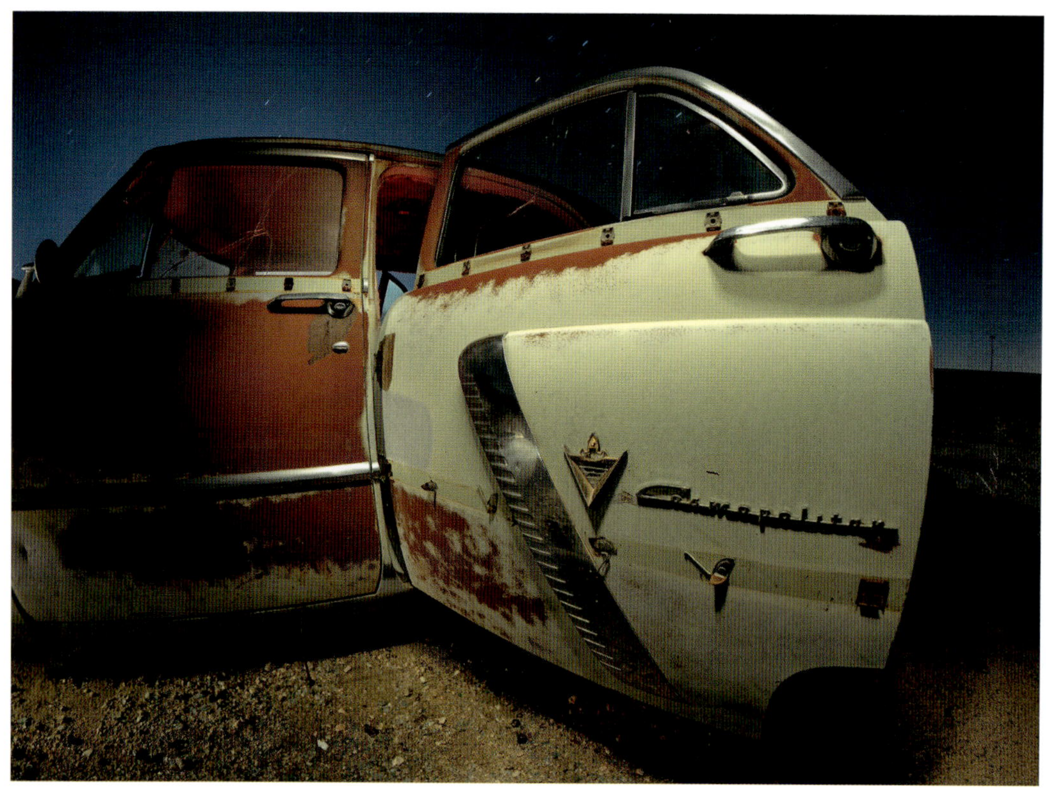

Cosmopolitan, 1950s Lincoln Cosmopolitan luxury car. President Truman and the White House leased ten black Cosmopolitans, which were modified to provide extra headroom to accommodate the tall silk hats that were in fashion at the time. Pearsonville.
Nikon D750/Rokinon 12-mm f/2.8 fisheye lens. Three minutes f/8 ISO 200. December 2019.
Full moon, warm white light from ProtoMachines LED2.

► **Compramos Botes**, bottle truck during a brutally hot and gusty night. I could also occasionally smell some of the smoke from the enormous Apple Fire in Cherry Valley. Pearsonville.
Pentax K-1/15–30-mm f/2.8 lens. Nine minutes total “stacked”; each photo three minutes f/8 ISO 200. Early August 2020.
Full moon, warm white and teal light from ProtoMachines LED2.

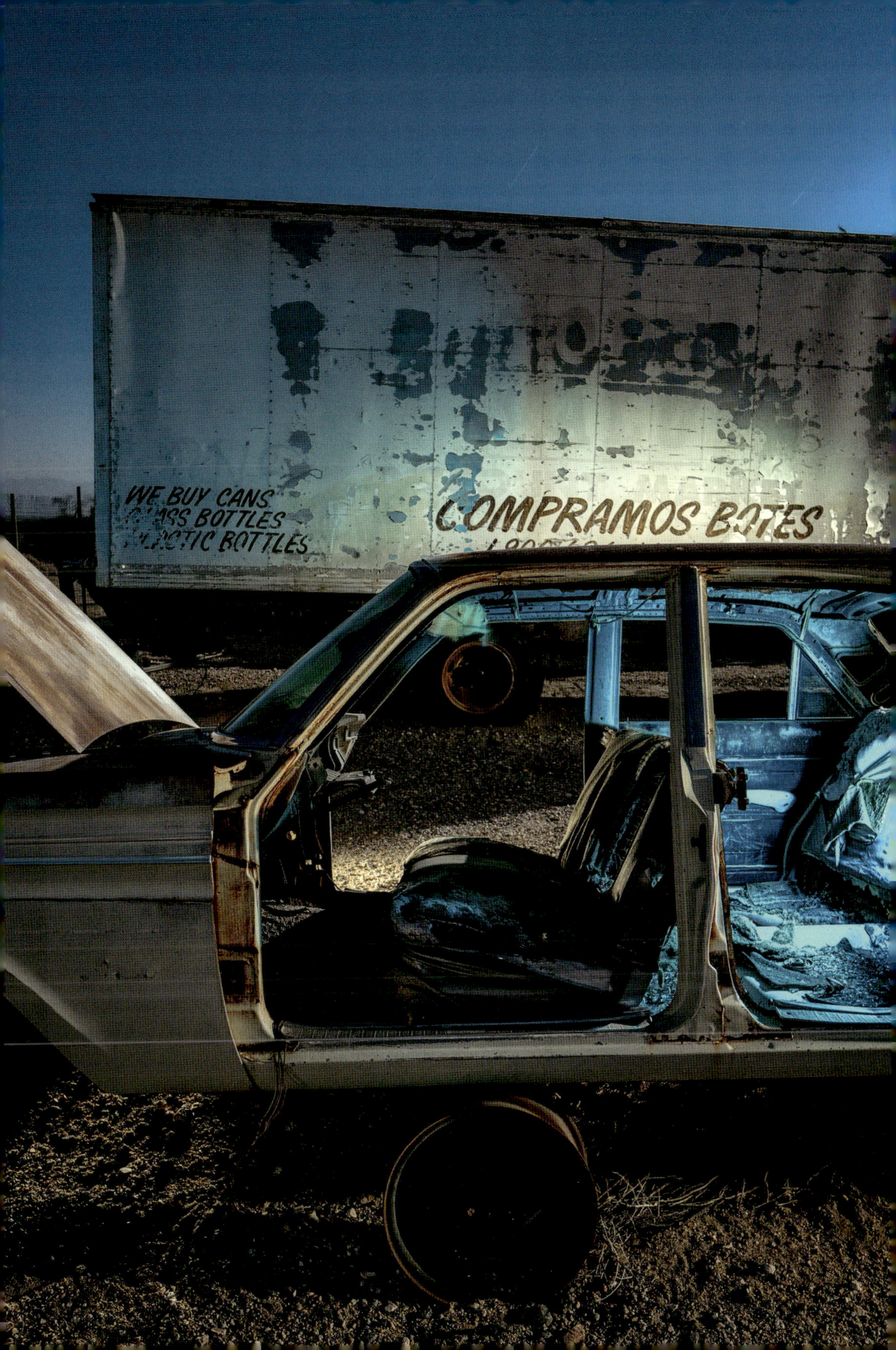
WE BUY CANS
COMPRAMOS BOTES

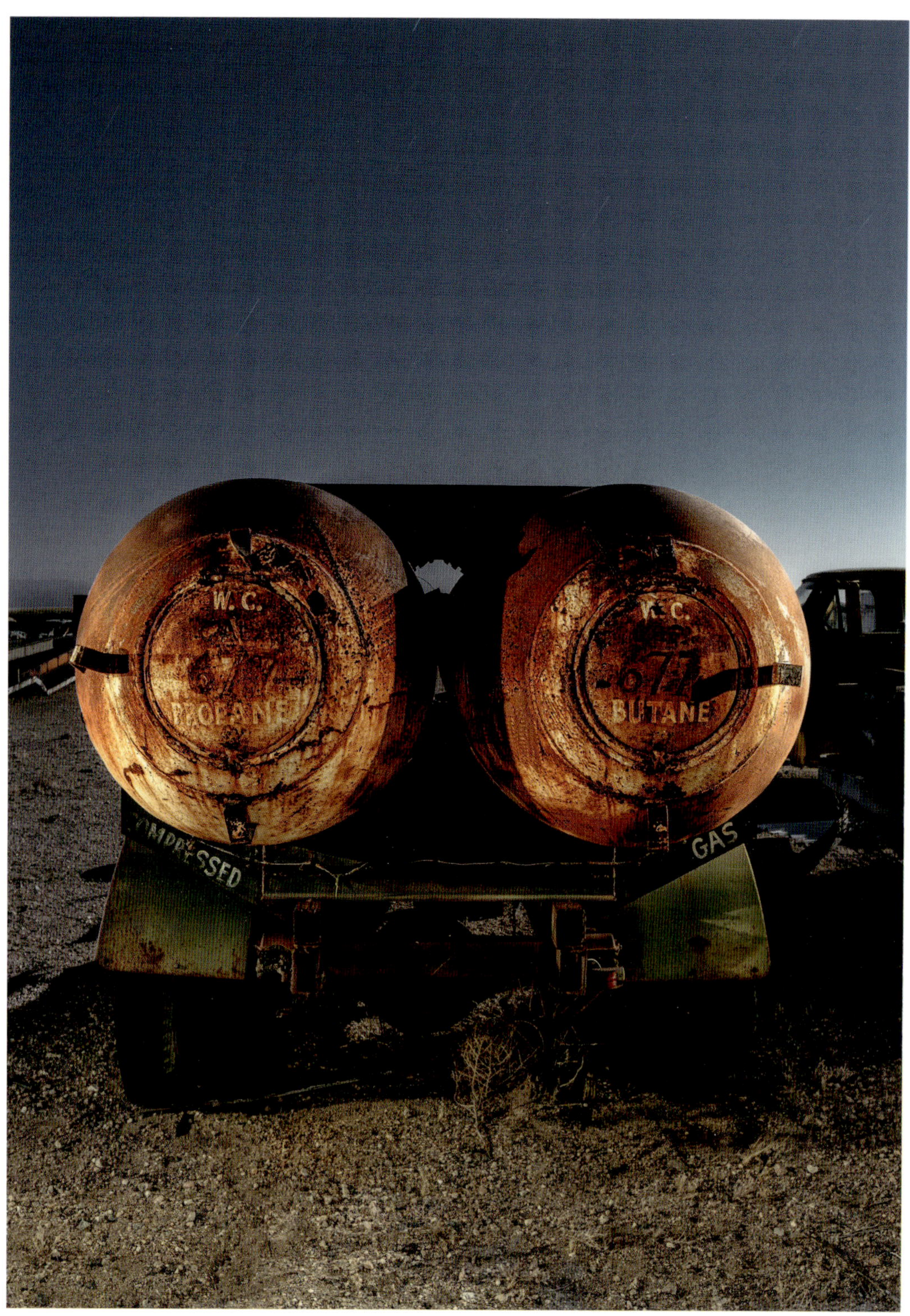

Weapons of Mass Distraction, a full-figured double-tank compressed gas truck underneath the faint trailing stars. Pentax K-1/15–30-mm f/2.8 lens. Nine minutes total "stacked"; each photo three minutes f/8 ISO 200. August 2020. Full moon, warm white light from ProtoMachines LED2.

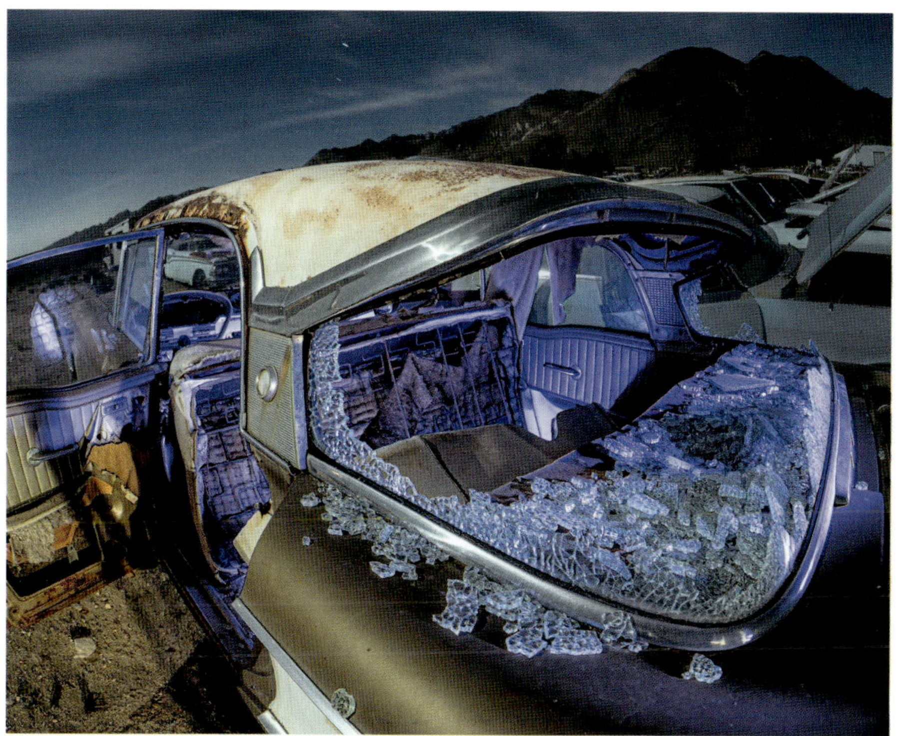

Blue Ice, a fisheye view of the seemingly crystallized back window of an old Edsel. Pearsonville. Nikon D750/Rokinon 12-mm f/2.8 fisheye lens. Two minutes thirty seconds f/8 ISO 320. October 2019. Full moon, warm white and blue light from ProtoMachines LED2.

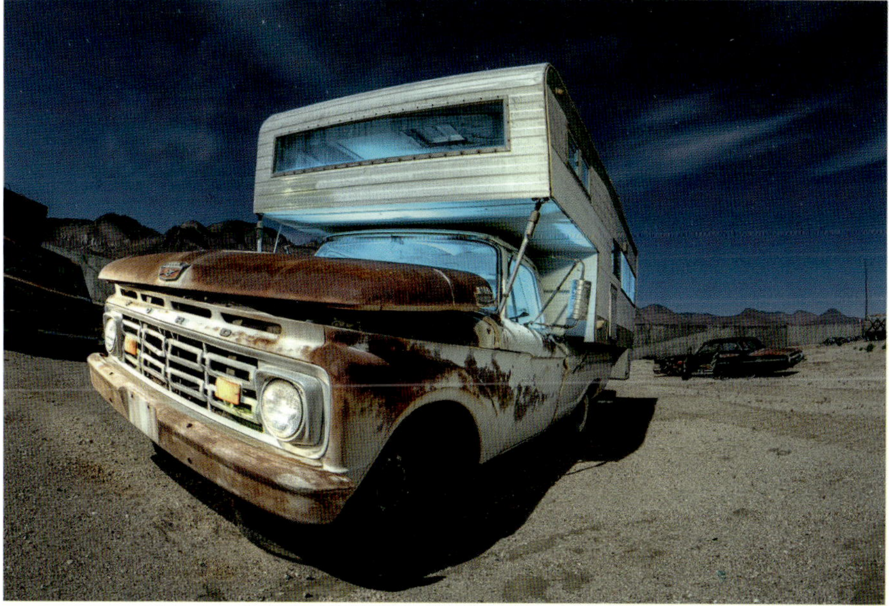

Blue Light Camp Night, old RV camper on a Ford truck on a beautiful cool desert evening. Pearsonville. Nikon D750/Rokinon 12-mm f/2.8 lens. One minute twenty-three seconds f/8 ISO 320. October 2019. Full moon, warm white and teal light from ProtoMachines LED2.

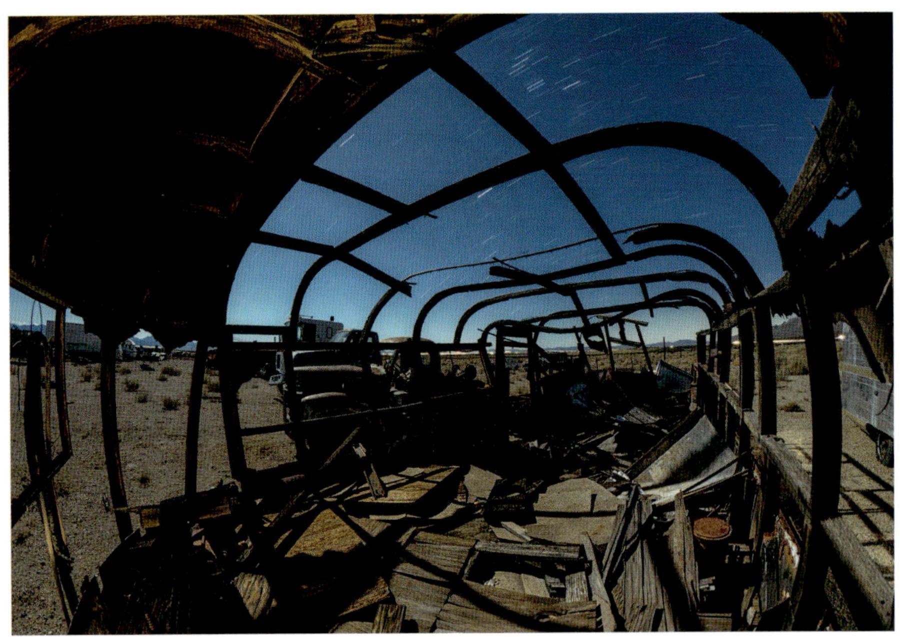

Ghost Riders in the Sky, long horse trailer. Pearsonville.
Nikon D750/Rokinon 12-mm f/2.8 lens. Twelve minutes total "stacked"; each photo three minutes f/8 ISO 320. December 2019.
Full moon, warm white light from ProtoMachines LED2.

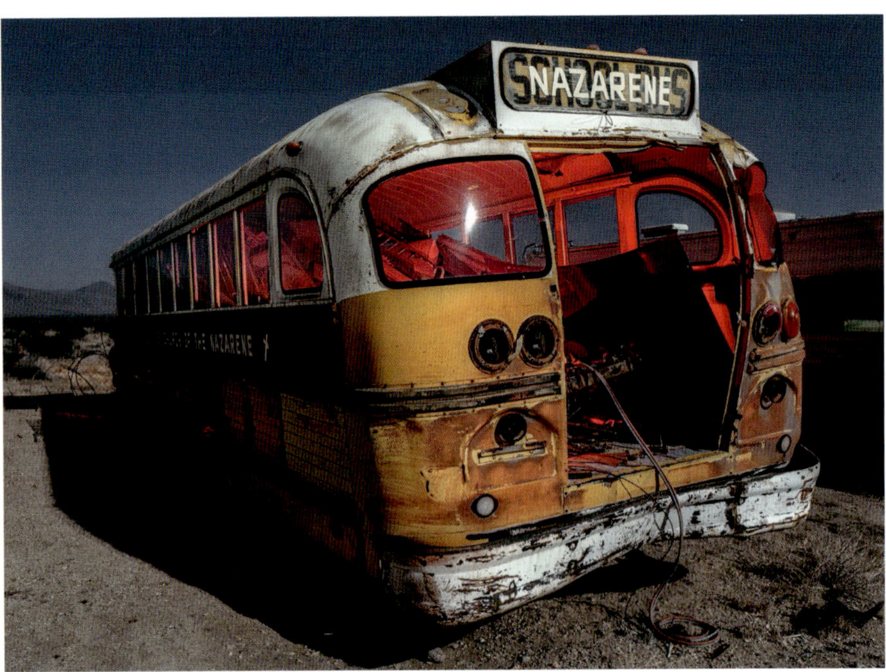

First Church of the Nazarene, former bus from the Roseville First Church of the Nazarene. Pearsonville.
Pentax K-1/15–30-mm f/2.8 lens. Six minutes total "stacked"; each photo three minutes f/8 ISO 200. August 2020.
Full moon, warm white and red light from ProtoMachines LED2.

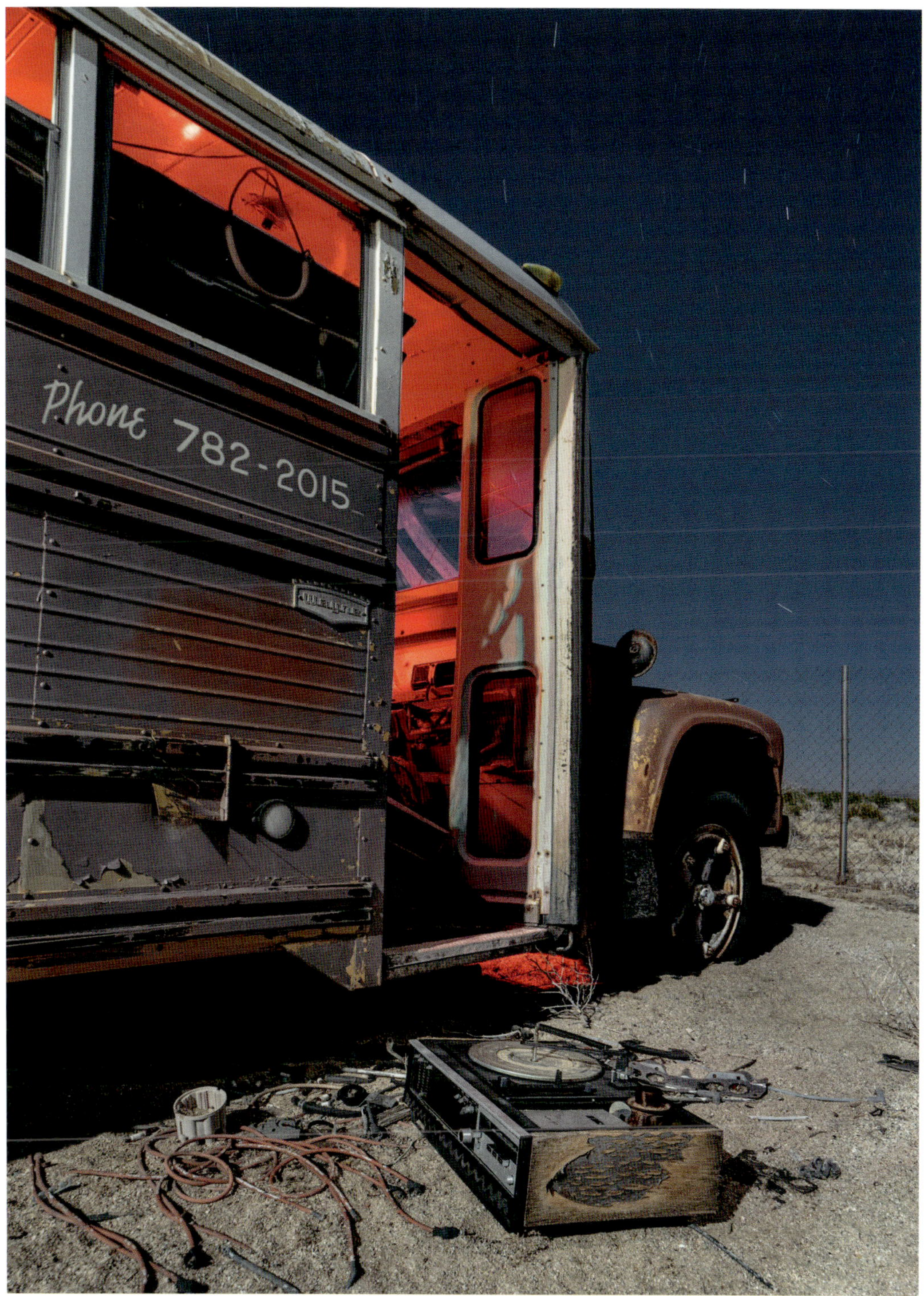

Long Play, Roseville First Church of the Nazarene bus and turntable. And no, I did not stage this! Pearsonville. Pentax K-1/15–30-mm f/2.8 lens. Nine minutes total "stacked"; each photo three minutes f/8 ISO 200. August 2020. Full moon, warm white and red light from ProtoMachines LED2.

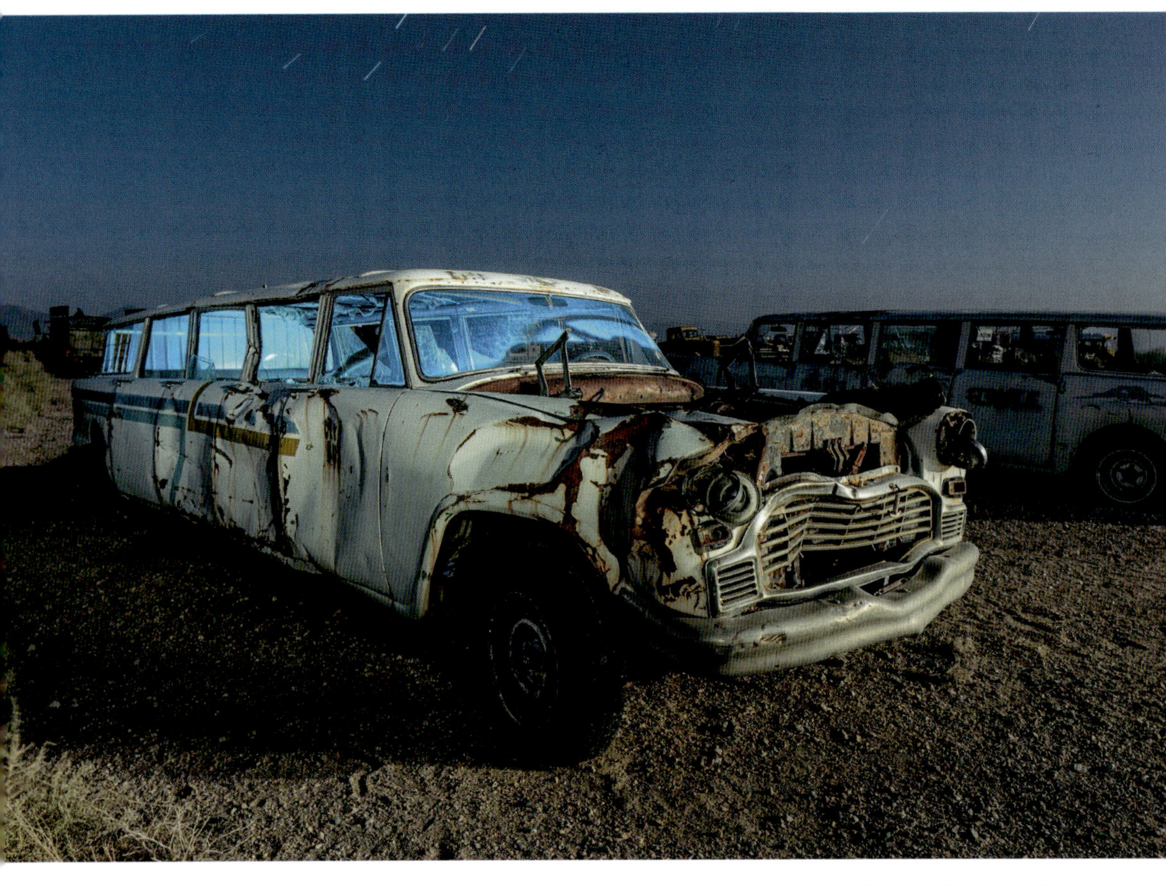

Long Ride, Checker Aerobus. You can see the haze from the enormous Apple Fire from Cherry Valley, which I could also occasionally smell. Pearsonville.
Pentax K-1/15–30-mm f/2.8 lens. Twelve minutes total "stacked"; each photo three minutes f/8 ISO 200. August 2020. Full moon, warm white and blue light from ProtoMachines LED2.

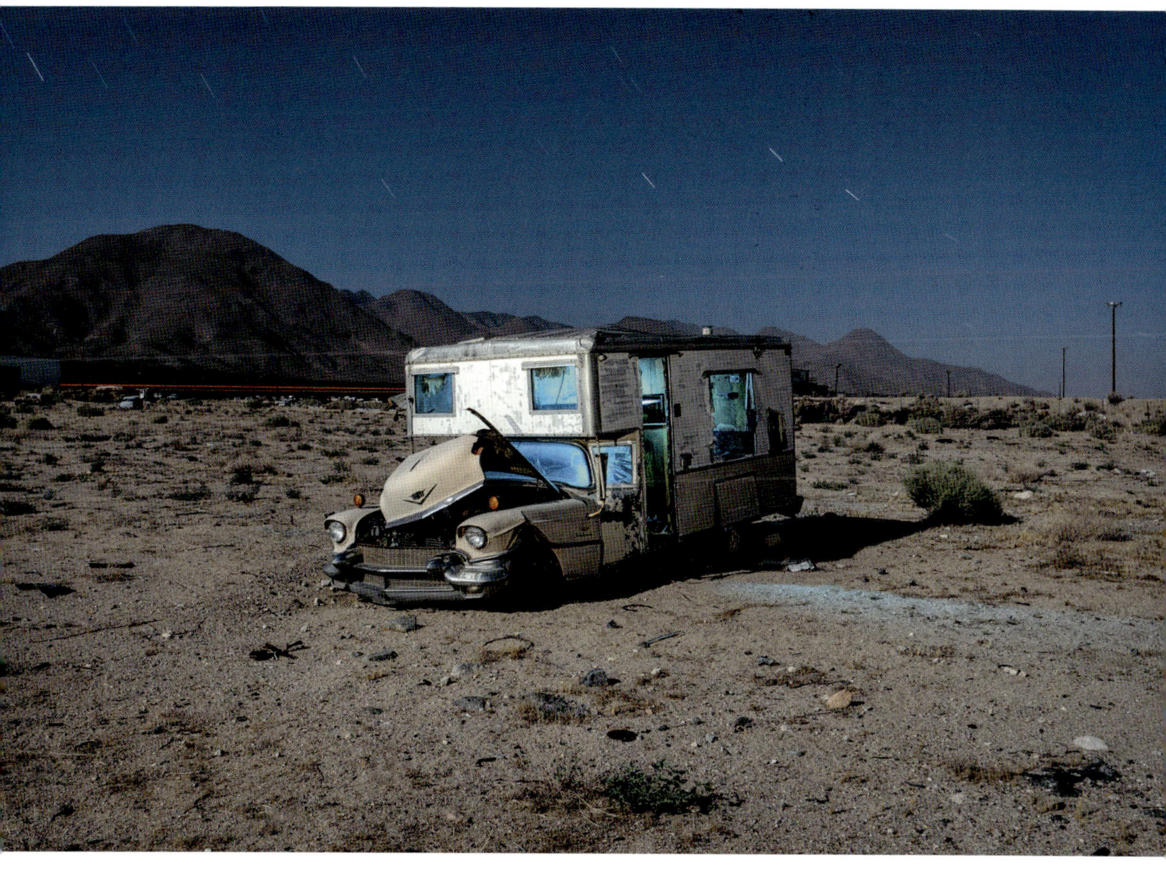

Alone Again, Cadillac Camper in what is now a largely barren auto salvage yard. Years ago, thousands of cars filled the yard. Pearsonville.
Pentax K-1/15–30-mm f/2.8 lens. Nine minutes total "stacked"; each photo three minutes f/8 ISO 200. August 2020. Full moon, warm white and blue light from ProtoMachines LED2.

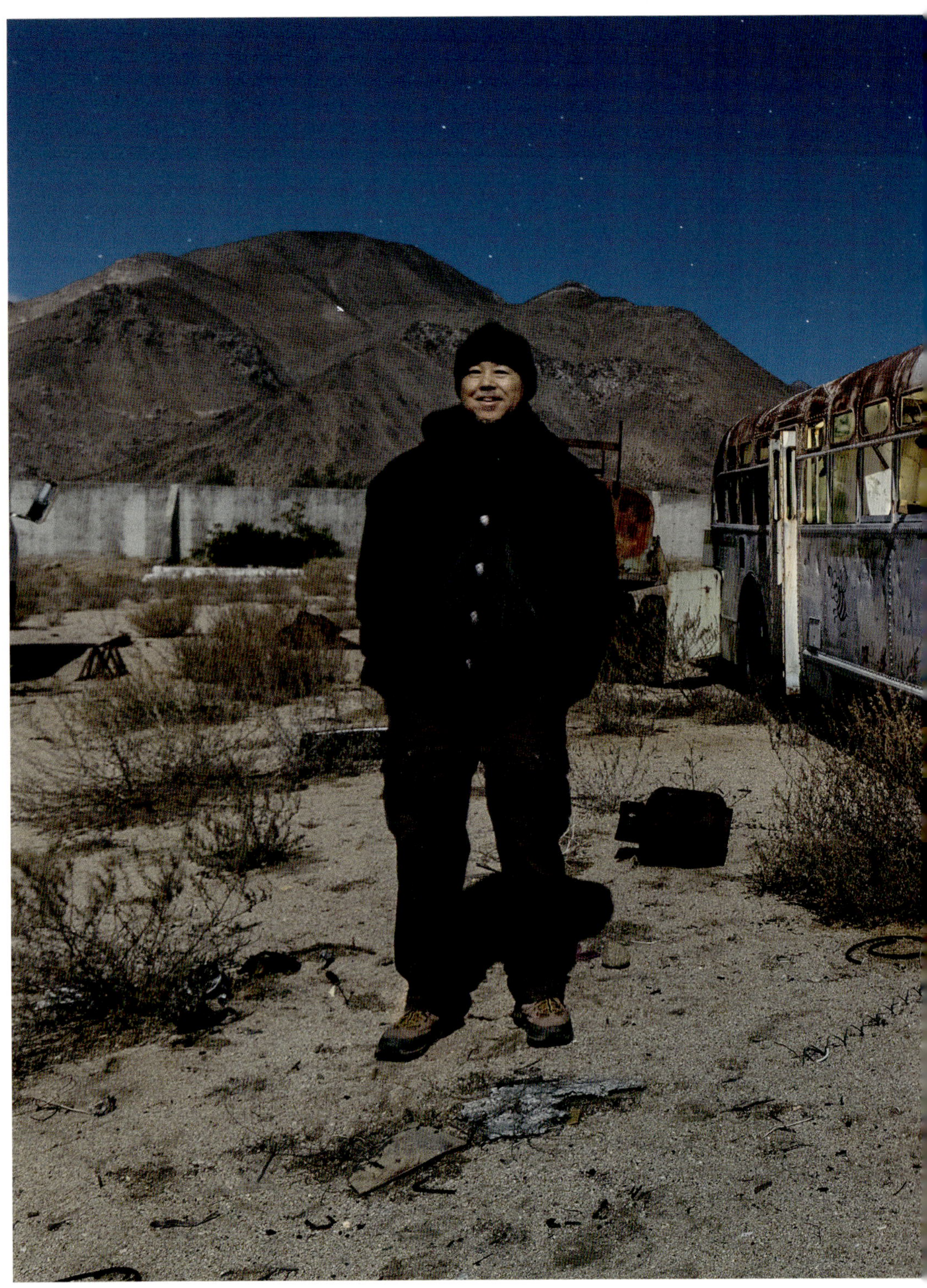

The Pearsonville Express, I did my best to stand still for fifteen seconds in front of "the bus." Pearsonville.

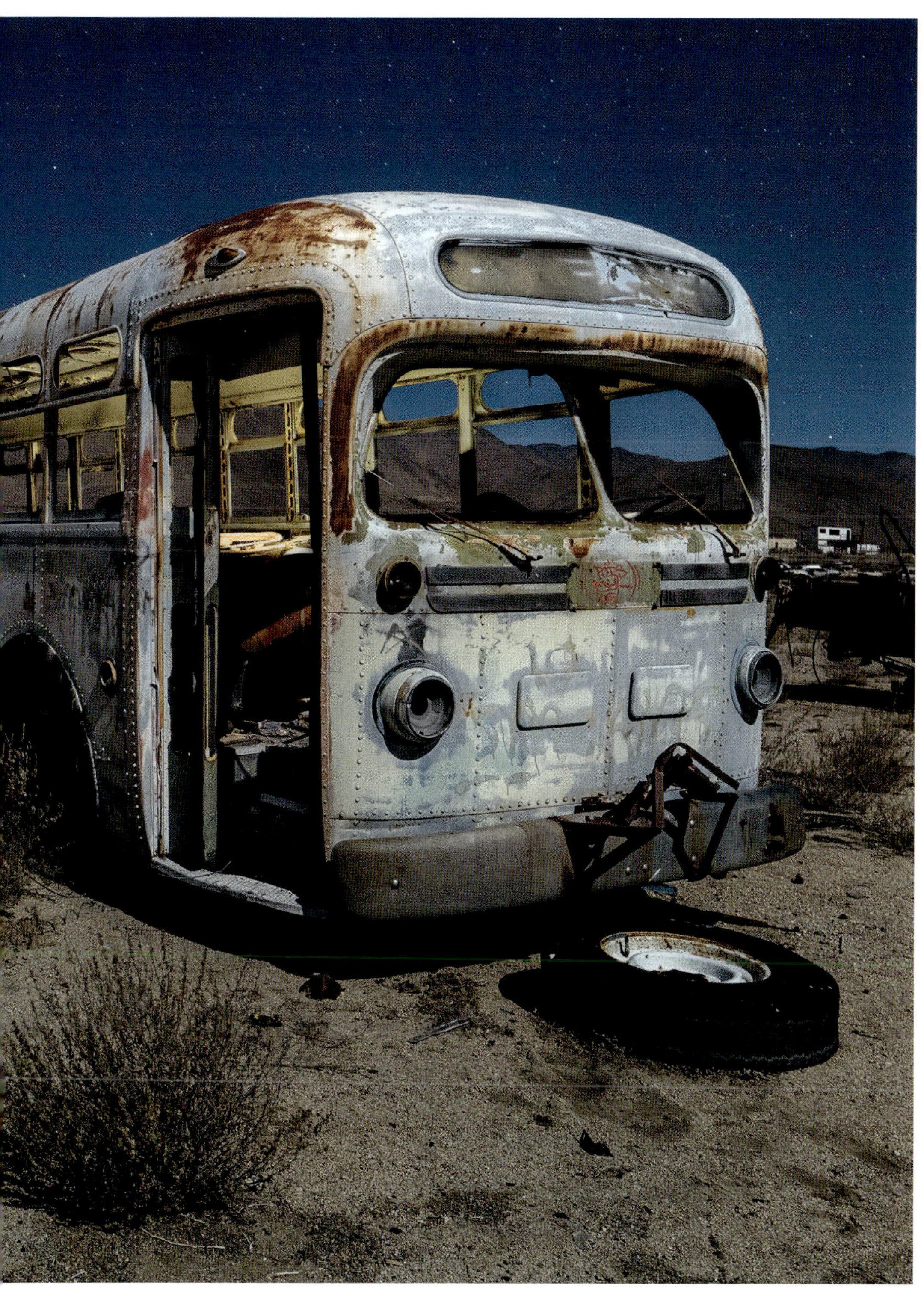

Pentax K-1/15–30-mm f/2.8 lens. Fifteen seconds f/5.6 ISO 1600. December 2019; the bus was light painted in a separate exposure at two minutes f/5.6 ISO 200 so it could be illuminated.
Full moon, warm white light from ProtoMachines LED2.

*M*A*S*H*

As a special education teacher, I had been purchasing from Derrick's education supplies store for years. One day, I surprise him by asking if he can laminate some Roscolux color filters to use for "light painting" the old *M*A*S*H* filming site in Agoura Hills, where the TV show with Alan Alda was made. It is late 2013, and it will be the first time I ever photograph abandoned vehicles at night.

Roscolux sells swatches of their colored lighting gel filters in a small booklet to aid people in selecting color or diffusion. I pull apart the book and select my favorite colors, but the gels are very thin. Knowing that they will not withstand the continual abuse of night photography, I ask Derrick if he can laminate these. He is immediately intrigued, and advises me to frame them in cardboard as well, almost as if they are old slide film. I also purchase some Velcro from him to attach the frames to my cheap LED flashlights. This will enable me to create colored lights more quickly. Also, I will not need to hold the gels awkwardly in front of the flashlight.

Several days later, on a very cold November night, I hike in to the *M*A*S*H* ambulances. I have one backpack for the camera equipment, and another for the various flashlights and gels. The trail winds through the mountains and opens into a beautiful valley, the site of the TV show's fictional Korean medical camp. At the time of filming, this was a movie ranch owned by 20th Century Fox. Between 1972 and 1983, most scenes were shot at this location. The site was later donated, becoming part of Malibu Creek State Park. Since that time, the ambulances have somehow survived the numerous wildfires that plague the region.

Two ambulances remain from the TV show. I set about photographing them with my new gels, storing them in an old audio CD pocket case to keep them from blowing away when I set them down. This is my first attempt at "light painting" vehicles of any kind. Despite the 40-degree temperatures, I am instantly hooked, and minutes melt into hours. During long exposure photos showing the movement of the stars, I run back and forth on the hiking trail to stay warm. I see a glow forming on the horizon. This reminds me how long I have been here. It is the first light from the sun. I arrive home well after the morning newspaper has been tossed on my driveway.

Derrick is quite excited by this project and asks me to email the photos to him. I send him most of the *M*A*S*H* photos featured in this book. He writes back immediately saying how cool they are, asking if he may use the photos for his educational store and his personal Facebook page. Of course I say yes. He writes the following caption: "Ken Lee, a special education teacher, used our laminator to strengthen and protect his color filters, which he then used to enhance his photography. Check out Ken's stunning results!"

The photography at the former *M*A*S*H* film location is a turning point. I have just begun doing night photography, but mostly Milky Way photos. I fall in love with this whole process of light painting near a full moon. It is actively creative and amazingly addictive. And it has ignited a passion that burns to this day. I am happy to leave you with photos from the beginning of my journey.

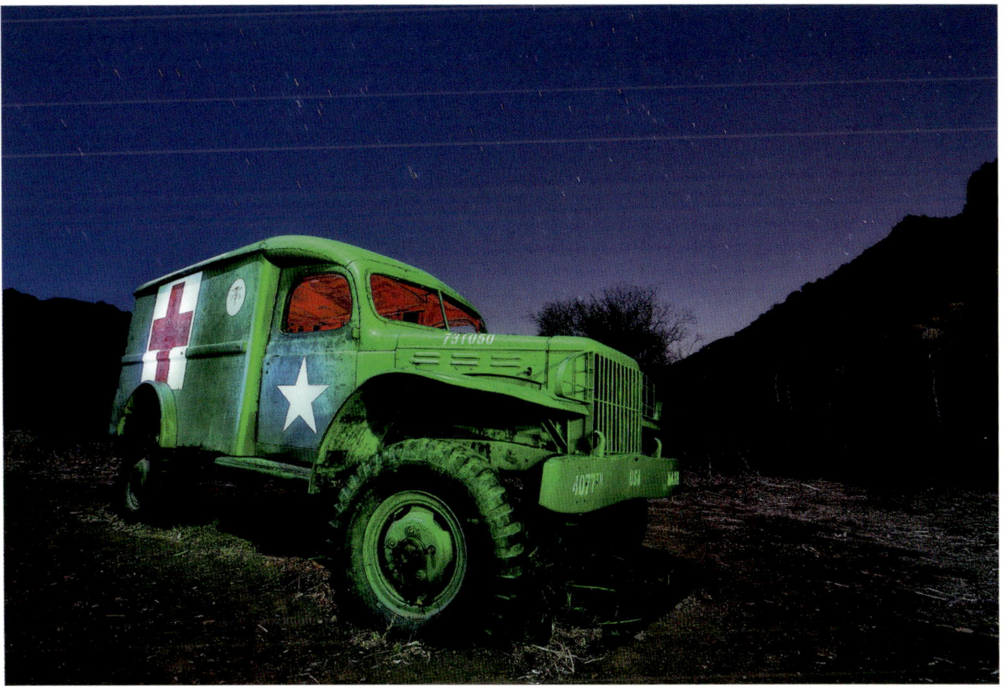

Suicide is Painless, *M*A*S*H* ambulance left at the old TV filming location, Malibu Creek State Park, formerly belonging to 20th Century Fox Studios.
Nikon D7000/Tokina 11–16-mm f/2.8 lens. Two minutes thirty-two seconds at f/8 ISO 200. December 2013. Full moon, white and red light from Streamlight 88040 ProTac HL flashlight and Roscolux color gels.

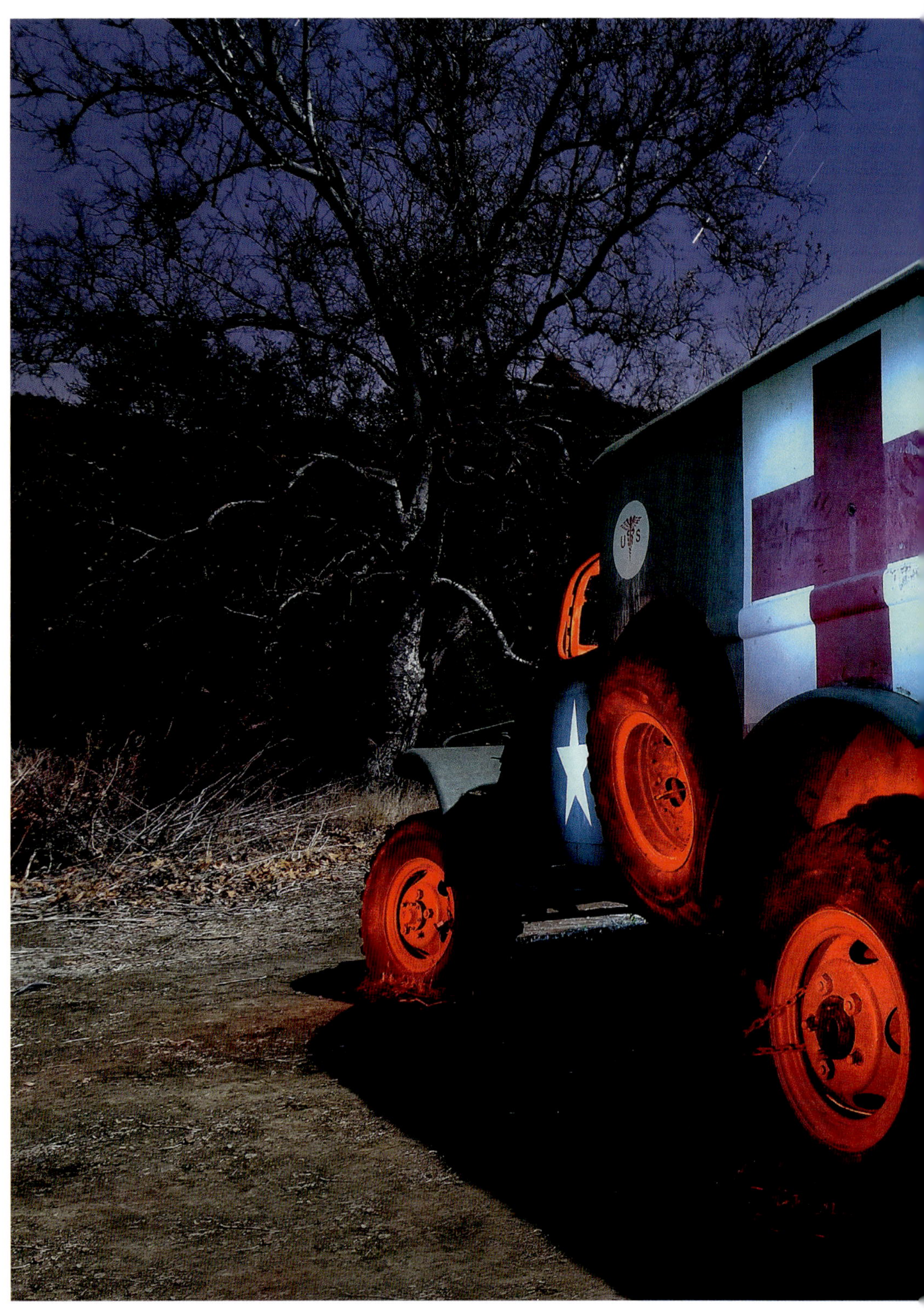

Haunted Ambulance, *M*A*S*H* ambulance left at the old TV filming location, Malibu Creek State Park, formerly belonging to 20th Century Fox Studios.

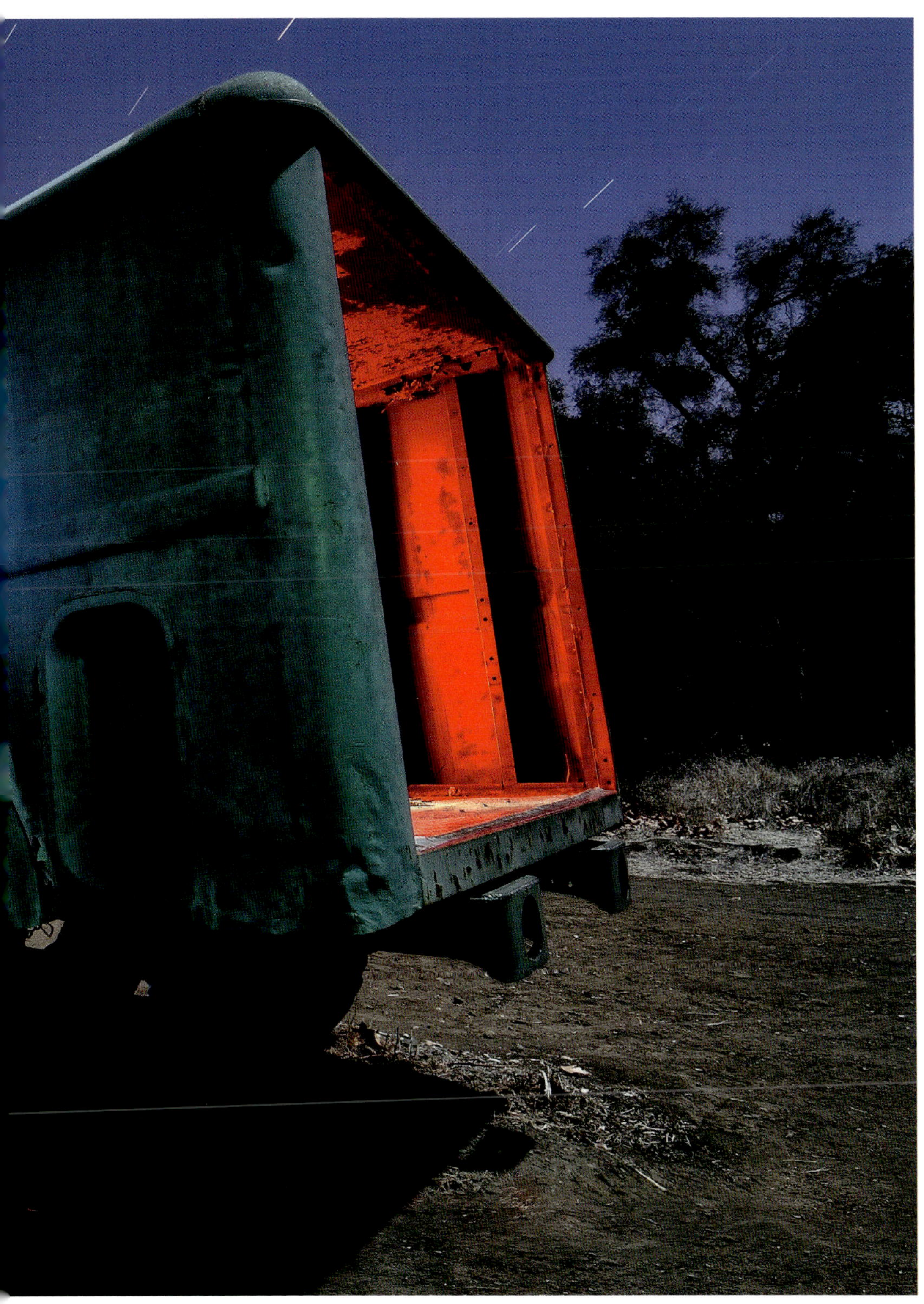

Nikon D7000/Tokina 11–16-mm f/2.8 lens. Six minutes thirty-one seconds at f/8 ISO 200. December 2013. Full moon, white and red light from Streamlight 88040 ProTac HL flashlight and Roscolux color gels.

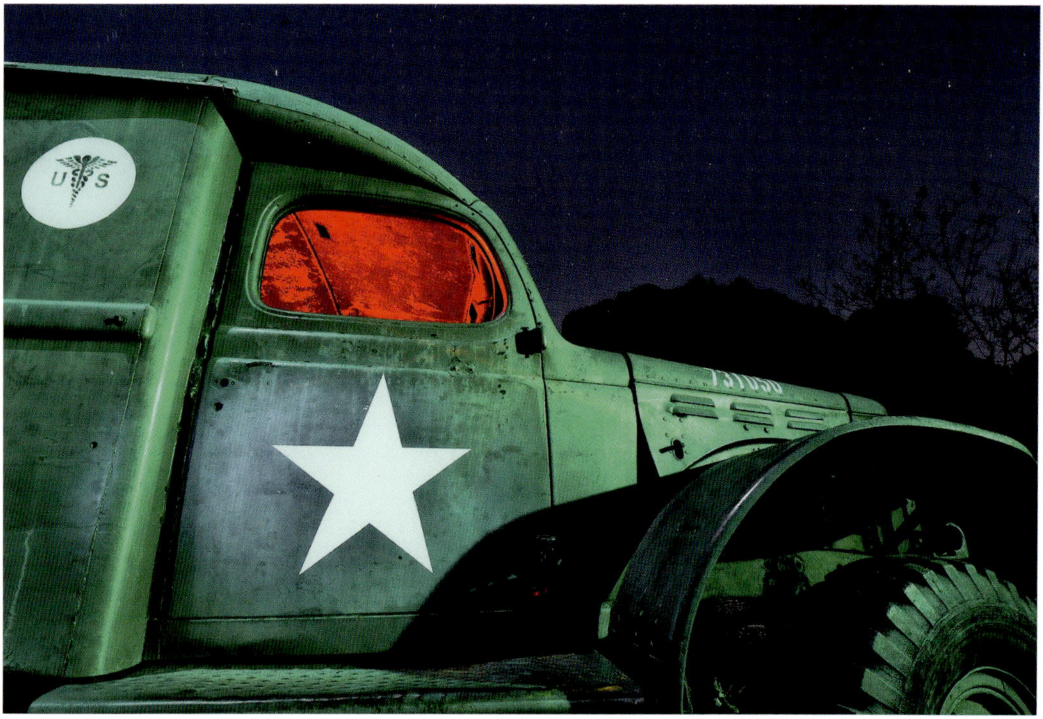

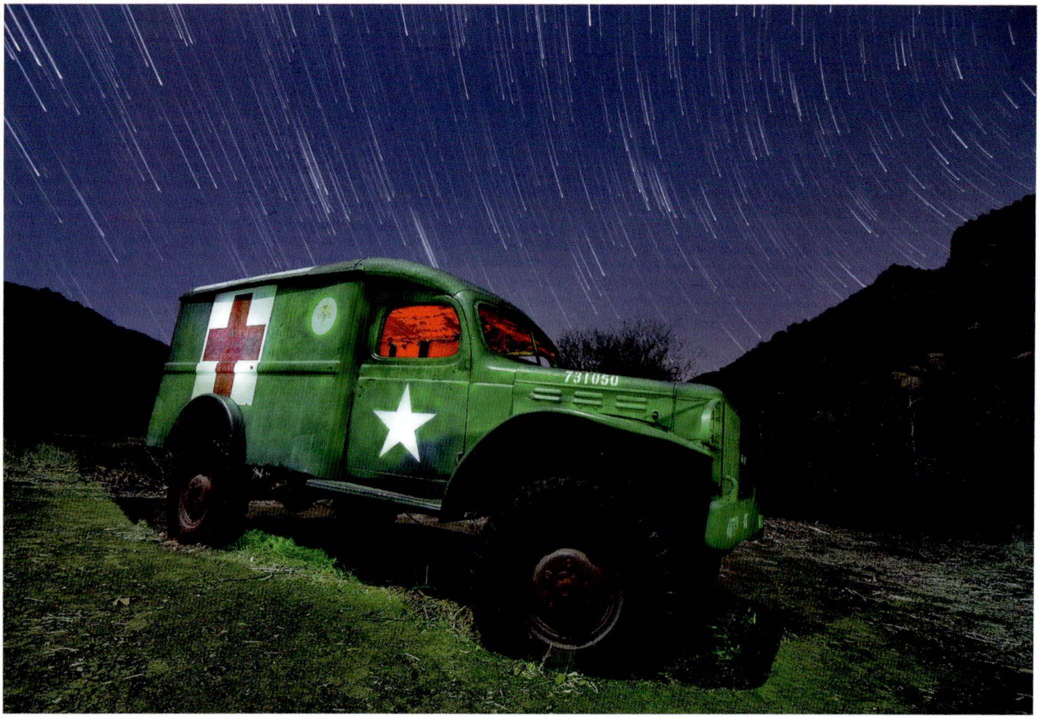

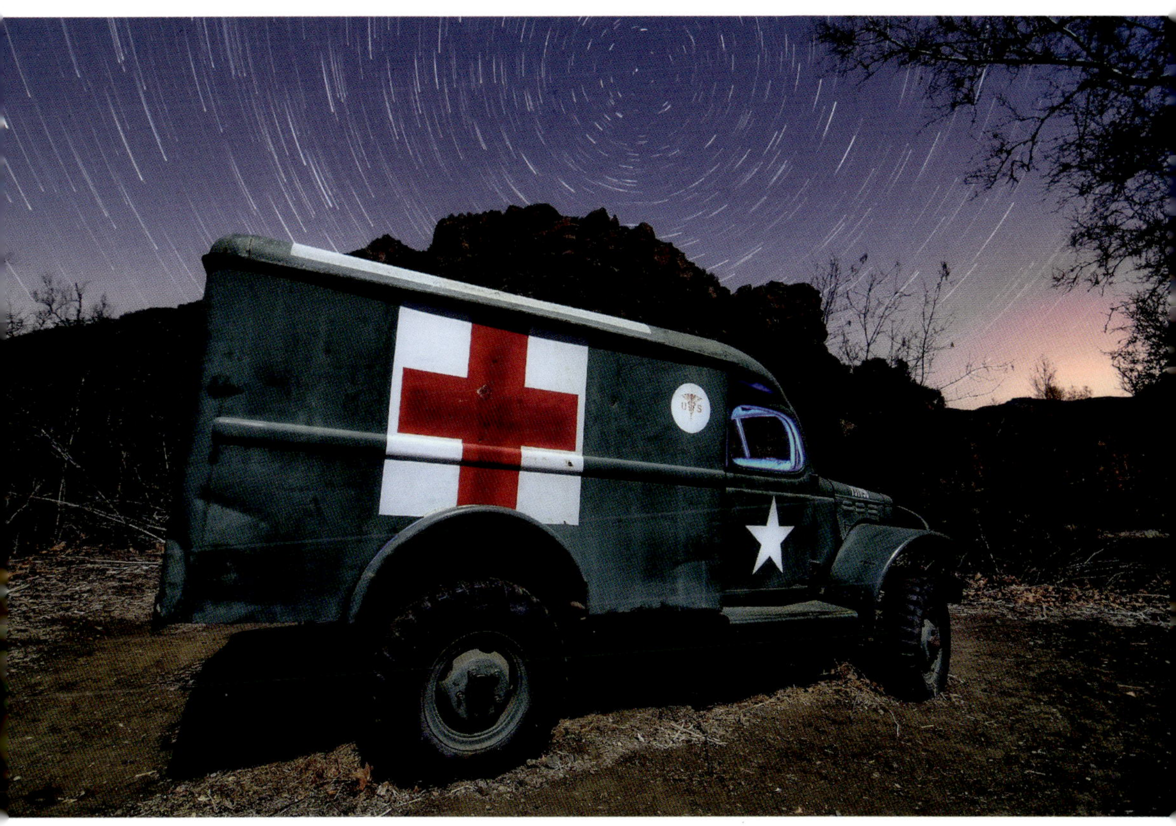

Guerilla My Dreams, *M*A*S*H* ambulance left at the old TV filming location, Malibu Creek State Park, formerly belonging to 20th Century Fox Studios.
Nikon D7000/Tokina 11–16-mm f/2.8 lens. Forty-four minutes total "stacked"; each photo twenty-five seconds f/4 ISO 400. December 2013.
Full moon, white and blue light from Streamlight 88040 ProTac HL flashlight and Roscolux color gels.

Opposite page

▲ **There is Nothing like a Nurse**, *M*A*S*H* ambulance left at the old TV filming location, Malibu Creek State Park, formerly belonging to 20th Century Fox Studios.
Nikon D7000/Tokina 11–16-mm f/2.8 lens. Two minutes twelve seconds at f/8 ISO 200. December 2013.
Full moon, white and red light from Streamlight 88040 ProTac HL flashlight and Roscolux color gels.

▼ **Hawkeye**, *M*A*S*H* ambulance left at the old TV filming location, Malibu Creek State Park, formerly belonging to 20th Century Fox Studios.
Nikon D7000/Tokina 11–16-mm f/2.8 lens. Thirty minutes total "stacked"; each photo thirty seconds f/4 ISO 400. December 2013.
Full moon, white and red light from Streamlight 88040 ProTac HL flashlight and Roscolux color gels.

4

CREATING THE IMAGES

The images in this book were created at night with long exposure photography techniques. Over the years that it took to create these images, I have used a Pentax K-1 and Nikon D750, D610, and D7000 with ultra-wide-angle lenses and even a Lensbaby tilt-shift-style lens, all mounted on a sturdy Feisol carbon-fiber tripod.

On or near a full moon, which is used as the primary light source, I set the camera for one- to four-minute exposures at f/8 at ISO 200. This is often long enough to show the stars streaking across the night sky, allowing the ambient light to "soak in" a bit.

Then I add light and color to the scene using a handheld ProtoMachines LED2 light painting device capable of creating any color in the RGB spectrum and offering controls for brightness and saturation. I usually walk around and light the foreground from multiple angles. I typically do not use light stands or other stationary lights. All the lighting is done in-camera at the time of exposure. These are techniques that are largely inspired by pioneering night photographers Troy Paiva and Lance Keimig. They were in turn inspired by Steve Harper and others.

If I photograph the Milky Way or the stars as pinpoints, I set the camera for fifteen- or twenty-second exposures at much wider apertures such as f/2.8 at ISO 3200 or ISO 4000. I photograph at a shorter exposure so that the stars appear as dots of light and do not begin to create star trails. Often, I will photograph the scene about twenty times in succession with identical exposure settings, keeping the camera in a fixed position. I will then use Starry Landscape Stacker, an app for Mac which uses "stacking" or "image averaging." This combines the group of images to create much less noise than I could achieve in a single exposure. After I photograph the sky in rapid succession, I photograph the foreground using a low-ISO setting on the camera, usually ISO 320 or ISO 400 for 150 to 200 seconds. As you might guess, this is also to reduce noise. The extra time also allows me to add light and color to the scene with the ProtoMachines light. Then I will blend this in with the "stacked" photo from Starry Landscape Stacker, creating a beautiful low-noise image.

Many of these night images are colorful. Some who are not familiar with night photography might regard this as odd since this is not the way night typically appears to our eyes. As night grows darker, our eyes become increasingly monochromatic. Our retinas widen to let in more light. But while our cones function well in brighter light and see color, our rods are monochromatic. However, our camera does not have the same limitations as our eyes, registering colors in low light far more vividly.

Not much equipment is needed to create these images. Indeed, all of it can fit in a small backpack, leaving me free to explore on foot easily. Typically, I have a camera, tripod, flashlight, batteries, snacks, water, and not much else. This allows me to move easily, create, and photograph these historic treasures before they are erased from history.

ABOUT THE AUTHOR

I am a night photographer. I drive long hours in a dusty car listening to weird music, stay out all night creating photos, get dirty, hang out with other creative sleep-deprived weirdos, see the stars drift across the sky, and always find the best taco stands. I have been exploring the Southwestern United States as well as parts of the East Coast for over six years, brandishing a camera, tripod, and colored flashlight. I especially love creating night photos of abandoned historical places, unique features, and beautiful landscapes. These are experiences that I absolutely cherish. I also currently have several books of night photography of abandoned locales that I am working on with a publisher. My images have appeared in *National Geographic* books, *Omni* magazine, *The Los Angeles Times*, *Westways* magazine, and many other publications. Keep up with me at www.kenleephotography.com and social media.